Polygamy and Sublime Passion

Sexuality in China on the Verge of Modernity

Keith McMahon

University of Hawai'i Press

Honolulu

© 2010 University of Hawai'i Press
All rights reserved
Printed in the United States of America
15 14 13 12 11 10   6 5 4 3 2 1

Library of Congress Cataloging-in-Publication Data
McMahon, Keith.
  Polygamy and sublime passion : sexuality in China on the verge of modernity /
Keith McMahon.
    p. cm.
  Includes bibliographical references and index.
  ISBN 978-0-8248-3376-3 (hardcover : alk. paper)
  1. Polygamy—China. 2. Prostitution—China. 3. Concubinage—China. 4.
Marriage—China. 5. China—History—Qing dynasty, 1644–1912. I. Title.
  HQ981.M36 2010
  306.84'23095109034—dc22
                          2009030299

University of Hawai'i Press books are printed on acid-free
paper and meet the guidelines for permanence and
durability of the Council on Library Resources.

Designed by the University of Hawai'i Press production staff
Printed by Sheridan Books, Inc.

Contents

Acknowledgments

I thank my wife, Deborah Peterson, for the many words and deeds that stimulated this book. I received tremendous impetus from the efforts of Ding Naifei and Liu Jenpeng, who arranged for me to give a three-part lecture series at National Tsinghua University, National Central University, and National Chiao Tung University in Taiwan in 2006, which gave me the opportunity to solidify the main points of my project. The three lectures were published in Chinese in the September 2007 volume of the *Tsinghua Journal of Chinese Literature*, in which "Cong Lagangde xingbie chayi lilun kan wanQing Zhongguo" [Lacan's Theory of Sexual Difference in Late Imperial China], edited by Li Yuzhen, overlaps with some of the introduction; "Qinüzide nanban yu nüxing qizhide bentilun" [The Male Consort of the Remarkable Woman and the Ontology of the Feminine], translated by Xu Huilin and edited by Li Yuzhen, contains parts of chapter 1; and "Xiandai Zhongguo qianxide xingxiang jiegou—Zhongguo nanxingde duoqi zhengzhi" [The Structure of Sexuality in China on the Verge of Modernity], translated by Liu Mengzhe, contains a digest of the introduction and chapters 1, 2, 5, 6, and 9. Giovanni Vitiello and François Wildt also vitally contributed to the conversation, and Chris Connery helped at various critical points along the way. I thank others who shared both published and unpublished work with me (especially Kang-I Sun Chang, Grace Fong, Andrea Goldman, Hu Siao-chen, Pan Suiming, Sophie Volpp, Ellen Widmer, Yuan Jin, and Paola Zamperini), the editors and reviewers who accepted earlier versions of other parts of this book for publication in books and journals (as recognized in the bibliography and endnotes to chapters below), and the conference organizers who made it possible for me to present parts of the book in public and later in print.

List of Frequently Cited Titles in English

Courtesan Chambers (*Qinglou meng*, 1878), by Yu Da.

Dream of the Red Chamber (*Honglou meng*, 1791–1792), by Cao Xueqin.

1839 Miscellany (*Jihai zashi*), by Gong Zizhen.

Flowers of Shanghai (*Haishanghua liezhuan*, 1892), by Han Bangqing.

Later Tales of Liaozhai (*Hou Liaozhai zhiyi*, 1884), by Wang Tao.

Nine-times Cuckold (*Jiuwei gui*, 1906–1910), by Zhang Chunfan.

An Old Man's Radiant Words (*Yesou puyan*, mid-eighteenth century, first publ. 1881), by Xia Jingqu.

Precious Mirror of Boy Actresses (*Pinhua baojian*, 1849), by Chen Sen.

Radiant Words (*Yesou puyan*).

Revisiting the Silken Chambers (*Qilou chongmeng*, 1805), by Wang Lanzhi.

Seductive Dreams (*Fengyue meng*, 1848), by Hanshang Mengren.

Shanghai Dust (*Haishang chentian ying*, 1904), by Zou Tao.

The Stone of Goddess Nüwa (*Nüwa shi*, 1905), by Haitian duxiaozi.

Tale of Filial Heroes (*Ernü yingxiong zhuan*, 1878), by Wen Kang.

Traces of the Flowery Moon (*Huayue hen*, 1858), by Wei Xiuren.

Tracks of the Snowgoose (*Haitian hongxue ji*, 1899), by Li Boyuan.

Introduction

The Male Consort of the Remarkable Woman

The Regimes of Polygamy and Prostitution

Until the early twentieth century in China, the prominent man was someone who deserved multiple women. This privilege mainly took the form of polygamous marriage and the patronage of prostitutes, two closely linked practices that legitimized the man who consorted with multiple women. The ideal example of such a man handled himself well in both the household and the brothel, and then likewise in the social and political world outside these two realms. For a man to have multiple women, however, was not a simple given, but always had to be justified. The order or lack of it in sexual relations could never be solely in his hands, and he could never assume that his authority was automatically acceptable to his women and other men. Even under the constraints of the polygamous order, women knew how to exert control and create status for themselves, while men on their part had elaborate fantasies about the power of women. Polygamy and prostitution were collective social formations that, in spite of their strict hierarchies, were shot through and through with struggle and interdependence and that addressed fundamental antagonisms of the sexual relation in serious and constructive ways.[1]

The central historical question of this book is how the dominant sexual regime of polygamy met its first stages of paradigmatic change in the nineteenth century, decades before the legal abolition of polygamy in the next century. No single word stands for both polygamy and prostitution, but I let polygamy sometimes stand for both, and I coin polygamist-philanderer to name the prominent man who had a main wife and one or more concubines and who also associated with expensive prostitutes. During the late Qing, China was just entering the scene of global modernity and beginning to define itself as a new nation among nations. Polygamy played a substantial role in this transition, although it has been drastically overlooked because of its marginalization in modern times as a backward and feudal practice. It was, however, a core feature of the master male's identity. It was a repository of cultural essence that at the end of the imperial era faced impend-

1

ing doom, for the decline of dynastic China was also tantamount to the decline of the polygamist-philanderer. It matters little that relatively few men ever had concubines (probably never more than about 10 percent of men could afford to do so) or patronized high-class prostitutes. Polygamy was nevertheless the superior goal toward which the successful man tended, while monogamy was for the rest—except the large numbers of poor men whose prospect was no marriage at all. What the privileged few desired constituted the supreme model by virtue of its prominence through millennia of history and by virtue of the socially productive effects of that prominence. Those effects included the market in women, who were bought and sold as maids, concubines, and prostitutes according to economic and aesthetic standards that determined the hierarchy among them. As it had been for millennia, among the relatively small group of polygamists was always the emperor, who as we see today was buried in the same tomb, sometimes the same chamber, alongside his empress (*hou*), that is, his main wife, and consorts (*fei*), his concubines. Just that one man is enough, I insist, to name polygamy as the dominant sexual regime.

Fictional, historical, and biographical literature projects an image of the masterful polygamist who wins the loyalty and harmonious service of multiple women. My approach to the fantasies of this literature, fiction in particular, is to emphasize not the masterful male, however, but the persistent theme of female agency, which I will examine in terms of a figure I generalize as the "remarkable woman." She defines female agency both within and outside the context of polygamy and prostitution. The temporal focus will be on the nineteenth and early twentieth centuries, which I call the verge of modernity. Female agency is especially clear in an age-old motif that emerges in the late Ming and again in the late Qing: female heroism in times of male failure, weakness, and despair. In dire times like these the man depends on the heroic woman for direction and self-definition, and they become involved in a love affair between just the two of them, which I label with the term "sublime passion." The man in this instance is what I will call the male consort of the remarkable woman, the paradoxical obverse of the master polygamist and his main wife, concubine, or prostitute. The accurate outline of polygamy and prostitution only emerges in subcurrents like this one, in which some form of female agency takes shape, or like the recurring scenario that I will call "passive polygamy," in which the polygamist is a passive and deferential husband whose remarkable women create and manage his polygamy for him. In this instance, the man and his multiple women act as if polygamy is as much for the women's benefit as the man's, if not more so. As if to apologize for and justify the existence of polygamy, passive polygamy is a contradictory compromise between polygamous mastery and the themes of sublime passion and the remarkable woman. It assumes male centrality while paradoxically fantasizing that the woman is not only a willing participant but also an active agent. Passive polygamy permeates Qing fiction and is a fundamental sign of the fact that polygamy was never a simple given but always incorporated behavior that compensated in direct and indirect ways for male privilege and its inequalities.

Numerous recent studies have revised blanket notions about a core set of Chinese phenomena that had previously been vilified as signs of traditional Chinese decadence and degradation, including opium smoking, footbinding, the connoisseurship of courtesans and boy female impersonators, and polygamy and concubinage. As the modern Chinese nation began to take shape, these signs of backwardness were supposed to disappear. In each case, however, we can go back and read them alternatively as signifiers of a type of cultural identity faced with extinction. Each in its own way embodied a precious essence that would soon be lost forever. The opium smoker was the last loose-robed, reclining Chinese in contrast to the tight-fitted, fast-paced Westerner. The peaceful addict was the last contemplator of human history as it hurtled toward industrialized modernity. The bound-footed woman stood for China's purity and sovereignty in an age of turbulence. She was an ideal woman in contrast to the grotesquely masculine Western one.[2] It was likewise with the polygamist-philanderer and his multiple women, who in certain works of late-Qing literature embodied the highest values of romantic love in an empire in crisis. To reexamine these supposedly backward characters is not to promote a kind of antimodernism, but to put them back into a dynamic whole in which they cannot easily be made obsolete or outmoded. The roles of the polygamist-philanderer and the main wife, concubine, and prostitute had a formative effect upon the entire field of sexual relations as China approached the verge of modernity. Whatever was on the verge did not simply disappear afterwards. It is especially revealing to consider how women exercised agency on their own and as partners of men, hence the emphasis on the remarkable woman as a model of feminine subjectivity that applies to both women and men. Agency, however, must be understood in a special sense that comes across in sources overwhelmingly written by men (the contrast with female-authored works will be saved for my conclusion) and that I will begin to discuss after first defining the concept of Chinese polygamy that will apply throughout this book.

Chinese Polygamy

It is necessary to examine the basic terminology of Chinese polygamy and briefly place this social formation within the broader context of marriage in general in China and in the context of polygamy worldwide. The word poly*gyny* (one man, many wives) is more accurate than polygamy (one individual, many spouses), though both imply that the multiple spouses are equal in status, which was not the case in China; I will nevertheless use both terms interchangeably. Concubinage is useful because it takes into account the critical distinction between a wife and a concubine, who could be acquired and expelled far more easily than a wife. The word "philanderer" is also useful because it names the man—in this book in particular, the patron of the elite prostitute—who is not necessarily married to the women he has sex with. Terms for polygyny and concubinage in modern Chinese include *yifu duoqi*, "one husband, many wives," which like polygyny is technically incorrect since the central model in China was to have only one wife, *qi*. Another term is *qiqie zhidu*, the "institution of wife and concubines," which comprehends the strictly lower status of concubines, called *qie* (among numerous other terms).[3] Standard marriage was between one man and woman of roughly the same social status who ideally stayed together until death; polygamy built on top of that by adding concubines. In this book polygamy or polygyny often stand in a broad sense for both marital and nonmarital relations, even including in chapter 3 the man who has sex with boys. The idea of potential polygamist or prepolygamist is also relevant, since adolescent males of elite families were expected to be polygamists as adults, hence the fact that elders supplied the young Jia Baoyu with a maid as a possible sexual partner in the famous eighteenth-century novel *Dream of the Red Chamber* (*Honglou meng*).

Calling polygamous marriage a dominant regime must further address the fact that it was mainly available only to elite and wealthy men, who were a small minority of the total Qing population. Monogamy was the practice of the vast majority of people, while the large surplus of single men, as I have said, meant that marriage of any sort was unavailable to them. Studies of Qing China have revealed a "skewed sex ratio" between men and women by the mid-eighteenth century, which meant that there was a shortage of women available as wives for poor rural men. One solution to this imbalance was polyandry, which Matthew Sommer has argued was more widespread than polygyny. Although it was likewise a minority practice, polyandry occurred in many forms, its two main categories being that in which a husband and wife of poor means arranged for the wife to sleep with other men for income, thus engaging in a form of prostitution, and that in which a poor, invalid husband or a poor husband with no sons contracted with a single outside man who moved into the household, shared the husband's wife, and supplied the family with his labor, income, and offspring. Although population numbers for single men and people engaged in monogamy and polyandry threaten to trivialize the topic of polygamy, the phenomenon of polyandry in fact helps clarify the pyramid-like structure of sexuality in late-Qing China. The key feature of polyandry versus polygyny is their lack of symmetry in that polyandry was not a sort of fair and just rebalancing of the phenomenon of polygyny. Polyandry was a strategy of survival driven by downward mobility and, though widely practiced and accepted, was never an exemplary model. A man did not enhance his masculinity by allowing another man to share his wife, and in the cases Sommer cites, women did not initiate or welcome the second husband. Polyandry grew out of a husband's economic and physical weakness, and to the Qing authorities was an "evil custom" that was strictly illegal and that those engaged in it always sought to hide from official eyes.[4] Even though polygyny often gave rise to moral disapproval, and was met with resistance from women, it was a sign of prestige and was fully sanctioned by law and ritual custom.

The practice of patronizing courtesans was closely linked with polygamy. Men bought concubines from the brothel and associated with courtesans on a long-term basis, treating them like temporary concubines. Courtesans and concubines were similar in status in that normally neither could become a main wife (even if a man's main wife died). Courtesans nevertheless acquired an aura of otherworldliness that distinguished them from the women of the polygamous household, a topic to be discussed in chapter 3. The theme of the male consort of the remarkable woman plays itself out elaborately in important late-Qing works in which the polygamist-philanderer seeks self-definition through his affair with the courtesan-prostitute. I use the words courtesan and prostitute interchangeably, where courtesan connotes the elevated status of the patron and the brothel, while prostitute, the lower-class word, persistently recalls the sexual relation and the financial transactions and calculations that occur between the customer, the seller, and her managers. No one word covers the man who is both polygamist and patron of prostitutes, thus the combined term polygamist-philanderer. Furthermore, polygamists did not necessarily frequent brothels, nor were patrons of courtesans necessarily polygamists. The most important factors joining the two practices of polygamy and patronage of prostitutes were the overlap in social status between concubines and prostitutes and the fact that both were bought and sold in the service of polygamy and prostitution.

I need also to note that my use of the term polygyny is a far cry from the sense used by anthropologists and sociologists who primarily study polygyny in the agricultural or hunting and fishing societies of sub-Saharan Africa, the Islamic world, and elsewhere. They conduct cross-cultural investigations of past and current societies to discover what factors "predict" or go strongly together with polygyny. These factors include such things as the economic value of women, the relative educational level and social rank of both men and women, and their occupations or modes of subsistence.[5] Two broad types appear frequently in this research: polygyny with co-wife autonomy and separate habitations for the man and his wives, and polygyny in which the husband and kin-related wives cohabit. There are numerous other factors and variations. Co-wife autonomy is related to the phenomenon of female participation in subsistence activities, to the point that wives increase the man's wealth or at least do not deplete it, unlike the model of cohabitation in which polygyny is costly to the man, as in the Chinese case.[6]

The polygynists I study roughly correspond to the model of polygynous cohabitation. They are prominent men in the form of prestigious merchants and literati, which vernacular fiction portrays prolifically.[7] According to prescriptive norm, Chinese men should take a concubine only to produce a male heir, thus valuing the woman by paying the appropriate price for her childbearing capacities. But although producing sons is a kind of subsistence activity, polygyny in Ming and Qing sources is in general vastly different both structurally and spiritually from the type of peasant polygyny primarily studied by sociologists and anthropologists. It mainly has to do with a man exercising privilege and prestige and, if possible, enjoying the sexual pleasures of having many women. My use of the term not only leaves peasant polygyny entirely behind, but also bends the conventional anthropological meaning by including the behavior of the man who seeks relationships with prostitutes. My definition, in short, is that a man is a polygynist simply because he is expected and allowed to have multiple sexual partners, regardless of whether he necessarily marries those with whom he has sex.

Female Agency in Polygamy

As for the topic of female agency in polygamy, "agency" as I use it must be divorced from the meaning that implies notions such as "empowerment" or "self-determination." The agency I am talking about takes place within the framework of a forced choice. Simply put, women have no choice but to submit to the order of polygamy. But within that order they exert influence and engage in struggle, while men on their part are not uniformly masterful and lead lives based on elaborate fantasies of female power. Women channel men's decisions and emotions, prop up or defuse men's self-image, and exercise control over selection of concubines and maids. The emphasis on female agency means that the construct of women as objects of male desire, however basic it may be, should not lead to the presumption that women are somehow tricked into the male fantasy as if they have no will of their own or as if the man is somehow purely, knowingly, and consciously in charge. Both men and women are caught in these fantasies, in which they play both subjective and objective roles and which they sometimes reverse, remold, and escape. The social formation of polygamy is ultimately bigger than the individuals involved. My focus is on the reality of this sexual fantasy mainly as transmitted in fictional texts written by men but in a few cases by women, whose characters, plots, motifs, vocabulary, and other thematic elements are my central materials. Even in the case of the biographical and autobiographical sources, whether by men or women, my emphasis is on sexuality as structure of fantasy. Shared by all subjects, the fantasy is something in which the sheer recurrence of patterns and themes, norms and exceptions is of prime importance. These are my numbers and case studies, from which I read the conscious and especially unconscious structure of sexuality in China up to the verge of modernity in the late Qing.

My method for analyzing polygamy as a collective social formation is to contrast what I call the classic polygamous love story with two main counter-narratives that depart from the portrayal of the potent polygamous philanderer. The master story is about a man who has sexual liaisons with a series of prostitutes and good women, most of whom he marries in the end in a grand polygynous marriage. This type of narrative, the classic polygamous love story, began to appear in fictional works in literary language in about the mid-Ming.[8] Of the two counter-narratives, one is that of sublime love in which there is a tortured affair between two people. The other counternarrative is the story of passive polygamy mentioned above. Both are subordinate and secondary to the main, classic narrative, and bow to the central notion that pleasure is primarily defined in terms of the male claim to polygamy. Sublime love resides in the realm defined by the term *qing*, which I translate as sublime passion and which embodies a form of feminine subjectivity that shuns the world of promiscuous male sexual drive. Passive polygamy, as I have said, is a compromise formation that in contradictory fashion combines elements of both master polygamy and the aesthetics of sublime passion. That is, it contin-ues to enforce polygamy while appropriating elements of the *qing* aesthetic such as the gentle, feminized man who never initiates concubinage and around whom remarkable women voluntarily gather.

Later chapters will further describe female agency in polygamy, but suffice for now to say that such agency is also apparent in situations that occur com-pletely outside or at the edge of polygamy in the figure of the remarkable woman. In quintessential form, she is the woman of the late-seventeenth-century Pu Songling's tales of the supernatural, the subject of the next chapter, whose model of female subjectivity will be an analytic tool for the entire book. This woman decides whether and when to have a relationship with the man and is the definer of the relation of love between two individuals, which I roughly label as egalitarian love. Sublime passion can only take place between two people. It is the marginal, the extraordinary, and the heavily idealized, especially in the sense that love between two is by rule sublime and transcendent. As recurrently portrayed, it occurs in missed moments, it is ephemeral, it hardly happens, it doesn't even happen, but it is profound and earthshaking. When it takes place in times of social and political turmoil, it defines lovers who experience the utmost willingness to die for each other and for loyalty to ultimate causes such as the threatened or falling dynasty.

The Psychoanalysis of Polygamy

Let me now engage in a temporarily deeper and theoretical consideration of Chinese polygamy, beginning with the example of the love story between man and prostitute in the last two decades of the Qing empire, the 1890s up to 1911. These stories culminate in a series of novels about prostitutes and their patrons in the flashy and bustling city of Shanghai. Accounts of street-smart Shanghai prostitutes fleecing gullible male patrons appear alongside accounts of anarchist-assassin-prostitutes who kill male leaders and force polygynists to liberate their concubines. What do these stories carry from earlier times as men and women become inhabitants of a new and foreign-run city like Shanghai, in an era flooded with ideas and disciplines from radically foreign sources, all of this taking place in a time of fundamental economic and cultural dislocation? This question is another version of the central topic of this book, how the regime of polygamous sexuality met its first stages of paradigmatic change at the end of the imperial era. The language of the rest of this chapter will be denser than usual, and signals an experimental use of Lacanian psychoanalysis to discuss sexuality in the late Qing. Although I will for the most part use psychoanalytic terms only here and in the conclusion, they will lurk beneath the surface and especially motivate the discussion of feminine subjectivity and the remarkable woman. Readers can, if they prefer, pass over this section and continue with the last three paragraphs of the chapter.[9]

The answer to the above question about what these stories carry from earlier times begins with the polygynist who says that he is the master of all women, but one of whose women is always having an affair with another man—hence the late-Ming novel *Golden Lotus* (*Jin Ping Mei*), whose Pan Jinlian is the proof, as it were, of the uncontainable nature of the woman. This example crystallizes the way this book defines sexual difference in general, which on the female side has to do with the failure of any set of rules or terms to fully contain the woman. This failure in turn indicates her exclusion from the universal rule to which the man must submit in order to qualify as a man among men under the rule of the ultimate and exceptional man, the polygynist emperor. If calling the emperor a polygynist seems to exaggerate a mere aspect of his special status as son of heaven, then my response again is to insist on the centrality of that feature in the entire scheme of sexuality in this society and to insist on its contribution to the understanding of the transition to modernity.

I define sexuality in a particular way that Lacanians refer to as the "radical antagonism between sex and sense."[10] Sex is never a simple case of biological or natural fact, nor is it simply a case of culturally constructed discourse, that is, "sense." There is no sex apart from talking about sex, but sex nevertheless exists in the gaps where talking about it either can't make sense of it or forces it to make sense. Forcing it to make sense means doing things like regulating social roles and sexual boundaries. "Gap" in this use of the word is best understood in terms of the basic notion of subjective gap or split, as in the psychoanalyst Jacques Lacan's notion of the "split subject." This is a notion long in use and frequently defined and discussed, but hardly ever in reference to premodern China. Since it is fundamental to the thinking underlying this book, a brief review is necessary in order to establish its usefulness in this context. To say that the subject is fundamentally split is a way of referring to the impossibility of full and present self-consciousness or self-understanding. In simplest terms, there will always be a gap between what subjects think they know of themselves and what is hidden from them. The subject can only fantasize that "I am what I say I am." The split or divided subject functions in the many ways in which people fail to grasp or coincide with themselves.[11] This situation is often illustrated in terms of the gap between the "I" who speaks and the contents of the statement that is spoken, which in Lacanian terminology is the distinction between the subject of enunciation—the I who speaks—and the subject of the enunciated, that is, the statement. There is the empty I that is the subject of enunciation and there is the self of the statement that is part of concrete reality. Lacan and others use as example the statement of Descartes, "Cogito ergo sum," "I think therefore I am," where in Cartesian terms "I think" designates a pure transcendental point of self-consciousness apart from the real world. But there is in fact no way to say "I think" without attachment to the whole of concrete reality. Such a transcendental "I" is inherently inaccessible, and is only purely possible, never concretely real. The I is a pure void, an empty frame only knowable through the predicates that make up the contents of what the I thinks. I cannot acquire consciousness of myself except through the endless series of predicates and statements that fill out what the I thinks.

Sexuality is the effect upon the sexual subject of the gaps and impasses that define the split subject and that point in general to the failure of the social order as an order of universal inclusion. Sexuality is the "sign of a certain structural faultiness," the effect of which is that it can never "find satisfaction in itself, because it never attains it goal."[12] The inherent faultiness of any social structure refers to the basic impossibility that any system—whether political, economic, religious, or kinship oriented—can shape order in a fully consistent way. No subject can be wholly spoken for by any social symbolic order, though some are always more at home than others. The fantasy of the harmonious polarity of yin and yang is the prime example of such an idealized sense of inclusion in terms of Chinese cosmology. The beauty-scholar romances (*jiaren caizi xiaoshuo*) of the seventeenth century portray this goal-attaining harmony through their fantasized ideal of symmetrical, conjugal love. Man and woman mirror each other in looks and attributes by having, for example, the same character in their names; or the man's father is dead, as is the woman's mother; or they exchange verse with matching rhymes. In what I am calling its most sublime form, however, love in terms of *qing* cannot entrust itself to such harmony. Instead, the central scene of sublime passion is one in which the perfect moment of love is always missed, as in *Dream of the Red Chamber, Precious Mirror of Boy Actresses* (*Pinhua baojian*), or *Traces of the Flowery Moon* (*Huayue hen*). The important point is that love is missed not merely because of external contingencies (the rules of arranged marriage, the pressure of social hierarchy, or bad karma), but because of the inherent nature of sexuality, which also means the inherently divided nature of the subject. The master philanderer is a good example of the split subject who denies that he is so, since he likes to be master of all women, like Ximen Qing in *Golden Lotus*. Although he likes to be master of all women, to repeat what I said above, one of his women is always having an affair with another man. The male consort of the remarkable woman embodies an alternate state of split subjectivity, especially as he identifies himself through the image of the talented woman, his romantic counterpart. Divided between his two cousins, Lin Daiyu and Xue Baochai, the young Jia Baoyu enacts another key scenario exposing the unconscious split that is inherent to polygynous mastery. He cannot marry the woman he loves, to whom he cannot even declare his love, nor can he marry both her and the woman his elders arrange for him to marry—though, as we will see in chapter 2, the idealizing sequels to *Dream of the Red Chamber* have him do so. Instead, he commits social suicide by becoming a monk because of the traumatic split he experiences between the two women.

If the example of the adulterous woman is the sign of the failure of universal, polygynist containment, then I define the man in turn as merely the concept or the thought of the totality of containment. That is, the totality or universe of men is a conceptual reality only. Any attempt to tie concept to reality—as in marrying one man to multiple women—involves the artificial construction of a set of master laws, which in this case amount to the symbolic order of polygamous sexuality. That order is inherently contingent and provisional, even if it held sway for thousands of years in China. It is inherently arbitrary and artificial because any attempt to tie concept to reality runs into the problem of the limitless and ungraspable series of particulars, just as happens in the case of the philandering man's affairs with woman after woman, many but never all of whom he can ultimately contain. Another key notion of manhood as conceptual totality rests on the idea of the exceptional subject who observes the social whole from an external, universal position. Such an exception—the son of heaven, the polygynist, but also the ascetic monk or the misogynist warrior—in turn rests on the idea of an inherent, inaccessible essence that, as it were, magically constitutes the universal male master. In other words, the man is master because of a magical essence that he supposedly harbors that separates him from all others, especially women, but also inferior men (including, for example, the men who must resort to polyandry or who can never marry at all). The universe that he governs, moreover, is one that he gains by either possessing all women or by severing himself from them. The polygynist possesses all women; the ascetic monk and the misogynist warrior sever themselves from all women.

The male master as universal exception is an idea I borrow from Lacanian theory. To be "Lacanian," as I interpret it, is to occupy the position of the analyst, the fourth of his four discourses of subjectivity, which are also crucial to this discussion and are as follows: Master and University (which comprise the masculine pole), Hysteric and Analyst (which comprise the feminine pole). In particular, the analyst is one who, like a Zhuangzian Daoist, engages in the continuous exposure of the arbitrary and self-enclosed nature of the Confucian master's discourse. Lacan points out that in the paradigm-shifting passage from one discourse or social formation to another, the discourse of the analyst always emerges for a brief moment. He is referring to the moments in history in which one master regime gives away to another, during which the inherently arbitrary and contingent nature of any regime is at least briefly revealed. The aim of the analyst is to expose the master-signifier, that is, to make visible the "'produced,' artificial, contingent character" of every master signifier at any time.[13] This moment of transition is especially apparent in the novels of the 1890s that take place in the international city of Shanghai and that feature the savvy prostitute who fleeces the gullible male patron.

As with split subject, many descriptions of the four discourses of subjectivity already exist, but it is necessary to describe them here in their bare minimum. Discourse in this sense is a structure that subsists in every speech act and human relation, and is fundamentally constitutive of the social order. It captures the subject both as speaking being and as object of the desire of others. The best example of the individual as object of the desire of the other is that of the child, who from birth is the object of the desire of parents and larger family, then society as a whole, including educational, religious, and legal and political forces. The position the subject occupies in relation to the desire of the other determines the way he or she experiences himself or herself and the surrounding world. As to Lacan's four discourses of subjectivity, the first is the discourse of the master, which assumes an autonomous and self-identical ego. The master acts as if there were no such thing as split subjectivity. He speaks from the position of a universalizing authority that at its ultimate expects unconditional obedience. His Law is the law because it is so, not because there have to be good reasons for it to be so. His followers—the "crowd"—are the ones who engage in the master's pedagogy, that is, the formulation and teaching of the master's rules.[14] Lacan calls the crowd's discourse the University, which besides the educational system also includes such things as religion and bureaucracy. The analyst illuminates what has been left out or excluded from the Master and University discourses. Contradiction, gaps in meaning, signs of anxiety and slippage, resentment, sense of alienation, and feelings of meaning-lessness—all such things indicate what is left out and excluded.[15] These signs are quintessentially apparent in the discourse of the hysteric. As a core model of the human subject in general, the hysteric is the inherently divided or split subject, the one who is fundamentally unable to grasp herself and to coincide with the way she is supposed to be—that is, the way the master tells her she should be. The hysteric is the protesting subject, the complaining subject, the resentful subject, or the one who feels guilt and shame and who is forever and inexplicably unable to conform and measure up. The hysteric both fails to satisfy the master and fails to be satisfied by the master's demands. She doubts the master but, unless suc-cessful in overthrowing him, remains bound and beholden to the master's rule. Hysteria is a feminine position, especially as found in a character like Lin Daiyu in *Dream of the Red Chamber*. But men also commonly occupy this position, thus the blank male in Pu Songling's tales, Jia Baoyu in *Dream of the Red Chamber,* or the literatus-philanderer in *Traces of the Flowery Moon* of chapter 4 who, during the catastrophe of the Taiping rebellion, dies a loyalist love-death together with the heroic courtesan.

The advantage of Lacanian theory is that it compels us to focus on the domi-nant elements of a discourse, whichever mode may happen to dominate at a given moment, and to distinguish between the senders and receivers of the discourse (that is, the active and passive factors) and between the overt and covert (or latent, unconscious) factors. Any discourse contains repressed and unnamable elements and produces predictable and unpredictable expectations in the receiver. The hys-teric, for example, addresses the master and demands an answer to a basic ques-tion: why do you expect me to be a certain way, and to play a certain role?[16] Psy-choanalysis is interested in the irrational, the paradoxical, the contradictory, the arbitrary nature of signification, and in general the unconscious effects that frame every conscious moment and structure. Psychoanalysis aims to "reduc[e] the priv-ileges of the consciousness," which it "regards . . . as irremediably limited."[17] The disadvantage of psychoanalytic terminology is that it can be heavy and hard going, and if narrowly used, it tends to reduce all phenomena to a single, static level. Another objection to psychoanalytic theory is its basis in modern European cul-ture and the supposed violence of applying it not only to premodern cultures but non-Western ones. To this I reply that "master" orders and "hysterical" reactions to them, as well as "analytical" exposures of the master's arbitrariness occur every-where and in all ages. Nevertheless, terms like these become unwieldy and awk-ward-sounding when used in other social and cultural contexts, and synonyms can easily be found. For this reason, as I have said, I will indicate my indebtedness to psychoanalytic theory mainly in this chapter and my conclusion, and let the ideas that I am now discussing serve as the basic scheme that I will otherwise describe in terms closer to both the Chinese texts and the more widely used language of literary criticism in general.

This book's focus on the role of the master polygynist is thus an example of the underlying influence of Lacanian theory without its being referred to each step of the way. The above statement about manhood as a conceptual totality rests on the basic idea of the masculine exception and upon the notion of the exception as that which constitutes totality from an external, universal position. The occupation of such a position only succeeds by an arbitrary act of exclusion and demarcation. It is normally socially prohibited to refer to the arbitrary nature of that exclusion, under which restraint and deprivation prevail for the rest of the men and women who lack the special quality of the master. Lacan never speaks about the master polygynist, but as a reference to the dominant male figure in the Chinese love story, it is as good a term as the Lacanian ones that stand for the same subject of the master discourse in other social and historical contexts. In a symbolic sense as played out in story after story in Ming and Qing China, both the remarkable woman—whether chaste-heroic or wanton-shrewish—and her male consort, the blank, feminized man, stand for the persistent questioning of the position of the master. The protesting woman in particular is as if to say that if there is one exception, that is, the male master, then his exceptionality should extend to her as well. She is as if to say that there is no one who is not exceptional, a key idea of the Lacanian theory of sexual difference.[18] In other words, the man is a polygynist only because he is an accidentally successful impostor. But since the woman can't effect a change in the social order by, for example, abolishing polygyny (though some female characters in Ming and Qing fiction imagine doing so), she can take the approach of appropriating the man's exceptionality to herself. She does so, for example, by affirming his exceptionality as if she were the one who granted it to him. She chooses his concubines for him. Or, like Pan Jinlian, after discovering Ximen Qing's secret affair with Li Ping'er, she will "allow" it, so to speak, if Ximen Qing promises to tell her about his visits with Li Ping'er and the nature of their sexual acts.[19]

The man, however, may also occupy a feminine position whereby he strongly identifies with the woman. In Ming and Qing literature the woman he identifies with is the remarkable woman, whose counterpart I call the male consort. When the man consorts with the remarkable woman, he especially identifies with her sense of the impossibility of fitting into the social whole. He shares her "hysteria," in other words. It is also the case, however, that the man may twist the fantasy of the remarkable woman in order to enhance his position as polygynist. As we will see in works like *Courtesan Chambers* (*Qinglou meng*) in chapter 5, he fosters and enjoys the woman's weakness and softness, which still translate into her mal-placement in the social order, but it is a mal-placement that contributes to her dependence upon the man. One of the most concrete illustrations of female dependence can be seen in the image of the bound-footed woman. Bound feet must in this case be seen in a special sense as a metaphor of the woman's need for the man. In this sense, the bound foot is the implantation in her body of the need for succor and fulfillment that only the man can deliver.[20] It is as if the heroic man guarantees that the woman needs him by creating a deformity that only he can appreciate and repair. Deformity and deficiency in the woman but not the man are the reasons for which woman after woman needs him—hence the story of the polygamous and philandering man and his easy liaisons with woman after woman, the bevy of whom he gathers into a final marriage in which no woman is jealous and all sex is enjoyable. Polygyny is as much for the benefit of the women as the man. In the scenario of passive polygamy as perfected by the last century of the Qing, it is even the women who arrange and manage the marriage, not the man.

In general, talking about polygyny must take into account the fact that both men and women accepted it. It came to them from the distant past. It had an erotic tradition in the form of the art of the bedchamber. Women could play major and decisive roles in it even though they could hardly enjoy the social privileges of men. Egalitarian love in the form of sublime passion, as I have said, was a concurrent though subordinate trope that at times was appropriated by polygyny, and in general existed as a romantic fantasy with ghostly effects that persistently haunted polygyny. Polygyny also coexisted and drew sustenance from the sexuality of the brothel. When domestic polygyny was lackluster or too restrictive, or when the man was far from home, he went to the brothel, the women of which, he might hope, were the only ones truly to understand him.

The book begins with two chapters dealing with seventeenth- and eighteenth-century precedents of the late-Qing love story, especially concentrating on the notion of *qing* in the sense of sublime passion. The precedents constitute a sort of mythical foundation for the literary manifestations of polygamous sexuality in the last century of the Qing, which takes up the rest of the book. I divide my study into three phases: the late Ming–early Qing (chapter 1), the mid-Qing period just before the Qing decline becomes obvious (chapter 2), and the nineteenth century from the era of the Opium War (1839–1842) to the end of the Qing (chapters 3–9). At the end of the Qing in the third phase I present two contrasting portraits. One is about the love affair of the polygynist-philanderer and his remarkable women as a trope of cultural essence faced with extinction. The other is of polygyny in a reformist mode that is outrageously dismissive of *qing* egalitarianism and that insists that philandering polygyny is still the right path for the modern Chinese man.

If polygyny was the dominant regime of sexuality in China as it entered the global scene of modernity, then the implication is that anything sexual we see even today must be viewed as having descended—however indirectly or unevenly—from the age of legal and faithfully practiced polygyny. Although modernity is defined in multiple ways, in sexual terms China became modern when it abolished bound feet and polygamy. But dominant social structures like these do not simply disappear, or if they disappear, do not do so without leaving a long history of psychic traces. How these traces play out in modern China requires knowing what the models of manhood and womanhood were as China approached the end of its imperial existence, hence the task of this study. The topic of polygamy in China is particularly compelling because it allows us to see male promiscuity in institutionalized form. The primary fact is that the man's promiscuity largely assumed a recognized, legalized, and proceduralized shape. Polygamy and prostitution functioned according to custom and precedent, though many men and women broke the rules. The embedded nature of these sexual practices made it such that in the face of epochal change in the nineteenth century, loyalty to China also included loyalty to polygamy and the patronage of courtesans. Given such history, and in particular given the intricate nature of Chinese polygamy, we should begin to wonder what remolding people had to undergo in order to assume post-polygamous identities. Dismissing polygamy as a relic of the past risks not only dismissing its possible operation in Chinese society today, but also what it can teach societies that were never so blatantly polygamous as to have it assume institutional form.

CHAPTER ONE

Sublime Passion and the Remarkable Woman

The Idealization of Women

The idealization of the woman has a long history in China, but in the late Ming it received a new burst of energy under the influence of the notion of *qing*, "sublime passion." The reason for this translation of *qing* has to do with the idea of *qing* as a leveler of boundaries, where it is beyond man and woman, high and low, subject and other. *Qing* evokes a sense of universality that lifts all burdens of social hierarchy and individual constraint. It is an equalizer, however, that does not extend to the real world outside *qing*'s glowing environs. Real women patterned their behavior after the prescribed models of feminine behavior, and they also suffered the pressures and condemnations directed at them in case of deviation from the norms. Their ordeals are the focus of *qing*-inspired male authors who create scenarios in which the inherent imbalances of social and gender boundaries fleetingly evaporate. This and the next chapter focus on *qing* and the remarkable woman in the late-Ming and early- to mid-Qing literature that is foundational for the late-Qing literature that is my main subject. The key linking this entire body of literature is the notion of a polygynous and philandering outer world surrounding an insulated and gender-fluid domain in which detachment and sensitivity are of supreme value. It is the notion of *qing* that best defines this realm.[1]

In its late-Ming formation *qing* was a concept of radical subjectivity.[2] By this I refer to its potential for signifying the subject's sheer evanescence and boundless connection with other beings and things. The remarkable woman is a kernel figure in capturing the sense of radical evanescence. From the mid-Ming to the end of the Qing, a long line of literary works takes the remarkable woman as the ideal subject in ultimate situations. In a moral sense she is innately superior to the man, as men in those times often actually spoke and wrote.[3] In an ontological sense she is the supreme figure when it comes to portraying the problem of subjection in the symbolic order. She embodies purity and transcendence, qualities that endow her with an ability to act decisively and in utter disregard of social and material constraints. Hence we have the famous courtesan and the chaste gentry woman in numerous works of drama, fiction, biography, and poetry from the Ming to the end of the Qing or the cross-dressing woman in both male and female-authored narratives who engages in social and political action beyond her normative role as bound-footed and sequestered woman and beyond the capacities of her male counterparts. The dramatization of radical subjectivity likewise persists in Ming and Qing literature about feminine young men like Jia Baoyu in the mid-Qing *Dream of the Red Chamber,* who is repulsed by the grossness of dominant masculinity. He is an example of the male consort of the remarkable woman, surrounding both of whom are the wastrel polygynists and philanderers who, to put it in a composite sense, "ride" many women but never love any of them.[4] If the remarkable woman could be reduced to a definition in a few sentences it would be as follows: She embodies a demand to commit utter self-sacrifice and to lift or cast oneself out of one's normative state of self-definition. In this way she evokes an existential condition of pure possibility.

The idealization of the feminine sounds like a static motif. It can be that, but at its passionate extreme it implies a kind of magic transformation best defined as the act of becoming feminine. If we take the example of lovers, then the true sign of *qing* love is shown when the partners at least hypothetically exchange with each other, that is, when they look alike and are both masculine and feminine. However, the more valuable direction of exchange is becoming feminine or subjectivizing oneself in the direction of femininity. The reason for this is that being feminine is more conducive to realizing the subjectivity of the other person, whether one's lover or friend, than being masculine is. In the normative social order, as I said in the introduction, masculinity is by rule the universal standard, the absolute position from which all else is perceived and directed, and perceived in a way that presumes its own exceptionality. By rule the masculine objectifies or instrumentalizes the feminine. In the literature of the Ming and Qing, the only way out of this one-sidedness is for the masculine person to try to know the feminine one from the inside. The understanding masculine figure's motto is thus something like "We are all women."[5] Such a motto crystallizes the egalitarianism that is inherent to the *qing* aesthetic. At the same time, as I note again briefly for now, there is a persistent and concurrent tendency of the polygynous formation to appropriate the subordinate discourse of *qing* egalitarianism. By this I refer to the scenario in which a charming and sensitive polygynist like Jia Baoyu wins the love of a remarkable woman but then does so with one remarkable woman after another, thus creating a kind of egalitarian polygyny, which should be an oxymoron. This is where the term passive polygyny applies, in which it is the women, not the man, who appear to serve as the agents and organizers of the polygynous marriage.

Qing and Its Negative Obverse

Calling *qing* a universal to which anyone could potentially have immediate access evokes the thought of the mid-Ming Wang Yangming and especially his followers of the Taizhou school, including Wang Ji, Wang Gen, and He Xinyin. They are behind a movement whose central theme was the shift from the reliance on external, canonical texts to a focus on the present and the internal, whether that be the innate moral mind or the spontaneity of *qing* enthusiasm. Late-Ming literati such as Li Zhi, Yuan Hongdao, and Yuan Zhongdao, inspired by notions such as "innate knowledge" (*liangzhi*), engaged in an intense campaign against cultured hypocrisy, the most ossified form of which they identified in rote memorization and slavish adherence to classical generic and stylistic models. They found the inborn "child-mind" (*tongxin*) in the unpretentious common folk, who were metaphorical cousins of the remarkable woman, both being figures of an authenticity that leveled the boundaries of standard social hierarchy. Feng Menglong gushed with "*qing* enthusiasm," of which he had been "endowed since youth" (*yu shao fu qingchi*) and which, when he saw it in someone else, caused him to "bow down before them." *Qing* courses through the cosmos; it is "indestructible" (*bumie*). "All phenomena are like scattered coins tied together by the string of *qing*" (*wanwu ru sanqian, yiqing wei xiansuo*). Feng's figure of coins in particular evokes the notion of the thoroughgoing equality and connectivity of all people, joined together like the strings of copper cash carried around by common folk. *Qing* is indiscriminate not only in its evocation of social continuity but in the sense that it is ever present. To restrain it is unnatural. "*Qing* arrives of its own, shapeless, sudden in its stirrings, which one can never predict." Like the wind, it is "always encircling and inextinguishable"; nothing can confine it.[6]

The idealization of *qing* also had its negative obverse in literature like the sixteenth-century novel *Golden Lotus* that focused on the powerful man's unfettered craving for sex with whatever woman he wanted at whatever time and place. Ding Naifei has made the best study to date of what I would call the *qing* obverse, focusing in particular on the obscene antithesis of the chaste remarkable woman, namely, Pan Jinlian, the "wanton woman," or *yinfu*. Both real and fictional figures of such women counter the chaste woman such as the virtuous widow or female "genius." As a woman who can be bought and sold, the unchaste Pan Jinlian is the female bond servant turned concubine (Ding's words). She is someone for whom grasping upward mobility is the only way to obtain a liberating sense of privilege. She can only ever eat off the permanently full plate of her polygynist husband, Ximen Qing. Her strategies exhibit a "parasitic mode of power that arises in regimes masculine, centripetal, and authoritarian." She can never transform the "host body" of the man like Ximen Qing, but she can at least pervert and erode it "from within and underneath."[7]

She is in fact a remarkable woman like the others, especially in her ability to vie with a powerful man like Ximen Qing. In his commentary to the *Golden Lotus,* Zhang Zhupo (1670–1698) views the wanton woman like Pan Jinlian as embodying a power that entraps and ruins the unguarded man. The implication is that if a man properly cultivates himself, he won't succumb to the wanton woman and will be impervious to *se* and *yu,* the terms used in these texts to refer to lust and sexual desire.[8] The invasive power of the wanton woman has an uncanny resemblance to the radical effects of *qing* femininity. As the obverse of the chaste female genius, does not the wanton woman accomplish the same dissolution of the man by making him explode from within, just as Ximen Qing literally explodes when Pan Jinlian gives him an overdose of aphrodisiac? No author that I know makes an explicit connection in this way between wanton woman and chaste female genius, who in general are rigidly separated. The wanton woman never sheds the stigma of baseness that is the rule in Ming and Qing society, even in authors such as Feng Menglong or Cao Xueqin, who unlike Zhang Zhupo generally refuse to vilify the wanton woman. The thread linking the wanton woman and the *qing*-inspired gentry woman like Lin Daiyu is that, whether sublime or base, *qing, se,* and *yu* carry within them the notion of the fundamental impossibility of love and pleasure, which are always missed and failed. *Qing* usually represents the chaste side of this truth, while *se* and *yu* serve duty as the unchaste and prohibited underside. Harmony is possible only as fiction, thus the idealistic beauty-scholar romances that end in perfect union, whether monogamous or polygamous.

The Real Remarkable Woman

Who in all this might be the actual "remarkable" woman who records her own voice in writings that are part of the Ming and Qing historical record? In Chinese terminology of the Ming and Qing, she is called the *cainü,* "talented woman" or "female genius," the *qinüzi,* "extraordinary woman," and the *mingji,* "famous courtesan." The term *nüxia,* "female warrior," can also be included. In terms of real historical figures, she is the poet-courtesan Liu Rushi (ca. 1618–1664); the poet, painter, and traveling scholar-educator Huang Yuanjie (ca. 1620–ca. 1669); the anthologist, writer, and educator Wang Duanshu (1621–ca. 1706); or the "three wives" of Wu Wushan, who wrote commentaries on *Peony Pavilion* (*Mudan ting*), to name a few.[9] She is the educated mother who taught both daughters and sons, including some of the most famous sons, such as Hong Liangji (1746–1809) and Gong Zizhen (1792–1841). *Guixiu,* "talent of the inner chamber," is the common term for the proper example of this type of woman, where proper in particular distinguishes her from the prostitute. In their writings and acts of writing, women like these formed a separate chorus, asserting their own sense of will in regard to love and marriage and emphasizing the strength of their talents alone or as partners with men. Their voice persists throughout the literature of late-imperial China, whether it comes from the woman herself or through the writings of men. The dramatization of the love affair between Du Liniang and Liu Mengmei in *Peony Pavilion* inspired many of these women. Du was a model of a woman who was both educated and sensuous and an exemplar of inner strength and determination. If there is one thing that emerges time and again in the writings of such women, however, it is complaint and resentment against the lot of the woman. The complaints are against things such as sequestration and isolation in the inner chambers, the authority of the mother-in-law, the boredom and incessant work of the inner chambers (child care and other women's work), and the lack of opportunity to do what men do in the political and military world. Some voices sound like women dying away; others are full of self-confident energy. They blame heaven, asking why they can't be recognized for talent and heroism. Why were they born as women? Why must women yield to men? Women writers dream of missions of heroism and vengeance, like Shen Shanbao (1808–1862), who after her father's unjust death wrote a poem at age eleven adopting the persona of a girl avenger who lived in the Later Han. At seventeen she wrote, "I bitterly resent the fact that I am a woman."[10]

A particular female-authored source that I will sometimes cite is the *tanci* rhyme-narrative, also called the plucking rhyme. As Hu Siao-chen writes, in their prefaces and narrative asides the female authors of these works speak of their freedom to write until marriage, after which they can write only during brief intervals of "escape" from women's work.[11] They resume only after the years of child rearing are over. Though men wrote *tanci* as well, the rhyme-narrative was essentially a woman's genre. Authors continued stories from earlier narratives by other authors. Girls and women copied and recopied the texts, passing them on and even including them as heirlooms in their trousseaus. If a woman could not inherit property, she could inherit the rhyme-narrative and all the common experience it represented both in terms of its contents and its passing-along as a written text. It was a form of female entertainment and pastime, and was read and recited in the multigenerational company of women within the household. Virtually every *tanci* author describes heroines who don male dress and enter the man's world of politics and struggle, making female cross-dressing probably the single most recurrent feature of the genre. A critical moment arrives in each narrative when the disguise is discovered. Will the woman return to her life as a good woman; will she remain a man, or hold on to her position in government even as a woman; or will the story abruptly end, as in the case of Chen Duansheng (1751?–1796?), author of *Zaisheng yuan* (*Bonds of Karmic Reincarnation*), who left the question dangling because it was too difficult to resolve? The woman who finally finished the narrative for her in 1821, Liang Desheng, took the cross-dresser Meng Lijun back to the role of good woman, which meant returning to a man who already had two concubines, Liang Desheng herself being married to a man who had several concubines.

The Affair of Sublime Love

Although the remarkable woman has a basis in historical reality, I prefer to think of her in terms of a fantasy figure who is a cross between supernatural woman (including goddess-immortal, fox fairy, and ghost woman) and courtesan-prostitute. This figure persists in the Chinese imaginary from early times. Although prostitute and supernatural woman seem drastically different, as idealized women they have much in common. As the next section will show, the most prominent feature of the affairs that men have with such women is their ethereality and instability. The man must behave in a way so as to deserve the woman's company; she leaves him at will; he does not know where she comes from or where she goes. He often abandons her because he is blind to her true worth. Her chambers are like a fairy realm. Being in her presence is a sublime, rarefied experience, an eternal present in the midst of the transitory effects of the outside political world. Whether or not she grants him her favors, whether he deserves her, and whether he realizes the rarity of the relationship—all these tensions are present in the literature of the man and the remarkable woman.

The remarkable woman, the prostitute in particular, plays an especially enhanced role in times of social upheaval—thus the famous prostitutes of both the late Ming and the late Qing, both real and fictional. In sublime terms, the brothel is a refuge from turmoil and is a source of militant sentiment and libidinal strength. As such, it provides its participants with an ethico-heroic stance that combines tender sentiment with dedication in the face of catastrophe. These scenarios generate a structure of feeling that reverberates from the late Ming to the late Qing and that centers on grand and passionate gestures involving such things as dedication to a lover but also to a cause such as the falling dynasty or, in the late Qing, the culture and nation in decline. The brothel is the central container of these sentimental and dedicated moments, whether in the late-Ming–early-Qing poetry of Liu Rushi, Qian Qianyi, or Wu Weiye, or in late-Qing novels like *Traces of the Flowery Moon* (*Huayue hen*) and *Shanghai Dust* (*Haishang chentian ying*). At the end of the Qing the polygynist consort of the remarkable woman becomes in effect the last imperial polygynist. He is the traditional male who meets his end in the face of epochal social and political dislocation. He finds refuge in what is left of the relationship with the traditional remarkable woman, or he gets fooled and fleeced by the woman who makes the leap to modernity faster than he does, thus the novels about Shanghai prostitutes of the 1890s and early 1900s. To provide the necessary foundation for that late-Qing prostitute, I now go to a basic scenario of *qing* subjectivity as exemplified in the seventeenth-century stories about remarkable women by the author Pu Songling. His portraits of female ghosts, immortals, and warriors capture the key elements of the female subject's transformative effects, beginning with her very entry into the fleshly world and including her effect on her male counterpart, whom I will call the blank male.

Strange Women and Foolish Men in Pu Songling's *Liaozhai zhiyi*

The scenario of the male consort of the remarkable woman is particularly visible in Pu Songling's (1640–1715) collection of supernatural tales, *Liaozhai zhiyi*.[12] The stories repeatedly portray men who are like consorts of strange and unusual women. Liminal, deficient, inhuman, half-human, and superhuman—this list describes the range of ghosts, immortals, swordswomen, and other radiant beauties that suddenly and magically appear to an unexpecting man. It is in particular the ephemeral nature of the woman's attachment to the man that makes the man, not the woman, a consort. He deserves her or he does not, not the other way around. She comes and goes as she wishes. He is weak and blank, even sexless, and thus beholden to her for love and self-definition. What does such an apparent reversal of the norm of male primacy stand for? I would say that Pu Songling is gripped with the problem of subjection in the social order and that his strange women are the better choice than the man when it is a matter of examining subjectivity in crisis. The woman or feminized man represents for him the human subject par excellence, as the hysteric and split subject represented it for Lacan, and to Pu Songling she is better than the man for illustrating subjective integrity.

To make sense of this female figure, let us recall the recent history of the remarkable woman in late-Ming and early-Qing drama and poetry, in which she is a hero who embodies supreme integrity in terms of loyalty to the Ming and greater valor than the male leaders of the late Ming who failed to act heroically in a time of crisis.[13] Compared to writers like Chen Zilong (1608–1664), Wu Weiye (1609–1671), or Qian Qianyi (1582–1664), Pu Songling did not experience the overwhelming magnitude of that trauma, but he still repeatedly featured the remarkable woman in the tales that he wrote and revised between the 1670s and about 1711.[14] As I have mentioned, the woman par excellence in the works of these other writers was the courtesan, who in the late Ming had become a figure in herself of the *qing* romantic ideal. Courtesans were famous independently, but were also known as the other half of famed love couples such as Wu Weiye and

Bian Sai or Chen Zilong and Liu Rushi.[15] A prominent feature of these love affairs, whether fictional or nonfictional, was the overlap of the romantic with the political. When Wu Weiye wrote about his failed affair with the courtesan Bian Sai, he used her voice to narrate her experiences and those of other women during the turmoil of the 1640s. He also confessed his weakness in failing to respond to her marriage proposal to him many years before when he pretended not to understand her intent. The close-up portrait of the man affected and incapacitated by his love for a woman was the topic of poems he wrote about prominent men of the time, including the famous "Ballad of Yuanyuan" about the Ming general Wu Sangui and his concubine Chen Yuanyuan, and "Praising the Buddha at Mount Qingliang," a subtle dramatization of the stages of the supposed love affair between the first Qing emperor and his favorite, Dong E. The cross between public duty and the waywardness of passionate love exemplifies Wu's and other writers' grandiose treatment of *qing* passion.[16]

What in particular is remarkable about the woman in *Liaozhai zhiyi*? In whichever of her various forms—the female immortal, the fox, the ghost, the woman warrior or female knight-errant, or the shrew—the nature of her attachment to the man is tenuous. As touched on above, she is brazen and willfully cool; she comes and goes as she wishes; she may educate the man and help him in times of crisis, if he deserves it (or in some cases to test whether he deserves it); and when necessary she acts strictly, valiantly, and resolutely. The man, on the other hand, does not know where she comes from or how she became the way she is, but can only watch her, gain benefit when possible, and otherwise respect or commemorate her as if doing so will perhaps enable him to join her ranks. Joining her ranks in turn would mean achieving the ability to suspend himself from the network of mundane cause and effect by means of an act of passionate self-negation. The notion of suspension recalls the ontological aspect of the remarkable woman that I have spoken of in regard to the *qing* aesthetic. She is the one upon whom Pu Songling focuses in her moment of entry into the world of sensual affects. In other words, she is the better focus than the man when it is a matter of symbolic and ontological crisis, especially in the case of grand refusal or headlong mission. The importance of *qing* in these cases has to do with that special tonality (grand, headlong) of the way in which the subject takes on her particularly chosen role. Her passage between presence and evanescence, attachment and detachment is ultimately the same in a figural way as her ability to open herself to moments of decisive gesture. In general, Pu Songling's use of the supernatural is closely bound with his superimposition of these various effects, that is, appearance and disappearance, entrance into the material world, and openness to decisive action.

The stature of heroic women and impassioned lovers, as I have said, reaches its greatest heights against the backdrop of the Ming dynastic catastrophe. In

Liaozhai, that event and its after effects frequently appear, but the social scene on the whole is relatively stable and mundane, although still capable of producing "strange" happenings.[17] Through the strange, Pu Songling takes the theme of *qing* with all its political and sentimental ramifications and passes it along as a kind of social and cultural inheritance, ready even in calm times and at the right moment to burst forth with its projections of radical possibility.

Entering the Fleshly World

Ontology in the sense I have been using the word has to do with the problem of the subject's entry into social and symbolic reality. This entry is most palpable in the liminal quality of the woman's appearance to the man. It is her appearance, with all its illusory effects, that captures the quality of liminality and that suggests a sort of primal formation and performance of subjectivity in general.[18] I will begin, however, with the opposite of appearance and display, the woman's withdrawal, a trademark of Pu Songling's and other writers' tales of the strange and supernatural. In a well-known type of story in *Liaozhai zhiyi* and elsewhere, a fox or an immortal warmly favors a man, then after a period announces that their time is up. Her withdrawal takes place against the man's desire to keep the woman for his own good. The crux of their failed relationship is the man's inability to tolerate the woman's mysterious nature and the woman's intolerance for being talked about among others. The recurrence of the woman's withdrawal gives these stories their particular character, as illustrated in "Xianü" (The Swordswoman, 210–216). A mysterious woman offers herself to a man in order to bear him a child in gratitude for his kindness to her and her mother. She presents him with a son, not long after which she shows him the head of her enemy, the murderer of her father. Having accomplished her revenge, she disappears forever.[19]

The swordswoman is the coldest of remarkable women. Warmer and more common is the fox or the immortal. In "Humeng" (Fox Dream, 618–622), the man's fox paramour teaches him how to improve his game of Go. When he later tells his male friends why he has improved, the fox leaves him forever. Stories about foxes who become lovers for only as long as the affair is kept secret have a long history, going back as early as the Six Dynasties. Secrecy is often part of a plot to take advantage of the man, but in Pu Songling's case it is more likely to provide a context for testing him.[20] The fox lover is for the one man only. She must not become what amounts to an appendage that he would display to others or who would become one woman among many, as in a polygynous marriage. In other words, being displayed to others marks a critical transition between the realm of the woman's control and that of the man's.

The divide between man and woman in *Liaozhai* in fact lies here, as played out in story after story. Once the woman crosses the line of entering into a permanent, public relationship, it is as if she is in danger of being placed among the infinity of other women with whom she will be compared and then potentially added or subtracted. The *Liaozhai* stories that focus on the sexual relationship can in general be said to weigh and reweigh this singular point. It is the obsession of Pu Songling to visit and revisit the scene of contact between lovers and either to hover around the unreality of that scene or to opt for the situation of order and stability (that is, family life with children). Whether or not the outcome is favorable to the man arrives only by means of specific conditions establishing the fact that he is deserving of the remarkable woman. In "Ainu" (1191–1196), for example, the ghost woman will not eat or drink and cannot be exposed to anyone else but the man. But he gets drunk one day and cannot resist forcing her to drink with him. She "immediately falls to the floor with blood gushing from her mouth" (1195).[21] In general, to be persuaded to accept her as a ghost or immortal is tantamount to accepting that she is a remarkable woman, something that the man in "Bai Qiulian" (1482–1488) succeeds in doing. Although he disobeys the woman's rule about trying to learn her true identity as a fish spirit, he uses that knowledge to rescue her from a jealous dragon and finally joins her in her homeland, far from his own. As in other stories, instead of being abandoned by the woman, the deserving man abandons his own world to join her in her unearthly one.[22] The constant in these tales is that the special woman belongs in a separate world, one that has ultimate priority over the man's, which is fraught with at least three main dangers: others will find out about the woman and will in some way profane her; the man will already have a wife, or else his family (who cannot see the spirit) will press him to take a wife; or the spirit will have to bear and raise children.[23]

The woman's loss of autonomy upon entering the world of sensual effects is best illustrated in "Jinü" (The Weaving Girl, 1221–1224), in which a beautiful young woman suddenly visits not a young man, but an old woman. The creamy softness of her skin excites the woman, whose lustful thoughts the girl immediately detects and warns against, but the woman cannot resist telling her friends about the girl. Eventually a famous scholar finds out about the girl and bribes the old woman in order to get a look at the girl, who accuses the woman of betrayal, but then acquiesces. In the most stunning scene of the story, she stands behind a curtain through which she sends a luminescent image of herself, spellbinding the young scholar. His only remaining wish, as he reflects to himself, is to see "the lower part of her body." Reading his mind, she exposes her tiny feet in their embroidered slippers. "Go away now," she says; "my energy is spent" (1223).

As he often does, Pu Songling approaches the problem of sensuality, or *se*, with no actual portrayal of a sexual affair. The old woman has lustful thoughts about the girl's body; the young scholar lusts to have her in bed. Instead of describing the scene of fleshly involvement, Pu Songling focuses on the frame that supplies the possibility of that scene. The frame first opens when the female immortal makes her appearance to someone who is seemingly the least likely to be attracted to her, the old woman. The girl realizes that she is guilty of "displaying her sensuous form to others" (*yi seshen shi ren,* 1223). What finally precipitates her departure is the "lewd poem" (*yinci*), as she calls it, that the man writes in which he fantasizes about touching "her phoenix-head slippers" and "turning into a butterfly and hovering by her skirt—one sniff of her fragrance, death would be sweet" (1223). In general, for her to remain detached, she would have to occupy a pure void of being. But she cannot do so because of the impossibility of watching her existence without actually inserting herself into it. The world of cause and effect, mobilized by the old woman, her friends, and the young scholar, nabs the girl by latching onto to the skin surface of her visible affects, which are captured most essentially in the scholar's love lyric. She is summoned to appear to others, an act that would eventually lead to sexual tryst and perhaps concubinage or marriage. The lassitude she expresses after displaying herself captures in miniature the advancing process of subjectivization, that is, of entrance into the world of social and sensual effects. In her case, she withdraws long before the women in numerous other *Liaozhai* stories who go so far as to have babies but finally leave them behind and entrust the exhaustions of motherhood to already living wives or concubines.

The Man Who Learns Sex from the Woman

The sexually aggressive man is central in Ming and Qing erotic fiction, and appears in miniature in "The Weaving Girl." In many other stories, Pu Songling instead emphasizes the man who weakens from his affair with a fox, or who has no sense of self-control, or who even has no knowledge of sex and must learn it from the woman. The gist of these presentations of the sexually weak or inept man is that he must undergo a transformation that only the woman is capable of teaching him. He is the blank male, and it is through his encounter with the strange woman that he learns not only about sex as a physical act but also how to have a relationship with a woman.

The man who learns sex from the woman appears in "Shuchi" (The Bookworm, 1453–1458) in the form of a student who loves the idea that "the beauty in the book will choose *him* as the one" (1453). That the fantasy woman will emerge not only from nowhere but the nowhere of a book crystallizes the scene for which *Liaozhai* is famous, the one in which a beautiful woman mysteriously appears to a suddenly deserving man. In Pu Songling's hands, the other half of this scene is that the wish-fulfilling woman turns into the one who sets the conditions of the wish. In "The Bookworm" the woman emerges from a book, but the man is so obsessed with book learning that he is ignorant of how to have sex (*buzhi wei ren,* 1454). As she tells him, his obsession with reading also keeps him from passing the civil exams. She educates him about both sex and effective book learning, but when she tells him that if he wants her permanently he must get rid of all his books, he refuses. Other people find out about her, including the district magistrate, who demands to see her and, when rebuffed, orders the student's books to be burned. She disappears, leaving a baby boy behind. The student passes the exams, attains office, and avenges himself on the magistrate, whose concubine he then marries.

When women bestow the capacity to have sex upon the man, they bring about his transformation into manhood. In "Xiaocui" (1000–1008), the sixteen-year-old man "still does not know the difference between man and woman" (1000). His transformation occurs when the girl Xiaocui suffocates him in a steaming bath, then revives him, after which he is no longer the foolish (*chi*) boy he was before. In general, the woman first exposes the man to lusty sex, but then through magic or persuasion compels him to restrain himself.[24] Without restraint, he would sicken from excess or try to have sex with one woman after another. Controlling his lust in this way is analogous to leaving him entirely. What all these situations have in common is the arrival at particularly conditioned situations in which the man has no control over setting the conditions. He gains the benefit of a son or a wife only because of a particular way in which he deserves them. He achieves high office, but he must abandon his obsession in order to do so. He achieves sexual capacity, but he must give it to the woman to control. He is united with what he loves, but must live a shorter life.[25] The idea throughout is that the transformation of the man is more important than that of the woman since she is already assumed to be more capable of acts of transformation than he.

The Shrew and the Spineless Man

No study of *Liaozhai* or Ming and Qing fiction in general can ignore the extension of the motif of the remarkable woman into one of its most grotesque forms, the shrew.[26] It is as if Pu Songling takes time out from idealizing the remarkable woman and joins ranks with fellow men in a collective sigh about the intolerable woman. If the blank male can eventually pass the strange woman's tests, in the stories about the shrew the man fails utterly. When the woman who arrives to a man is a shrew, not an immortal, he turns from a blank man into a spineless one.

The shrew is "like an abscess on the bone" (1273), says the Historian of the Strange in his comment at the end of "Yunluo gongzhu" (Princess Yunluo, 1264–1275). "There is a yaksha [female demon] in the bed of every household in the land" (353), he says at the end of "Yecha guo" (Yaksha Kingdom, 348–354). In his commentary following "Ma Jiefu" (721–736), he emphasizes how intractable a problem she is by appending two essays made up of allusions to famous shrews. "Hearing the roar of the angry lion, one can only look helplessly to the sky," for example, refers to a poem by Su Shi about a friend whose wife flew into a rage when the friend held a banquet to which he had invited singing girls. "He urged his oxcart with a deer-tail chowrie, but the stupid animal wouldn't go fast enough!" comes from the account of Wang Dao (A.D. 276–339) of the Eastern Jin, who kept concubines in a secret location. When his wife found out, she rode there herself as Wang raced to get there first, thus the desperate urging of the oxcart. Men observing these women shake their heads in dismay. In the worst cases, the shrew's husband finds himself deserted by his friends, condemned by public opinion, and finally abandoned by his own family, thus "Ma Jiefu" and "Jiangcheng." The commentator Dan Minglun (1795–1853) scolds the man for being spineless and "unmanly" (*wu zhangfu qi*, 725) and decries "the utter disintegration of the social code" (721). Another commentator, Feng Zhenluan, is gleeful when the shrew is punished: "This is the best thing that could happen in the whole world!" (724).[27]

The husband's loss of nerve before the shrew parallels the young scholar's illness and death from sex with the fox or the ghost. The man is like this because, as he says, he is "afraid of the woman's beauty."[28] The woman's jealousy, her abuse of her husband, father-in-law, and in one story the murder of her own son ("Lü Wubing," 1110–1118) align her with the swordswoman and other remarkable women in that they are all women for whom no accommodation exists on earth. They all share the determination to take their defiance to ultimate limits. Severing themselves from familial bonds and staking their entire existence on such severance is what most distinguishes this otherwise varied group of women. Their defiance is even evident in the fantasy flip side to marriage with the shrew, that is, the story of the successful polygynist, which Pu Songling also writes and will be discussed in the next chapter. In these cases the shrew is as if invisibly present in that the man arrives at having more than one wife only if he fulfills certain conditions: he must not be coarse or lustful,[29] and he may even forgo sexual contact with one of the wives;[30] he cannot favor one woman more than another; and the women may form alliances or otherwise exert some form of control over their positions vis-à-vis the man.[31] Such control is akin to that of the woman who terminates the relationship with the man when he fails to live up to her stipulations.

The Edge of the Frame

The woman's display of herself to the man is a centrally defining moment in Pu Songling's stories. The appearance of the woman frames the very condition of subjectivity in general, that is, the subject's entry into and placement within the social-symbolic order. The momentous nature of the woman's entry and exit, of her attachment or detachment, and of her choosing to accept or refuse her mandated role evoke the quality of radical subjectivity that I spoke of above. Having now examined the framing of the remarkable woman, what can we finally say about why these renditions are so important in Pu Songling's work? What is the significance of the remarkable woman insofar as she arrives to us from the perspective of the male subject who produces this image? Another way of asking these questions is, if the emblematic woman in Pu Songling is the one who comes and goes at will, who finally is the emblematic man?

He is the blank, foolish, sexless subject who through his encounter with the woman learns what sex is, that is, what being human is, which is also what the human relationship is with all its attachments, expectations, battles, and separations. Marriage or love only work in *Liaozhai* if the man is in some way foolish and blank, the best example of which occurs when a woman literally bestows sexual capacity upon the man. In general, such a man must act according to the highest standards of *qing*. As advocated in Feng Menglong's *Anatomy of Love*, people of deep passion will brave extremes of self-sacrifice, including death. They will sacrifice sexual contact altogether, like the man who castrates himself to prove his devotion to a courtesan.[32] Dying or severing a part of one's body constitutes ultimate devotion to a sublime goal in complete negation of conventional necessity. Ultimately, *qing* involves an experience of abyssal nothingness, whether sacrificial death, castration, or the severing of one's flesh, all being forms of the dissolution of the self.

In "A Bao" (233–239), a young man with six fingers is betrothed to a haughty girl who rejects him unless he cuts off his sixth finger. When he does so, she tells him to get rid of his "foolishness" (*chi*, 234). Eventually she loves him after she realizes the purity of his love. "Liancheng" (362–367) is about a young woman who falls ill when her parents betroth her to someone other than the man she desires. When a monk says that only "he who is willing to sever his own flesh to heal her will marry her" (363), the betrothed man scoffs at the idea, but not the young poet she loves, who finally marries her and a second woman. In "A Xian" (1380), the husband loves his wife even after learning that she is a rat spirit. In "Ruiyun" (1387–1389), a courtesan loves a talented but poor young scholar. A mysterious patron suddenly leaves a mark on her face that ruins her looks. The young scholar, a man of "deep passion" (*duoqing*, 1389), marries her anyway, after which she regains her original beauty. These stories all feature the gesture of severing a part of one's self, whether one severs actual flesh or endures some form of loss of social face, which may have to do with looks (tolerating the mark on the courtesan's face) or social status (marriage to a rat or someone of low class). The gesture of severance can be defined as a kind of absolute negativity through which one must pass in order to progress in one's identification with *qing*.

In her study of *Liaozhai,* Judith Zeitlin has rightly drawn our attention to Pu Songling's focus on boundaries.[33] Boundaries are frames for "the display of sensuous form," to use the Weaving Girl's words. The crossing of a boundary or even just the approach to its edges evokes the sensation of the nothingness of the frame. Such crossing marks an edge of things and an approach that, so to speak, has just left the nonplace of the frame. Stories like "Weaving Girl" evoke that same edge in their dramatization of the inevitable linkage between the first step into the frame and the concrete effects that follow. What such scenes evoke is the very aspect of "framedness," where the frames in these cases are always ajar or awry, never lining up with each other. The man in "Le Zhong" (1540–1547) has a nonsexual relationship with a prostitute who one day he has rub his thighs. Scars from where he once severed his flesh in order to cure his mother's illness rise up from the surrounding skin (1544). The scars are ugly asexual things aroused in a sexual manner. They are in a place, the thighs, that is next to but not at the conventional place of sex, the genitals. The man has no sex with the sexiest of women, having previously divorced his wife after deciding that sex with her was "filthy" (1540). At the end of "Le Zhong," the Historian of the Strange says that Le Zhong and the prostitute "slept together for thirty years somewhere between *qing* and no *qing.* This is the true face of the Buddha. How can earthly people fathom it?" (1546).[34] Somewhere between *qing* and no *qing* is the ultimate space for the blank male and the strange woman. The man's foolishness, the literal and metaphorical acts of the self-negation of severing the flesh, and the liminal quality of the remarkable woman—all these are signs of the negativity of the frame, and in themselves amount to the empty core of the individual subject.

CHAPTER TWO

Qing Can Be with One and Only One

The Perfect Moment of *Qing* in *Dream of the Red Chamber*

The two common threads between the seventeenth-century Pu Songling and the eighteenth-century Cao Xueqin are the focus on the exquisitely ephemeral nature of *qing*, especially as captured in the perfect moment of love that is fleeting or just missed, and the figure of the young man in his blank state, in particular as incarnated in the version of this man in *Dream of the Red Chamber*, Jia Baoyu. Cao Xueqin's novel stands as the main node of passage between *qing* in its late Ming–early Qing manifestation and the late Qing during the period of Western incursion. Nothing written in the mode of *qing* in the nineteenth century can ignore the powerful effect that *Dream of the Red Chamber* exerted right from its first publication in the 1790s. But whereas Cao Xueqin illustrates *qing* in its radical mode as inherited from authors like Tang Xianzu and Feng Menglong, other authors claim the same *qing* inheritance but deradicalize it by plugging it into situations of polygynous marriage, something that would be impossible in *Dream of the Red Chamber*. Moving into the mid-Qing period and after, this chapter begins with *Dream of the Red Chamber*'s influential presentation of sublime *qing* passion, then details ways in which *qing* becomes deradicalized, first focusing on the mid-Qing novel *An Old Man's Radiant Words* (*Yesou puyan*), which reverses the blank male of Pu Songling and Cao Xueqin by transforming *qing* into radiant masculine energy, and then examining the mid- to late-Qing sequels to *Dream of the Red Chamber*, which in their perfection of the scene of passive polygamy erase the gap between sublime love and its real and practical fulfillment. I finish with a special instance of polygamy in which authors construct a marriage that paradoxically allows the man more than one, but only two, remarkable woman, thus adhering as closely as possible to the *qing* aesthetic without relinquishing the hallowed practice of polygyny.

The mid- or high Qing can be referred to as the "long eighteenth century," to use Susan Mann's words, an age of relative stability and prosperity extending from the 1680s, after the final pacification of Ming loyalist resistance, to the Opium War in 1839 and the massive changes that began to occur around that time.[1] But the word stability is deceiving since Chinese society in this period was in fact characterized by high and open social mobility and intense competition for status and material gain. A novel like *The Scholars* (*Rulin waishi*) crystallizes this atmosphere in its rapid shifts from one character and scenario to another, to paraphrase Shang Wei, where all that the participants experience (the noise and commotion, the rumors and scandals) "inflames desire, enhances vanity, and motivates them in the competition for worldly gain."[2] For women the situation can be broadly characterized as one that "put daughters at special risk" because of the fact that virtually all of them were expected to marry. Girls of lower-class families or families in severe distress were commonly sold as slaves, maids, and concubines, while the daughters of elite families risked that their husbands would take (or already had) concubines. As played out in *Dream of the Red Chamber* and as recorded in biographies by men and in poetry and other writings by women, unhappy marriage was a "constant theme."[3] These same sources, including *tanci* rhyme-narratives by women, reveal that stories of gallant women were especially attractive to young female readers. Female heroism and martyrdom provided them with grand images of strength and independence. In this chapter, the unhappy woman appears alongside the blank male in *Dream of the Red Chamber*, while strong and happy women marry successful polygynists in *An Old Man's Radiant Words* and the sequels to *Dream of the Red Chamber*. The stories of two-wife polygyny that the chapter ends with do away with the unhappy woman, keep the blank man, and match him with two remarkable women who agree to rise above jealousy.

The *Dream of the Red Chamber* begins with the famous statement by the male narrator about how all the "remarkable girls" are "vastly superior to me" (1.1).[4] Like Pu Songling, Cao Xueqin chooses never to portray such women in the mode of the erotic and polygynous romances that are legion since at least the mid-Ming, whose main male character is the successful libertine who "rides" many women without becoming attached to any one. Versions of that man appear in *Dream of the Red Chamber* in the form of Jia Lian, Xue Pan, and Jia She, all of whom are unworthy of remarkable women. Thus when the elder Jia She exercises his patriarchal authority to ask for the young maid Yuanyang as his concubine, he is rebuffed both by Yuanyang herself, who would ultimately commit suicide rather than comply, and by the matriarch, Grandmother Jia, whose withering criticism of Jia She puts an end to his request. In general, sex in *Dream of the Red Chamber* is reduced to an act of clowning, as in Jia Lian's tryst with Duo Guniang, whose name connotes the "great number" of men she sleeps with. The description is as minimal as found in Pu Songling: "they loosened their clothing and set right to it" (21.295–296). The scene of Jia Baoyu's sex in a dream with the goddess Keqing, on the other hand, harks to the high erotic tradition in its dense and sensuous but nongraphic imagery, culled from some of the most famous sexual affairs in Chinese history. The density and allusiveness of the scene provide it with the quality of suffusion that makes the sex in this instance a case of *qing:* not quite attainable and inherently insubstantial.

Thus the perfect moment of *qing* between lovers in *Dream of the Red Chamber* is the one in which they cannot say what they wish to say. The narrator at one point even addresses the reader to say: "It looks as though the two are of one heart, but they have so many misgivings that they always end up arguing" (29.414). Then they are suddenly enlightened when they hear Grandmother Jia utter the words of the famous proverb: "love never comes without rancor and bitterness" (*bushi yuanjia buju tou,* 29.417). The commentator in the Gengchen edition writes: "She hereby enunciates the main theme of the entire book!"[5] Later they have a thousand things to say but can only "gaze mutely at one another" (*zhengzhengde wangzhe,* 32.447). When Baoyu finally musters himself to articulate his feelings, he is so confused that he blurts them out to Xiren instead of Daiyu, who has just hurried off.[6]

In scenes like these, it takes the blank male like Baoyu to constitute the male half of the relationship between just two lovers. Blankness in Pu Songling and other authors means such things as "foolishness" (*chi*), lack of blatant lustfulness, feminine features, and willingness to go to extremes of self-sacrifice. In *Dream of the Red Chamber,* it includes these but also reaches the level of what would qualify the man as a wastrel—hence Baoyu's appearance in his father's eyes as being "dull and listless," with "sullenness and secret depravity written all over his face" (*weiwei ruirui, yituan siyu choumen qise,* 33.452).[7] He fails to live up to the classic model of masculinity in the figure of the *dazhangfu,* the "great man," who as master of himself and others is characterized in Jia Zheng's words as "expansive and full of lively energy" (*kangkai huisa tantu,* 33.452). In light of the *qing* aesthetic, however, Baoyu's supposed wastrel qualities are a sign of a kind of primordial virtue that he shares with the young women he worships as superior beings. Perhaps it looks as though he sees in them something that he lacks that, presumably, could fulfill him if he possessed it—hence his "foolish obsession" (*chiqing*) with the daily activities of the girls in the garden, that is, their hair combings, ablutions, wakings, sleepings, hurt feelings, illnesses, and poetizings. The girls ideally constitute a kind of collective set of Women, with no one more individualized than the other, and ultimately no one—including Baoyu—more male or female than the other. In other words, as many have pointed out, the ideal state of fulfillment in the garden is defined by the dissolution of the normative boundaries that outside the garden assign them the roles prescribed by the social order of marriage for women and career for men.[8]

But the joyous life of the garden also carries a voidlike undercurrent that keeps Baoyu from ever being satisfied. His blankness and failure as a full masculine self may be something for which he compensates by seeking the company of idealized Women, but it is also a deficiency that he ultimately shares with them, above all with Daiyu, the person who in this light is no longer simply an idealized Woman. Baoyu and Daiyu are in other words two versions of the same subject defined by a fundamental flaw or deficiency that they always unclearly realize they hold in common, thus their love for each other in spite of the fact that they can never utter or fulfill it. In the terms of the mythic beginning of the book, love is a debt that can be repaid only with tears, which is to say that it can never be repaid. To put this message about love on such a mythic level is precisely to make of it something primordial that is fundamentally at odds with the inertia of the normative social order. It is precisely such an untenable position that evokes the aura of sublime *qing* passion.

Qing's Transformation into Radiant Masculine Energy

Dream of the Red Chamber is exceptional in its rendition of the *qing* aesthetic because of its emphasis on the "dull and listless" (*weiwei ruirui*) hero who refuses to become "expansive and full of lively energy" (*kangkai huisa tantu*). Jia Baoyu is the most celebrated listless male in all of Qing fiction, a model for romantic heroes up to the end of the dynasty and after. As if he produces his own opposite, a radiant counterpart appears at about the same time—though probably not by direct textual influence—who undoes the radically feminizing aspects of the *qing*-inspired male. No longer defined by fundamental flaw, Wen Suchen of *An Old Man's Radiant Words* would never consume himself in love with one and only one woman. Love no longer causes lovers to quarrel and misunderstand each other. The female voice is still strong as both vehicle of moral authority and a force motivating the male subject. But man and woman are now united in transparent, well-run households that embody the essence of the values of high culture whose invigorating effects extend beyond the household to society at large, even to realms outside the core of civilized China. *Qing* thus turns into radiant masculine energy.

An Old Man's Radiant Words, by Xia Jingqu (1705–1787), is of about the same mid-Qing era as *Dream of the Red Chamber,* although it was not well known until the 1880s.[9] It merges two types of hero into one, the "brave and righteous" (*xia*) hero on the one hand, and the handsome, talented scholar on the other. The result is to deradicalize *qing* by turning it into a charismatic masculine energy scrupulously observant of Confucian orthodoxy. It is through this convergence that *qing* undergoes its deradicalization.[10] A key term in defining the new inflection of *qing* is *ernü yingxiong,* which can be translated as "childlike hero," where *ernü* in effect displaces *qing,* although the word *qing* is still often employed. I will call it the *ernü* kind of *qing.* In this new blend the author of *Radiant Words* envisions a man who is both a confident and valiant hero but also full of "deep feeling" (*duoqing*). The *ernü* kind of *qing* is no longer liminal and unfulfillable. Instead, *ernü* indicates pure and innately correct love on the part of valiant men and women. Unlike Baoyu and the remarkable women of the garden, the characters of *Radiant Words* take their childlike purity into adulthood, which consists of healthy polygyny and successful participation in the management of family and empire.

The *qing* hero in *Radiant Words* is the hardly fallible Confucian superman Wen Suchen. Confucian superman should be a contradiction in terms given the Cheng-Zhu orthodoxy that the novel professes.[11] No mortal and nonimperial self should act like Wen Suchen in outdoing the emperor and his Confucian ministers and generals. His sagely mother's periodic rebukes are as far as the novel goes to signal his excess. She is a self-proclaimed representative of Cheng-Zhu orthodoxy, but she only succeeds in rendering Suchen temporarily abject. As Martin Huang puts it, Suchen is a kind of Wang Yangming activist in Cheng-Zhu disguise. The novel makes no mention of Wang Yangming and vociferously denounces the earlier representative of Wang's brand of Confucianism, Lu Xiangshan, but nevertheless models Suchen's life on Wang's in numerous ways. In general, even though Suchen repudiates decadent late-Ming culture, his larger-than-life self harks back to the same one that populated the mid- to late-Ming imaginary. He does so by reducing the emperor to a virtual token, becoming China's "de facto ruler" as he battles sexual deviants, especially lecherous Buddhist and Daoist monks and wastrel polygynists, their wanton concubines, snake monsters, evil eunuchs, and traitorous members of the imperial court.[12]

Suchen's female cohort undergoes a parallel transformation. The remarkable woman now takes shape in plural form first in Suchen's sagely mother and then in his numerous wives with their various fields of expert knowledge. The wives are said to be his *zhiji,* "soul mates," one of the chief terms in late-Ming literature for designating *qing*-inspired lovers. Their plurality, however, renders them distinctly lower than Suchen and his mother, and none becomes Suchen's exclusive *qing* companion. Filial piety takes precedence over loyalty to a lover. The key to sexual harmony lies in Wen Suchen's definition of sexual pleasure, the model for which is the method of intercourse once a month according to the woman's menstrual cycle. As Suchen states, the pleasure of sexual love lasts up to the commencement of "congress," a defining edge beyond which pleasure self-destructs.[13] The important point in all this is that the *ernü* kind of *qing* acknowledges the same void celebrated in *Liaozhai zhiyi* and *Dream of the Red Chamber,* that is, the void of pleasure that dissipates or that is impossible to perfect. But the characters in *Radiant Words* do not succumb to that void. Instead, what is elsewhere void is now called dissipation, which is something that the correct individual can simply bypass.

The energy of the *ernü* kind of *qing* takes its primary form in the therapeutic yang strength of Wen Suchen's body. Hardly a strongman in the tradition of *Romance of the Three Kingdoms* (*Sanguo yanyi*) or *Water Margin* (*Shuihu zhuan*), he is strong simply because of the radiance of his yang energy, which he frequently uses to cure physical and sexual deficiencies in others.[14] The wavelike effect of Wen Suchen's energy even operates at the level of China as a whole, vanquishing all forms of yin heterodoxy, Buddhism in particular, and bringing about the Confucian conversion of Europe through the efforts of one of his friends. China becomes a great *ernü yingxiong*, spreading its yang energy within and without and taking in both male and female allies. Although yin is the primary defining characteristic of evil in the novel, men, not women, are the main villains. Shrews and wanton women, prominent scourges in novels such as *Golden Lotus* and *Tales of Marriage Destinies* (*Xingshi yinyuan zhuan*) are absent, replaced instead by heroic women who besides Suchen's mother and co-wives also take the form of women warriors, armies of women, and spectacularly skilled female acrobats. Strongwomen are constants in military romances of the same period as well as later novels sharing the *ernü-yingxiong* theme, such as *Routing the Brigands* (*Dangkou zhi*), *Tale of Filial Heroes* (*Ernü yingxiong zhuan*), and the female-authored rhyme-narratives throughout the Qing. A summary distinction between *Radiant Words* and novels such as *Dream of the Red Chamber* and *Scholars* is that if, in Shang Wei's words, the latter two are engaged in a "constant vigil against assuming the voice of narrative authority," *Radiant Words* is instead determined to embody that voice, constantly vigilant against decadent detractors.[15]

Female talent and authority still draw all these works together—*Dream of the Red Chamber, Radiant Words, Routing the Brigands,* and *Tale of Filial Heroes*—and ally them with writings by and about women throughout the Qing. The women in *Dream of the Red Chamber* who write better poetry than Jia Baoyu, who out-debate him, and who deliver the scathing criticism of Baoyu's male elders Jia Zheng, Jia She, and Jia Lian distantly echo the talented wives and matriarchal sage of *Radiant Words*. All represent remarkable women whose talents rival or excel men's. In the literature by and about them, they educate their daughters and sons and in general serve as models of female creative and intellectual self-confidence. When they educate their sons, they do so in the absence of fathers who are dead or away from home. They represent the "civilizing process" of China as a whole, directly participating in what Susan Mann calls a "familistic moralism" through both their management of households and their role as learned moral instructors and confidants. In general, such a woman thrives best on her own or with a comparably reliable husband. She is ineffective if faced with a wastrel, as the example of Xue Pan and his mother and sister shows in *Dream of the Red Chamber*. Xue Pan's mother is a failed matriarch who might elsewhere have succeeded in exerting her moral authority, while Baochai is an example of the educated sister on whose superior wisdom a brother should have relied, but in this case failed to.[16] In contrast, Daiyu is the chaste female genius who writes melancholic poetry, like the spurned courtesan or the mistreated concubine. She will not become the wife or mother who speaks confidently and with moral authority (except in the sequels to be discussed momentarily). The confident female paragon such as Baochai lectures men such as Jia Baoyu, who in this light is a genteel version of the outright wastrel Xue Pan. In short, female moral authority does not ally itself with marginalized men such as Baoyu, whose female counterpart is instead the frail and melancholic poet who like him is crushed by the civilizing process.

Nostalgia for *Dream of the Red Chamber*

Starting with this section, let us now move to the question of how the deradicalization of *qing* subjectivity fares in literature of the last century of the Qing.[17] The role of historical reality, especially from the Daoguang period on (1821–1850), assumes major importance as the trope of the male consort of the remarkable woman gets taken up in what can retrospectively be called the fantasy of cultural destiny at the end of the Qing. Like the famous courtesans and literati at the end of the Ming, lovers become symbols of high-cultural sensibility in times of social and political crisis. They assume these roles as they become enveloped in large-scale events such as the catastrophe of the Taiping Rebellion and the social and economic suffering resulting from imperial weakness and foreign incursion. I approach the historical reality of late-Qing China, however, by first looking at a group of works that luxuriously insulate themselves from harsh reality by cloaking themselves in nostalgia for *Dream of the Red Chamber*. Together they recall what was just demonstrated in *Radiant Words* in its foregrounding of the achievement of social order through healthy polygyny. They also provide the first extended examples of passive polygamy, the situation in which women helpfully arrange and manage the man's polygamy.

    Radiant Words's three main accomplishments can be summed up as rejecting the notion of the unattainable nature of *qing*, desentimentalizing the talented woman, and energizing the polygynous male protagonist, which amounts to rejecting the blank male of *Liaozhai* and *Dream of the Red Chamber*. The same restorative trend occurs in the series of sequels to *Dream of the Red Chamber* written between about 1796 and 1877. The difference between these and *Radiant Words* is their avowed loyalty to the memory of *Dream of the Red Chamber*, about which the author of *Radiant Words* shows no awareness. The sequels do everything that

I have just said *Radiant Words* does, but in turn show no awareness of *Radiant Words*. If we take *Radiant Words* and the sequels as making an unconsciously collective statement, then it is that a worthy man must be a polygynist in order to ensure domestic and social order. As the sequels demonstrate, Baoyu must marry more than one of his cousins, maids, and other women in order to resolve the love crises of *Dream of the Red Chamber*. Given the sequels' loyalty to the original novel, such a resolution still requires subscription to the *qing* aesthetic. The sequels, however, drastically soften that notion by constructing pragmatic solutions to problems that were unresolvable in *Dream of the Red Chamber*. The result is that men and women stay whole and do not evanesce, or if they do so, only in vestigial and reductively sublime ways.

The sequels collectively evoke nostalgia for the good times of the original novel. Let us conceive of nostalgia in this case as a psychic mode that reproduces for the sequel writer and reader the perspective of lost innocence. Readers identify with the masterpiece's original world in a way that excludes the intrusion of discordant, ironic distance. Authors desublimate the "mind-lust" of the original Jia Baoyu. They eliminate the unbridgeable gaps between male and female, adult and child, earthly sorrow and heavenly bliss, or life and death, and in doing so render these pairs transparent to each other, with the boundaries between them made permeable and easily traversable. The readers thus enter an eternal mythic present. If *Dream of the Red Chamber* was likewise nostalgic in its celebration of the idyllic premarital life in the Grand Prospect Garden, it nevertheless undermined that world by introducing dystopic and traumatic elements throughout. In the sequels, on the other hand, nothing too drastic happens, and whatever went wrong in the original novel is now corrected, mainly in the form of the Jia household's regained prosperity. The sequels, in short, crave safety and stability, and dread an overdose of the realities of adulthood.[18]

Three main strategies characterize the way in which the sequels sustain their nostalgia: (1) the healthy improvement of Baoyu, (2) the vindication of Daiyu, and, most important, (3) the resolution and simplification of their complex love affair, which the majority of sequels accomplish by having Baoyu become polygynous. The theme of female talent is paramount in all sequels, particularly in the figure of the educated gentry woman, who we know was a common reader and lover of *Dream of the Red Chamber* in those times and who in Gu Taiqing, the author of *Honglou meng ying* (*In the Shadow of the Dream of the Red Chamber*), became the first known woman to write a vernacular novel.[19] Female readership possibly compelled some of the authors to write with a mixed-gender reading audience in mind, though it did not impede them from turning Baoyu into a polygynist. With one exception, he is a polygynist in all the sequels I discuss, Gu Taiqing's included.[20] As nineteenth-century *tanci* rhyme-narratives by women also demonstrate, female authorship does not preclude the portrayal of trouble-free polygyny. This fact leads us to the conclusion that, if each sequel is in its own way a correction of the original novel, then having Baoyu be a virtuous polygynist is inherent to this correction, and resolving the contradictions between polygyny and the *qing* aesthetic is one of the main practical tasks of these works.

In defining what constitutes a sequel to *Dream of the Red Chamber*, I confine myself to a dozen that were republished by Beijing University Press in the 1980s and 1990s. The earliest of these—and the earliest of all sequels—is *Hou Honglou meng* (*The Later Dream of the Red Chamber*), which was completed no later than 1796, while the latest is *Honglou meng ying*, which appeared in 1877 but was written in the years before and after 1861, the date of a preface referring to its incomplete form.[21] All claim to be direct continuations of *Dream of the Red Chamber*, whether by using the same characters or by combining original characters, families, and settings with newly created take-offs. They continue the original work from either chapter 97 (the death of Daiyu) or the very last chapter (120). The first nine were published in fairly close succession up to 1824, after which three more appeared by 1877. A gap in the production of new sequels ensued, with more finally appearing in the early 1900s and continuing up to the present, hence my focus on the particular group between the 1790s and 1870s.[22]

The Improvement of Baoyu, the Deserving Polygynist

The sequels improve upon Baoyu's original character by having him return happily and healthily to his family either as himself or in another incarnation. He no longer lacks the will to pursue study and career; he is no longer prone to decadent activities like reading racy books or associating with actors;[23] he is no longer "clinging" (*zhanzhi; Honglou yuanmeng*, 3.16); and he will no longer "drown himself in women's makeup rouge" (*ni yu zhifen; Honglou huanmeng*, 2.21). The majority of sequels deemphasize passion and sexual love and have characters engage in nonromantic pursuits. Baochai is a general who participates in the defeat of pirates; Daiyu helps Baoyu quell bandits; the men and women devote hours to leisure, especially poetry writing; they practice philanthropy; or the focus is on Baoyu studying for the exams.[24] *Honglou fumeng* (*Return to Dream of the Red Chamber*, the longest sequel, at one hundred chapters and almost one million characters) goes so far as to create what amounts to a form of male chastity as a counterpart to female chastity. Its preface, written in 1799 by Chen Shiwen, the younger sister of the author, Chen Shaohai, states that the book is devoid of lewd contents and thus appropriate for both men and women (3–4). Even though Baoyu now has twelve wives, he is fair to all, harboring no favorites. Reborn as Mengyu, he is all "sentiment" and no "lust" (that is, all *qing* and no *se*), as the narrator describes in a stunning take-off on the motif of gender fluidity, such that when he consorts with his wives and maids, "he is not even aware that he is male and they are female. As far as he is concerned, someone else's body is mine, and mine is someone else's. . . . Even if one of the women is sponging herself or taking a bath, he comes and goes as he pleases and no one minds" (26.287).[25] In this carefully established atmosphere of chaste intimacy, Baoyu hugs one woman, helps another put on her shoe (19.213), becomes mesmerized as he watches the group of them (20.223), and licks the rouge off someone's lips (28.309–310). The author takes gender fluidity to the extreme of gender-oneness and transparency, erasing the difference between male and female and thereby removing the tensions inherent in the relationships in the original novel. He thus makes polygyny appear natural and unproblematic, devoid of jealousy because the man is supposedly no longer a man, and therefore the women supposedly have no more reason to be jealous.

The method of two sequels, *Qilou chongmeng* (*Revisiting the Silken Chambers*) and *Honglou huanmeng* (*The Illusion of the Dream of the Red Chamber*; and to a certain extent *Xu Honglou meng*), on the other hand, is to eroticize the interactions between Baoyu and his wives. They emphasize sexual love that is robust and problem free, with no one engaging in *qing* exclusivity. In both, Baoyu resembles the sexually active polygamist of Ming and Qing erotic novels who enjoys cozy and harmonious relations with all his wives.[26] He is a correction of both Ximen Qing the profligate, who let women destroy him, and the original Baoyu who, by implication, failed to be sexually valiant when by implication he should have been. In *Qilou chongmeng*, Baoyu's original precociousness inflates to the point that he is both a civil and martial *zhuangyuan* (first in the imperial examinations) by age ten, at which point he accomplishes military feats with the aid of some of his future wives. He has five wives by age sixteen (43), including Daiyu (now reborn as Shunhua), preceding which he has sexual relations with numerous young women except Daiyu. Before marriage, he learns the trick of having sex with prepubescent girls, especially maids, so that none will get pregnant. He learns erotic arts from a nineteen-year-old female acrobat, after which he practices the arts with a new group of twenty-four maids, of whom he takes four each night (35). Both sequels attempt to achieve the difficult if not impossible goal of a type of pornographic art that tries to balance between the genteel love story and the explicit description of sex. In general in Ming and Qing fiction, the rule is that the more explicit the description, the more grotesque the detail and the less sublime the affair. In *Dream of the Red Chamber*, Baoyu's sniffing Daiyu's sleeves, threatening to tickle her, and otherwise trying to avoid hurting her feelings or making her angry were the rarefied nonversions of actually having sex with her. These two sequels instead insist that the rarefied can be made concrete in the form of uncomplicated sexual relationships that are supposedly as sublime as the original not-quite-sexual ones.

The Vindication of Daiyu, the Female Manager of Polygyny

Most sequels vindicate Daiyu, in general replacing the sentimental and melancholy woman with one who represents the voice of strong and familistic moral authority. In seven cases she becomes the primary wife of the polygamous family in which she is superior in rank to Baochai and other wives.[27] She reemerges fuller in flesh and happier in temperament, "completely abandoning her former pettiness and her tendency to dark melancholy" (*Honglou huanmeng*, 3.31). She draws a clean slate, saying, "I should stop making cutting remarks" (*wo bugai yuyan jianli*, 4.53). A key gesture of the female management of polygyny occurs when she arranges the addition of concubines. In *Hou Honglou meng*, for example, she requests that her parents-in-law add Baochai's maid Ying'er as concubine, doing so not because Baoyu had any prior dalliance with her, as it is said, but to parallel the fact that Daiyu's maid, Zijuan, is also about to become Baoyu's concubine. In this way, says Daiyu, "everyone works closely together" (*dajia bangzhe ban shi*, 19.251). Like other main wives of fictional polygamies, she then calls a household meeting at which she announces strict regulations, including rules against luxury. For she is Baoyu's number one "soul mate" *zhiji* (19.256), which, instead of meaning that she is his sole partner in love, means that she is the one who best understands his refined temperament.[28]

In general, the combination of unjealous deference with a sort of female directorship undoes the portrait of Baoyu and Daiyu as lovers of *qing* passion, though most sequels still retain traces of that image. In *Honglou huanmeng*, for example, Daiyu pointedly states that their former difficulties arose because of the "selfishness of their love" (*sixin aimu*, 4.52). Now they are openly in love, but they also share themselves with Baochai and other wives. *Honglou huanmeng* is the most fine-tuned of all sequels in its painstaking attention to the question of how Baoyu will divide himself between his wives. Daiyu designs an arrangement in which he gives her his entire "innate, original fool's heart" (*xiantian benxing chizi zhi xin*), after which he should divide his "external worldly heart" (*houtian de xin*) into ten parts, shared among five others, including Baochai, who gets two-tenths (4.53).[29] But she then urges him to return to Baochai's apartments, for "he must be fair in every regard" (*yiqie dou yao gongping*). He must not abandon Baochai, and, moreover, he must tell her everything that Daiyu and he have discussed so that Baochai will not think that Daiyu is trying to "monopolize" him for herself (*longluo*). Her ultimate goal is for "the three of them to be of one heart" (*sanren tongxin*, 4.54), which is borne out in the eventual routine according to which Baoyu, Daiyu, and Baochai sleep together in the same bed each night. When they finally achieve this routine, the question of fairness is dropped, as if resolved and in no more need of attention.

Passive Polygamy and the Resolution of the Love Affair between Baoyu and Daiyu

The deliberations about the ranking of wives in some of the sequels demonstrate the notoriously sensitive nature of ranking, but the truly sensitive issue is the relationship between just two people, that is, Baoyu and Daiyu. The original *Dream of the Red Chamber* appealed to readers precisely because Baoyu and Daiyu's love was so deep but also so deeply bound to fail. The sequels in general cannot support such failure, hence their avoidance of the portrayal of tortured love in this or any couple. The scenario of passive polygamy is their key method of resolution, which *Qilou chongmeng* and *Honglou huanmeng* illustrate in their eroticization of the relation between Baoyu and his wives. *Qilou chongmeng* engages in a brazen parody of Baoyu's precociousness, making women the glad recipients of his sexual mastery, while *Honglou huanmeng* focuses on female agency both in managing polygyny and in enjoying sexual love. Both are instrumental in identifying the features of passive polygamy that apply in novels up to the end of the Qing.

Qilou chongmeng is a farcical tour de force in its untrammeled exaggeration of Baoyu's precociousness and attractiveness to women. It grants him the knavish capacity to turn all women into loyal and gratified followers. If empathy means something like putting oneself inside someone else, then *Qilou chongmeng* takes this original characteristic of Baoyu and engages in a relentless series of scenes in which Baoyu demonstrates his mastery of female bodily and especially sexual functions. As soon as Baoyu is about to be reborn as Baochai's son, he expresses delight at the opportunity to "return to familiar territory" (1.3). As a child, he displays precocious lust when he peeks at a naked girl (6.35), plays intimately with girls in bed (11.66, 13.91) or while bathing (20.130, 41.265–266), teaches a girl how to kiss (15.96), or has girls look at animals copulating (17.109). He loves to demonstrate concern for women during illness or menstruation, in one case delightedly inspecting a young woman having her first menstruation and explaining it to her (20.131). When a young female cousin is ill, he immediately knows she needs to sit on the chamber pot and helps her do so (9.53–54).[30] The ultimate effect of this farcical repetition is the opposite of *Honglou fumeng*, which hyperrarefies male and female sexual difference in order to erase the rawness of actual sexual contact. *Qilou chongmeng*, on the other hand, hypernormalizes sexual promiscuity, turning the young male into the masterful and benevolent leader of women who automatically follow his lead. The effect in both novels is to collapse the distance between female and male, doing away with the scene in the original novel in which Baoyu empathized with women and gained their sympathy but remained a fundamental outsider. *Qilou chongmeng* makes him a perverse insider who stages and manipulates the woman's agency by making himself indispensable to her and therefore becoming her master.[31]

A contrasting attempt at seamless harmony occurs in *Honglou huanmeng*'s construction of a practical, forthright, but also sexy female agency. In playing the role of manager of the polygamous household, Daiyu openly manifests her love for both Baoyu and his other wives. She tells Baoyu how she enjoys sex with him, and she engages in erotic play with Baochai and Qingwen.[32] Polygyny thus incorporates exuberant sexuality among the wives, including female bisexuality. In general, men and women have overcome their former blockages and now manage sexual and romantic relations in practical and problem-free ways. When two characters fall in love but can't communicate their feelings to each other or anyone else, Baochai steps in to join the two. She compels the woman to admit her feelings by directly asking her, "Now, do you or don't you love him?" to which the woman answers, "I love him" (*Ni ke ai ta?. . . . Wo ai ta*, 9.132). Such a direct declaration of love could never have occurred or succeeded in *Dream of the Red Chamber*.

The sequels in general reduce and undress their predecessor, squeezing balder and more-explicit messages out of its originally subtle ones. For example, no matter how we look at him, Baoyu was indeed a polygynist—or, at least, a prepolygynist pressured and expected to be a full-fledged polygynist.[33] With only one exception, the sequels merely push this assumption to fruition by mapping out variations of possible polygynous arrangements in the original novel. Likewise, Baoyu was indeed an obsessive admirer of women. *Qilou chongmeng* parodies that obsession by taking it to a perversely repetitive extreme in which Baoyu tends to women's physicality in a way that makes them beholden to him for their very entry into womanhood. Echoing the masterwork's emulation of remarkable women, other sequels create capable women who join men in grand actions outside the home and direct their marriages within. Sequels also attempt to resume the sublimity of the original novel, especially in their variations on the blank male. Hence *Honglou fumeng*'s creation of a Baoyu who "is not even aware that he is male and they are female," or *Honglou huanmeng*'s portrait of a Baoyu who cedes the directorship of his polygamous marriage to Daiyu, to the point of appearing to yield control over how he distributes his affections and arranges his preferences. *Honglou meng ying*, authored by a woman, even creates a refined realm among women that excludes the melancholy Baoyu. It fantasizes the enduring survival of talented women in spite of the harms caused by men and their female allies of lesser moral stature.

Sequel writing treads a fine line between critical revision, even travesty, and respectful re-creation. *Qilou chongmeng* provokes the accusation of travesty, creating a polygynist who confidently satisfies all women. *Honglou meng ying* demonstrates that no woman conforms to what the polygynist wants her to be. What the two hold in common with other sequels is the attempt to make happen what they wish would have happened in the original work: returning the Jia household to prosperity, passing the exams, creating harmonious marriages, foregrounding the momentous event of childbirth, and having successful children.[34] Making possible what was originally impossible amounts to imposing transparency where it could not have existed before. The best examples of such transparency are *Honglou fumeng*'s attempt to erase the divide between male and female, *Bu Honglou meng*'s (*Patching the Dream of the Red Chamber*) elision of the divide between supernatural and earthly worlds, and *Qilou chongmeng*'s farcical usurpation of female agency. Usurping female agency, in other words, makes the female subject transparent to the male. The elision of supernatural and earthly makes each transparent to the other by allowing a single eye to behold them both at once. Erasing the difference between male and female likewise demystifies sexual taboos and creates a situation of transparent gender-oneness. The will to carry out such acts of elision and erasure draws the sequels into a composite whole.

The Man with Two Wives

Since the fantasy of passive polygamy is a crucial part of the picture of polygamy and sublime passion in general, it is necessary to clarify it further by means of a strikingly recurrent form of it in Qing fiction, the man with two wives, which is notable for the way it appears to seek a balance between the relationship of two lovers and that of the master polygamist and his multiple women.[35] The most famous version of two-wife polygyny appears in *Dream of the Red Chamber* and its sequels in the form of the triangular knot of Baoyu, Baochai, and Daiyu. Having Baoyu marry both women as equal co-wives would have been impossible in *Dream of the Red Chamber,* and could have happened in real life only under special conditions.[36] The sequel *Honglou huanmeng* stages three instances of a man's marriage to two wives and uses wording in each case to indicate the special predestination of the double marriage.[37] As a kind of relay between polygynous hierarchy and *qing* egalitarianism, marriage to two wives can be summed up as follows: For the man to deserve two wives, he must show willingness to forgo sexual contact and in general be unlustful or even asexual. For a woman to be willing to join such a marriage, one or both women must initiate the marriage. The rationale for such a marriage wants to imagine that two-wife polygyny is fair to both women, this being key to passive polygyny in general. The most common feature of two-wife polygyny is that the man acquires an air of subservience in the relationship to the two women. Numerous works show the man agonizing over his split between two women, some works denying him two at once, others allowing this limited form of polygyny. In the latter case, the man discovers the trick, as it were, of playing the subservient one in order to disguise or erase the compromises that the women must make. He gives them the power to decide that he may have two wives, while he himself acts as if he never initially wanted two.

To understand the basic construction of this motif, it helps to go back to Pu Songling's *Liaozhai zhiyi*. Passive polygamy in the sequels is a reaction to the crisis of the threesome in the original novel, but *Liaozhai* precedes *Dream of the Red Chamber*, already providing numerous analogs to the triangular knot of Baoyu, Daiyu, and Baochai. In *Liaozhai*, the man with two wives is known for his gentleness.[38] In one case, the man is "like a eunuch" until an older female fox magically sexualizes him, after which he marries both her daughter and a ghost ("Qiaoniang," 256–264). The formula, in short, is that in not lusting after women, the man therefore gets two of them. The women may be rivals at first, but then they ally with each other to help the man in a predicament (e.g., "Lianxiang" and "Xiaoxie"), or else they simply choose to accommodate themselves to each other by way of achieving harmonious stability with an unlustful man. As the Historian of the Strange says, "Such harmony in the inner chambers is rare even for a king" (1503), and "only the man who is not always lusting after women will meet with such fortune" (779).[39]

The fact that the women solve the problem of rivalry implies an alliance that of necessity distances them from the man and makes of him a minor member of the marriage. Some stories formalize this detachment by assigning equal or greater importance to the female alliance than to the alliance between the women and the man. The main love affair is between the two women, an immortal and a mortal.[40] The women are originally Daoist nuns who manage to stay together by marrying the same man; one sleeps in the mother-in-law's bedroom and concentrates on household chores, only occasionally switching with the other woman, who sleeps with the husband. Or the two women are flower spirits, one his "sexual" (*yin*) companion, the other his "sentimental" (*qing*) companion.[41] There is a kind of draw between sexual and sentimental, with the emphasis on women, not men, deciding upon the marital arrangement. The division between sexual and nonsexual relations is another version of the split between *yu* and *qing*, or between two people in love who always miss the perfect moment. Missing that moment is like not being able to stay with the immortal lover who finally disappears. The difference between the immortal who disappears and the mortal wife who raises the man's children reproduces the same division. Even though only one wife remains, such stories could also be said to be about a man with two wives. In other variations of such splitting, one woman is a ghost, the other a fox ("Lianxiang" and "Qiaoniang"); or one is concubine while the other is main wife (as in the stories about shrews in which the shrew finally accepts the concubine, e.g., "Shaonü" and "Da'nan").[42]

Pu Songling's companion stories, "Wang Guian" (1632–1637) and "Jisheng" (1638–1644), are case studies of the motif of two-wife polygyny in which the women are of the same social status, like Daiyu and Baochai. To take the second one first, in "Jisheng" two young women vie to marry a certain young man and eventually overcome their rivalry by becoming his co-wives. It is as if two love stories run into each other, leaving triangular marriage as the only viable solution. As the story goes, the young man loves his cousin, Guixiu, but her father rejects their marriage (Guixiu being the term for a proper, educated woman). Another woman, Wuke, sends a go-between to promote herself, but Jisheng declines (Wuke meaning "perfect in every way," a daring counterpart to the name Guixiu). He dreams of Wuke telling him it is "not fair" to favor Guixiu over her, then swears to marry Wuke, only to find that she has just been betrothed to someone else (a move that she had faked in order to see whether he would fall ill over her as he had over Guixiu). He finally manages to rebetroth himself to Wuke, but on the day of the marriage, Guixiu's mother (his aunt) puts Guixiu in Wuke's place—somewhat like Baoyu's marriage in which he thinks he is marrying Daiyu but discovers he is marrying Baochai. But Wuke's family agrees to marry her to Jisheng anyway, and the two women become friends. Reading back to the companion story, "Wang Guian," we see that it predicts two-wife polygamy, but narrowly avoids it. "Wang Guian" begins with the marriage of Jisheng's parents, shortly after which the father, Wang, suddenly tells the mother that he already has a wife. Hearing this, she commits suicide by throwing herself into the river, although it turns out that the father was joking. Unbeknownst to him, the wife survives and, already pregnant, bears their son Jisheng. At the end of "Wang Guian" they all reunite.

The contrast between the companion stories recalls Pu Songling's fascination with the woman's appearance and disappearance in his stories of the supernatural. Choosing a form of disappearance, Jisheng's mother commits suicide and avoids subjection to the order of polygyny. Wuke and Guixiu choose appearance and marry the same *qing*-inspired man as if that were not a compromising thing to do. The reader can imagine what the members of such a marriage might do in order for some kind of harmony to prevail. The pressure of equivalence would perhaps have a kind of creeping effect that displaced the man's centrality. That is, as a member of a triad, he would become one of three rather than one over many. Perhaps Wuke, the more remarkable of the two women, would become the de facto head of the family who would lead the other two in their common goal of self-refinement.

What is the explanation for two-wife polygyny, for which no designation exists in Chinese literature, but which is strikingly recurrent nevertheless? *Liaozhai zhiyi* and the sequels to *Dream of the Red Chamber* answer that in general polygyny is a scenario that must be created and that creating it is a matter of obtaining the willingness of women. In short, polygamy must be negotiated. *Qilou chongmeng* shows the man obtaining the willingness of the women in the most blatant and knavish way, which is to appropriate agency from women by creating a man who virtually drives them from within. On the other hand, Pu Songling and other authors of two-wife polygyny portray a naïve man of *qing* to whom women arrive through no effort of his own except that of being a harmless and unlustful male. Stopping at the number two is as if to mark the limit of difference between the blank male and the polygamist master or the limit up to which the story can still adhere relatively well to the spirit of the *qing* aesthetic and the motif of the remarkable woman. Adhering "relatively well" means abiding by the principle of equivalence and being fair to two equal women who marry the same humble man and agree to avoid jealousy by rising above it. Rising above jealousy is the prime feature of the fuller-blown forms of passive polygamy that we see in the sequels and other late-Qing novels to be examined later on, in which I will read this scenario in light of the history of the end of the Qing.

CHAPTER THREE

The Otherworldliness
of the Courtesan

Qing and Opium Smoking

In the High Qing landscape of worthy female figures, as I have said, the learned gentry woman is the voice of stability and moral authority, remaining so until the end of the Qing. *Dream of the Red Chamber,* its sequels, and *Radiant Words* all illustrate this woman, as does much of the literature by women. Beginning around the time of the first Opium War (1839–1842), however, the courtesan-prostitute reemerges as the focal female presence in numerous fictional and auto-biographical accounts that are the subject of this and all but one of the rest of the chapters of this book—the novels *Seductive Dreams* (*Fengyue meng*), *Precious Mirror of Boy Actresses* (*Pinhua baojian,* in the form of the boy female imper-sonator), *Traces of the Flowery Moon* (*Huayue hen*), *Courtesan Chambers* (*Qing-lou meng*), *Flowers of Shanghai* (*Haishanghua liezhuan*), *Shanghai Dust* (*Hai-shang chentian ying*), and *Nine-times Cuckold* (*Jiuwei gui*), and autobiographical accounts such as Gong Zizhen's (1792–1841) poetry collection *1839 Miscellany* (*Jihai zashi*) and Wang Tao's (1828–1897) fictional and autobiographical *Later Tales of Liaozhai* (*Hou Liaozhai zhiyi*). The courtesan is a special form of the remarkable woman. She is a wanton and base woman who is permanently stig-matized by orthodox morality. If she marries a patron, as often happens, she in general can marry only as a concubine, not a main wife. But she can also be like Pu Songling's supernatural woman who sets the terms of the relationship or, like Xiaoqing or Daiyu, melancholic women with heightened sensibilities. The man's relationship with the courtesan—especially the classy or pseudo-classy ones of the works just listed, often called "famous courtesans" (*mingji*)—is a special case of otherworldly *qing* involvement. This chapter defines the otherworldly qualities of that relationship in the historical context of the Opium War and after, at first comparing an autobiographical and a fictional source of approximately the same period and geographical region, Gong Zizhen's poetry collection, *1839 Miscel-*

lany, and Hanshang Mengren's 1848 novel, *Seductive Dreams,* then focusing on an extravagant portrait of sublime passion and male same-sex love in Chen Sen's 1849 novel, *Precious Mirror of Boy Actresses.* Although my sources for this book are mainly fictional, Gong Zizhen's autobiographical poetry, like other biographical and autobiographical sources I cite, verifies for us that the motifs of the *qing* aesthetic and the regimes of polygamy and prostitution apply in both fictional and nonfictional contexts.

The patron who visits the brothel in nineteenth-century literature divides into two types. He is the wastrel and opium addict who symbolizes the decadence of his times, or he is the pure soul who represents the finest essence of China in the midst of social decay and political fragmentation. In either case, the brothel harbors an otherworldliness like that of the relationship with the female ghost or immortal in Pu Songling, except that in this case the woman is real and the man goes to her, not she to him, and except that the story needs to be reidentified now that new historical conditions apply. Those conditions have to do with the fact that from about the Daoguang period on, the Chinese way of life is threatened at a root level by political corruption, widespread opium addiction, banditry, rebellion, and the forces of Western encroachment. The Opium War is the convenient historical event marking the approximate beginning of the period of the literature I will now examine. That event and other realities of China at the level of the imperial state make little or no appearance in *1839 Miscellany, Seductive Dreams,* or *Precious Mirror of Boy Actresses,* which can nevertheless be read in a historically symbolic way. As I have argued elsewhere, the mere presence of opium smoking in these works is integral to the larger picture of conditions from the Opium War onward.[1] Opium is a sign of grand decline and disintegration, and as such a critical signifier in the distinction between those who smoke it, who are supposedly wretched and decadent, and those who never would, who are supposedly pure and unsullied, especially as embodied in the *qing*-inspired heroes of *Precious Mirror of Boy Actresses* in this chapter and *Traces of the Flowery Moon* in the next. The boy actress in the former and the prostitute in the latter are the most intense embodiments of sublime purity in a time of ugliness and decay, hence the extravagant portrayals of these figures in the two novels.

The Courtesan and the Courtly Lady

What do men seek in the courtesan's other world? In whatever period, men like to be connoisseurs of these women and to write about scenes and events in the brothel. They like to know about how the woman entered prostitution and to demonstrate sympathy with her over her unfortunate fate. Her chamber is a "soft and warm" (*wenrou*) home away from home. It is a place where men meet and play games, recite poetry, and carouse. The chambers may contain erotic toys and illustrations. Some women are known for their *neimei,* or "sensual charm," that is, their ability to please men sexually. Men favor the famous courtesan for her purity and refined tastes and seek in her a soul mate who affirms their true talents and provides them with charming solace. In the most highly charged image, the courtesan is distant and difficult to approach.[2] She is unpredictable, demanding, and even tyrannical in temper. The patron distantly recalls the male "I" of the medieval European troubadour's love poem, who presents himself as being at the mercy of the unpredictable and powerful courtly lady. The Qing courtesan is not powerful in a political sense, but like the courtly lady, she is a figure who delights the male patron by appearing lofty and unattainable. In the Occitan language of the troubadours, the lady is typically "too far away from me." The attempt to satisfy desire is even pointedly missing at first, as with the blank male of Pu Songling's stories or the refined men of *Precious Mirror of Boy Actresses* and *Traces of the Flower Moon.* The troubadour fantasizes intimacy with the lady but nevertheless foregrounds the difficulty or impossibility of getting through to her. The Qing patron eventually sleeps with his courtesan, but he begins the relationship politely and observes the ritual propriety of the high-class brothel or at least the brothel that has pretensions of being high class. Some form of impasse is paramount.[3]

As this distant person, the courtesan-courtly lady is a kind of fictional figure who is chaste even though she is supposed to be sexual with the man. In Chinese literature, an example of this fictional chastity occurs when the man asks about how the woman entered the brothel. He thus learns about the harsh realities of her life and the purity of her young soul. The patron acquires an air of benevolence that supposedly makes the woman beholden to him for more than just money. Like the courtly lady, the ideal courtesan plays a role that expels the negative attributes of real women, whom troubadour literature assumes to be lacking in reason and the noble sense of love. In fact, if such a woman is too ready to receive the man, she incurs the troubadour's contempt. Chinese patrons are similarly contemptuous of the overly made-up woman of the vulgar brothels, such as those of the Canton region in the eyes of men of Jiangnan, or the dirty and vulgar barber boys of Beijing in *Precious Mirror of Boy Actresses.* Men like to vilify the woman who cheats her patron and doesn't love him enough. Even if the courtesan is inherently unchaste, the ideal image of her is of a woman who, as in *Traces of the Flowery Moon,* sacrifices everything for her lover who on his part identifies with her as a being utterly above the negative attributes of worldly reality. In the sublime mode of literature about patrons and courtesans, sex and marriage are contaminated with vulgar realities, hence the motif of the courtesan's imaginary distance from the real world, especially the world of marriage and procreation.

The man and woman in the brothel are in fact real, however, and are in fact at cross interests. The brute reality is the market in female slaves, maidservants, boys, prostitutes, and concubines. These people are in a position of needing to survive and advance themselves against great odds, while the patron, if he wants, can enjoy the inherent advantage of playing their benefactor. Already by the High Qing, as I have said, women were a commodity in especially short supply, a situation that gave rise to extreme flux in the buying and selling of women.[4] Girls were commonly kidnapped into brothels, then later bought out as concubines (as reported in *Seductive Dreams*). The demand for women made brothels prime sites for men to shop for concubines. Women could be leased for terms after which they returned to their owners or families. They could free themselves only by paying off their owners or meeting patrons who would pay to redeem them. Demand for boys was also strong, especially the ones called *dan* who were indentured by opera troupes in which they sang female roles and were expected to serve as prostitutes, as in *Precious Mirror of Boy Actresses*.

Given such conditions, courtesan and patron are at cross interests in that she, for example, wants him to buy her out of prostitution and marry her, but the patron, however he may depend upon her, cannot finally commit himself to buying her out. The relationship with her is too tempestuous, as the poet and New Text hero Gong Zizhen discovers. Neither his autobiographical poetry nor the novel *Seductive Dreams* attains the rarefied heights of novels such as *Precious Mirror of Boy Actresses* and *Traces of the Flowery Moon*, which hark back to the stories of loyalist figures such as Qian Qianyi and Liu Rushi in the late Ming and early Qing. Gong Zizhen cuts his relationship short before it affects him too much; the addicts in *Seductive Dreams* run themselves into the ground rather than turn into martyrlike loyalists. But all partake of the impulse to engage in the escapism of a love affair with an immortal courtesan. The man becomes the woman's consort against the backdrop of what was then commonly acknowledged as an era of social decline. The reason he fails in life is the same reason he loses, in a metaphorical sense, against the remarkable woman. He depends on her to instill in him the ethical energy either to die nobly or to recover and regenerate, hence Gong Zizhen's *1839 Miscellany*, or else he spends his time in dissipation until she fleeces him entirely and replaces him with a new patron, hence Hanshang Mengren's *Seductive Dreams*. These two texts take place in roughly the same social milieu, the brothel in Jiangsu Province north of the Yangzi River, an area also known as Jiangbei. Qingjiang in northern Jiangbei is the site of Gong Zizhen's affair, while Yangzhou in southern Jiangbei is the site of *Seductive Dreams*. Prostitutes travel between the two places in *Seductive Dreams;* both are stops on the Grand Canal that men such as Gong Zizhen traveled between Jiangnan and government posts in Beijing.

Gong Zizhen, the Migrating Goose

One of the most famous intellectuals of his day, Gong Zizhen was known for his erudition in paleography and etymology and his fine poetry and essays. He was also an unabashed lover of courtesans, dying in 1841 two years after an affair with a woman known as Lingxiao, whom he first met briefly in the spring of 1839 and with whom he spent ten tumultuous days in the following autumn. He came to her at a failing point in his career, in a historical age that he characterized as an "era of decline" (*shuaishi*). "Patriotic worry, righteous outrage, ability to think and take action, sense of shame, and sense of decency"—all these, he said, were blocked in this age.[5] He scorned the Qing government's literary inquisition, its corrupt system of taxation, and its inability to deal with foreigners. He scoffed at the dire state of the army and the moribund institution of the civil examinations.[6] It is against this background that, on his way south from Beijing, he met Lingxiao, who impressed him so much that he wrote a quatrain hailing "historians to take the trouble to add the colorful touch, that I, Gong Zizhen, at forty plus years of age have met Lingxiao!" (poem 97).

Lingxiao in turn is the formidable, unfathomable, and relentless courtesan, against whom Gong with his entire intellectual prowess and experience in government and philology has only one countermove. He leaves her without saying good-bye, which makes him feel miserable until he finds solace by a lamp in a quiet inn (poem 278). A number of features qualify Gong Zizhen as a male consort of the remarkable woman, beginning with his relationships with educated women early in life. His mother, who was the daughter of the famous scholar Duan Yucai, educated him in poetry. As a young man he was a friend of the poet Gui Peishan, and once confided in her about his foolish attraction to courtesans. His record of a brief Platonic affair with a woman in 1826, his fifteen poems grieving about a woman who died leaving gifts for him and longing for his return, the affair with Lingxiao, and the apocryphal stories about both Lingxiao poisoning him to death and about his affair with another woman, the Manchu poet Gu Taiqing—all of these, whether fictitious or real, form a romance in themselves even if they do not take the shape of a continuous narrative.[7] Gong Zizhen stands alongside figures like Qian Qianyi and Wu Weiye, who likewise wrote poetry about their love affairs with famous courtesans. They in turn fit alongside Pu Songling, Cao Xueqin, Chen Sen, and Wei Xiuren, all of whom take part in a kind of common relationship with talented and remarkable women, or in Chen Sen's case, famous boy actresses.

Based on Gong's poetry, which includes his own narrative notes, the story of his affair with Lingxiao is as follows: Lingxiao lived in Yuanpu, also called Qingjiang, which was along the Grand Canal upon which Gong traveled in spring 1839. "Verse from Deep Sleep" (Yici) is the name Gong gave to the group of poems about his affair with Lingxiao, who soon upon his return to Qingjiang in the fall of 1839 proposed that he redeem her from prostitution (poem 245). To paraphrase his response: How could a hermit (*chushi*) like him marry such a stunningly beautiful woman like her? Still, at a time in his life when his "courage was exhausted," the sound of her voice instilled him with new energy. He would gladly "serve at her makeup table, anticipating her every wish" (poem 252).[8] She is "an immortal whom his fleshly eyes can hardly take in" (poem 257). When she asked about his family, he declared that he had a wife, but wondered if Lingxiao "would be willing to lead an army of the flowers of the right," his euphemism for offering her a position as concubine.[9] Then he wrote of her formidable skills of argument and debate. She was too hard to fathom; she left him in a fog. So he used his own "Book of Arcane Strategy" and flew away like a "migrating goose" (*zhenghong*, poems 263–265). When she sent him a letter of apology, he was so impressed that he rejoined her. "If heaven can calm these pains of love, and if the gorgeous woman should settle herself at my Yuling villa [his home in Kunshan County], then the castles in the mountains of the immortals would be like nothing to me. I'd gladly put off Buddhahood for as many ages as it takes" (poem 268). But then it was all over, and after a sleepless last night, he left the next day without waiting for her to see him off (poem 271).[10] Thirty-five *li* away, he wrote a poem on a wall and sent her another, telling in both of his regret at leaving her and his inability, unlike the flying geese, he says, to keep from "looking back" (poems 272, 273). Upon his return to Yuanpu two months later, he learned that she had stopped seeing patrons and had left for Suzhou. Two sketchy pieces of evidence suggest that he traveled to Suzhou a year later and redeemed her.[11]

An intellectual biography of Gong Zizhen would note that he was a follower of New Text Han learning, in which he was a student of the famous Duan Yucai (1735–1815), his maternal grandfather. The New Text school was a scholarly formation among well-connected men in the Jiangnan region beginning in the late eighteenth century. It sought to undermine the brand of Confucian ideology supported by the Manchu rulers, whose increasing corruption since the time of Heshen in the late Qianlong era reminded many among this Han elite of the eunuch-based corruption at the end of the Ming. Gong came under the influence of this school because he was from a Jiangnan family of high scholarly pedigree and thus enjoyed contact with many of the major intellects of the period. But in political terms, his success was limited. He won the *jinshi* status in 1829 after several tries, and served in a series of offices in Beijing before withdrawing in 1839 and returning south.[12]

Gong Zizhen hardly resembles the male admirer of remarkable women embodied in the delicate, melancholic man like Jia Baoyu. Gong was a political activist in line with the New Text school's idealization of that role, unlike the young Jia Baoyu, who despised the adult men's world and who, failing in love, took refuge in monkhood. Gong Zizhen's refuge is his ideal self-image as a man of the political world, constantly busy with political and intellectual affairs, hence his excuse that it is impossible for him to consider involving himself in the redemption of a courtesan (poem 241). He also views himself as a "hermit," except not like a monk who "leaves the world" (*chu jia*). His hermitage is the image of himself as a seasonal migrating bird; or it is the feeling of unperturbed calmness he experiences when climbing high places, which allow him to "escape the charms of outings with women," as he once wrote (*bi yeyou*, poem 238). Nineteen years earlier he wrote similarly of cutting himself off from courtesans, in this case in an 1820 poem to Gui Peishan. His first wife having died in 1813, he traveled with his new wife of 1815 to Suzhou, where he first met Gui in 1817. She was his slightly older confidant with whom he engaged in an exchange of poetry about his attempt to discipline his obsession with "romantic love" (*fengqing*). He alludes to a famous motif in the *Vimalakirti Sutra* in which a celestial maiden periodically scatters flower petals upon boddhisattvas and lesser Buddhist disciples. The petals fall off the boddhisattvas but stick to the others, who have not yet formed their "inviolate body" (*jieti*), a term for the one who is immune to wanton female demons.[13]

In the poetry about Lingxiao, Gong Zizhen presents the affair as an open testimony to his admiration of such a splendid woman, as if to congratulate himself, but he also foregrounds his feelings of inadequacy and remorse. Here he embodies the essential traits of the high-cultural polygamist-philanderer's admiration of remarkable women. Like other such men, he would not think of vilifying Lingxiao for toying with his emotions and leading him to perdition. But nor is he overly sentimental, since he refrains from melting into self-annihilating sorrow, like Baoyu, the young male lovers of *Precious Mirror of Boy Actresses,* or Wei Chizhu of *Traces of the Flowery Moon.* In all this, Gong is like other elite men who have a wife and possibly a concubine or two at home, but who freely associate with courtesans during their travels away from home. Given his elite pedigree, it is safe to assume that his first and second wives (like his mother) were highly literate. Although he imagines Lingxiao fitting perfectly into his Yuling villa, as he writes in poems 200 and 201, it goes without saying that, like his passion for gambling, his interest in courtesans is most happily indulged when away from elders and wife, and that in front of them and women like Gui Peishan, he feels ashamed of his involvements with prostitutes.[14] As he says in a note appended to poem 245, the notion of actually marrying Lingxiao "is more a case of drunken dreaming than sober consideration." It was up to those who spread apocryphal stories about Gong Zizhen to vilify Lingxiao by saying that she poisoned him to death. Yet another set of tales alleged that he had a secret affair with Gu Taiqing (1799–1877), the author of *Honglou meng ying,* whose husband sent murderers to kill Gong, and that, years later, to avenge his father, Gong's son Gong Cheng (b. 1817) colluded with foreigners and betrayed the Qing government.[15] In these gossipy tales, the intimate link between the important man and the famous courtesan shades into the story of the femme fatale and scheming prostitute (Lingxiao), or the talented concubine turned wanton woman (Gu Taiqing).

Eroded Dreams, a Prelude to Shanghai Modernity

The year in which Gong Zizhen met Lingxiao, 1839, is also the year in which the 1848 Yangzhou novel *Seductive Dreams* ends.[16] Though still a bustling city, 1839 Yangzhou showed signs of decline that both inhabitants and visitors like Gong Zizhen noted and that characters in the novel observe in scenic spots that were taken care of years before but are now barren and rundown.[17] The word "dream" in the title is the telltale sign of the novel's inheritance of the love story of *Dream of the Red Chamber*, but it is an eroded replica that takes place in brothels and teahouses visited by opium-smoking wastrels. The brothels are at the mercy of opium-addicted "protectors" called *bashi*, a kind of mafia who practice loan-sharking and trumped-up lawsuits to take advantage of wealthy young men, brothel managers, prostitutes, and each other. Motifs from *Dream of the Red Chamber* still survive, but only as designs in the prostitute's clothing or themes in her songs. Opium is the central allegory of erosion and degradation; no relationship escapes it. It is the sign of a new state of affairs in China that has completely taken over and that figures prominently in literature from now to the end of the Qing.[18]

The Yangzhou of *Seductive Dreams* is an infant prelude to the Shanghai of a few decades later, which appears tangentially in the novel but in the 1840s had not yet grown into what it would soon become: the city of cheaters and connivers and the home of the most fashionable and savvy prostitutes in all of China. Yangzhou is still a Chinese city, unlike the international part of Shanghai that is the setting for the literature about prostitution in Shanghai of the 1890s and early 1900s. But *Seductive Dreams* uncannily predicts that later literature, beginning with the motif of the naïve young man's arrival in the city. One of his incarnations in *Seductive Dreams* wears cotton clothing, shoes, and socks, not the fancier materials of the fashionable crowd (6.35–36). Shocked at the casual way his Yangzhou cousin treats a certain woman, he doesn't recognize that she is a prostitute (6.39–40). Staring at the bizarre features of a Western clock, he has no idea what it is (7.43). Nor does the new arrival know how to smoke opium, which is de rigueur for the true Yangzhou initiate.

The constant movement and interaction that pervades *Seductive Dreams* also predicts the novels of the 1890s and mirrors the "bustling splendor" (*fanhua*) of the cities in which they take place. Men and women have to master this bustle in order to survive; many are swallowed up by it, as in the case of Lu Shu, another new arrival, who eventually turns into a destitute addict who is cheated by his prostitute girlfriend and the brothel protectors. Let us examine the atmosphere of bustle as presented through his eyes, which provide a vignette of the splendid but devouring world of decline that now prevails. Having arrived in Yangzhou to look for a concubine, as many men did, he takes his first stroll in which he looks at Western pictures and peep shows, listens to the songs of female impersonators (2.10), and plays a gambling game, the prize for which is a book of erotic pictures (2.11). Later with his group of friends, he sports a Western watch, a fan, a lotus bag, and a small knife (3.14). The lid of his friend's opium box has a lion with movable eyes and tongue (made in Shanghai because the silversmiths of Yangzhou lack the necessary skills). His friend is an expert at smoking opium, which he teaches to the clumsy Lu Shu (3.17–18). Lu becomes infatuated with a prostitute whose clothing and fan bear motifs from *Dream of the Red Chamber* (5.28–29), and she sings a song about the melancholy Lin Daiyu (5.30). On his girlfriend's birthday, he and his friends arrange performances that include a comedy act; in its final skit, a man hangs a curtain from behind which he makes the sound of cats mating, thus beginning a skit about an old woman who asks her daughter-in-law to give her a massage and sing her a song. When the old woman goes to sleep, the daughter-in-law lures a reluctant young monk inside, but just as she pulls at his pants, her husband comes home and discovers the monk, ending the skit (13.95–99). It is against this constantly moving backdrop that *Seductive Dreams* situates its descriptions of the ruthless dealings of Yangzhou brothels, the corruption of which no one escapes.

As is common in literature about prostitutes in general, the male author provides details about the unfortunate lot of the woman, which is the source of sublime misery in *Precious Mirror of Boy Actresses* and *Traces of the Flowery Moon*. In contrast, *Seductive Dreams* portrays her lot in graphic detail, thus implicitly justifying her need to constantly look out for herself and making the *qing* aesthetic appear unlikely and impractical, two key points tying the novel together with the later fiction of Shanghai, especially the 1892 *Flowers of Shanghai*. Sensational "news" (*xinwen*) is heard at the beginning of *Seductive Dreams* about a woman leased from a brothel who commits suicide by swallowing opium because of the harassment of her patron's jealous wife. In another piece of news, a man sells his daughter to a brothel, from which she escapes to a neighboring family who turns her over to the yamen and sues the father, who has already fled.[19] Vestiges of the sublime now merge into the sordid. The opium-abstaining prostitute, Shuanglin, is loyal to her patron, Yuan You, who when he dies provides her with the means to support herself for life (31.217). At his death, however, she commits suicide, after which people lay their corpses together on a bed, but Yuan's angry wife orders

Shuanglin to be put on the floor and her good clothes changed for the worn-out ones of an old servant (31.222–223).

Another eroded version of the *qing*-inspired couple is Jia Ming and Fenglin, both addicts, who separate when she leaves him for a man who pays a large sum to redeem her. Jia Ming is like a lesser Gong Zizhen whose New Text erudition and fondness for gambling transform in Jia Ming into average literary talent and opium addiction (Gong to our knowledge did not smoke opium). Fenglin is a lesser Lingxiao whose story contains the details about a prostitute's harsh life that are missing from Gong's "Verse from Deep Sleep." Like Gong Zizhen, Jia Ming pours his attachment to Fenglin into a set of poems about their affair. He calls her "the Immortal Fairy Erudite" and himself the "Great Fool" (*Taichisheng*, 28.197). When they met in 1837, he writes, he was impressed with her "utter lack of the vulgar airs of the world of misty flowers" (*jue wu yanhua sutai*), an old trope in literature about courtesans. During his illness in 1839, he continues, she cared for him daily. Compared to Gong's poetry, Jia's is plain in diction and full of romantic clichés. "For years I lived in fear of lovesickness. But when we met out of the blue I couldn't help but lose control. It must be, it has to be, a predestined love. For how could such infatuation result from mere love at first sight?" (poem 1). In a self-rebuke common in such poetry, he asks why she loves him so much when "I know full well that I have treated you shabbily" (poem 5); and he has wronged her because he "has no mansion in which to settle her" (poem 6), using the same word for "settle" (*zhu*) that Gong Zizhen used when he envisioned settling Lingxiao in his Yuling villa (*Seductive Dreams*, 28.197–199; *Jihai zashi,* poem 268). The present life for which he hereby apologizes is the one in which he has a wife at home who approves of Fenglin, whom Jia Ming retains as an opium-smoking companion for a periodic fee that he pays Fenglin's husband and mother-in-law, from whom he has no plans to redeem her. The end of their affair replays the willful departure of Pu Songling's fairy immortal who leaves the man because of his failure to realize her worth. When a wealthy Hanlin scholar from the north seeks a meeting with Fenglin, Jia Ming encourages her to accept the invitation so that she can earn money to buy more opium (29.202). But she returns announcing the man's generous offer to redeem her. In the parting songs Jia Ming and Fenglin then sing to each other, her theme is "I have no choice but to harden my heart and take another man" (*gai jia*). His is "How could I have known that I would be so wronged by pure devotion" (*duoqing*, 29.206–207). He weeps pitifully at her departure and retreats into the petty man's resentment at the cold-hearted woman.

In sum, *Seductive Dreams* predates the 1892 *Flowers of Shanghai* in the way it allows the harshness of the prostitute's life to balance with the man's foolishness. Lu Shu's girlfriend, Yuexiang, is the epitome of the heartless woman, who, like women in *Flowers of Shanghai*, openly declares that it is her business to "fool" (*hong*) the man (21.149). Fenglin is one of the least heartless, but she takes the decisive step of joining the Hanlin scholar, opting to change her life completely rather than stay with the noncommittal Jia Ming. In Pu Songling's stories, the woman's bondage takes the form of her very entrance into the fleshly world, from which she maintains independence by escaping it at will. She is an idealized model of *qing* subjectivity, against which the concrete details of her life easily fade away. In sticking to those details, *Seductive Dreams* creates an explicit connection between the *qing* imaginary and the prostitute's daily reality, here epitomized by the advent of opium smoking and its link with the world of conniving and extortion. Shanghai soon replaces Yangzhou as one of the most sought after places to patronize brothels and purchase concubines. Especially after the Taiping Rebellion in the 1860s, Shanghai becomes the new center whose initiates shed their local origins and learn the methods and fashions of the modern international city. Just beginning to gain importance in the 1840s, Shanghai appears tangentially in *Seductive Dreams,* once as a place where fancy opium utensils are made and another time as a place to which Fenglin might have gone but didn't for fear of "being sold in Shanghai" (*mai zai Shanghaile,* 25.178). The anticipation of Shanghai is accidental at this point, but in retrospect it is accurate in predicting the star figure of Shanghai modernity, the larger-than-life prostitute who brazenly names herself Lin Daiyu and over whom no man can prevail. In literature of the 1890s and 1900s, she becomes not only a representative of strong Chinese womanhood in the modern, international setting, but also a model of the subject in general who is adept at adjusting to new realities.

Sublime Love in a Homoerotic Novel, *Precious Mirror of Boy Actresses*

First published in 1849, *Precious Mirror of Boy Actresses* (*Pinhua baojian*) takes the theme of unattainable love into the realm of the same-sex romance, where sublime passion displaces the degradation that overwhelmed *Seductive Dreams*.[20] The central characters are handsome young scholars who love boy impersonators of heroines in Kun opera, that is, "boy actresses," called *dan* or *xiaodan*. The otherworldliness of the courtesan now takes the form of the exquisite beauty and talent of the female impersonator, whom vulgar patrons assume to be available as a prostitute, but whom refined patrons, even if in love with the boys, would never take as a sexual partner. Thus one of the brilliant scholars, Mei Ziyu, has an earth-shaking but resolutely chaste affair with the boy actress Du Qinyan. At the end of the novel, Mei surrenders this romance to marry a virtuous and talented wife who understands the profundity of his affair with Qinyan but who politely and confidently demands that he now dedicate himself to her. For she is no less talented and beautiful than the *xiaodan,* who, as everyone must finally accept, is only a boy actor. The author Chen Sen (ca. 1796–1870) rarefies the otherworldly, same-sex affair in at least three ways: by declaring that sex profanes the relationship of sublime same-sex lovers, by noting that the affair can only exist in an oblique and unreal form since in real life men can only marry women, and by concluding that the indentured boy actress, if truly loved and respected, must ultimately be allowed to become a free man and himself marry a good woman. This last point is where Chen Sen engages the egalitarian implications of the *qing* aesthetic by extending them into the realm of practical, ethical realism. To be the boy's lover means to act upon an ethical obligation to help him "leave the profession," *gai hang,* that is, redeem himself from his indenture to the opera troupe and allow him to become a peer of the young scholar himself.

The novel emerges from a theatrical milieu with a vast body of texts: plays, literature of connoisseurship, and accounts of the lives and characters of people who inhabited this milieu.[21] The most idealized relationship in this literature is between the young and upcoming scholar of privileged background, in *Precious Mirror* called the "famous scholar" (*mingshi*), and the fifteen- or sixteen-year-old boy at the peak of acting perfection, in parallel terms called the "famous *dan*" (*mingdan,* which also resonates with *mingji,* "famous courtesan"). In this heightened realm, the *dan*'s true lover understands the *dan* from the inside, as if the lover had been himself thrown into the human market and sold as a helpless boy into the opera troupe. Between them there is no behavior on command, such as serving the patron his opium pipe (neither scholar nor boy ever smokes opium), giving him massages, and satisfying him sexually. The *dan* can tell the literatus everything that he feels, and the literatus will hear him, especially when the *dan* talks about how trapped and unhappy he feels. If the young scholar truly loves the boy, then he can no longer expect the boy to be a *xiaodan*. The end of the novel thus portrays the star boys burning their acting paraphernalia, now liberated from servitude and having succeeded in maintaining their virginity (59.767).[22]

To briefly summarize the plot, the story is about a group of elite young friends who, besides preparing for the marriage and career that are appropriate to their class, have a keen fascination for Kun opera. Each of them has a special boy whom he loves most, but Mei Ziyu loves the actor Du Qinyan in a way that surpasses all others. They first see each other only fleetingly, but immediately feel an overwhelming love. An opposite cast of characters consists of ugly and untalented men, the most profligate of whom is Xi Shiyi, whose craving for Qinyan forces the boy to seek refuge as a retainer in the household of Hua Guangsu, a wealthy and benevolent opera connoisseur who is nevertheless incapable of appreciating the true feelings of someone like Qinyan. The love between Ziyu and Qinyan is constantly thwarted, meanwhile, until they finally spend their most intimate time together for one chaste night. This occurs after Qinyan has obtained his freedom by becoming the adopted son of a famous literatus. Ziyu has by then married a talented woman who looks like Qinyan and who implicitly acknowledges the ordeal that Ziyu has experienced with Qinyan.

Precious Mirror echoes earlier Qing literature that experiments with the volatility of social boundaries by dissolving the distinctions between high and low, active and passive, and masculine and feminine. The liminal aspects of the boy's feminine role parallel those of the extraordinary woman in Pu Songling. Sublimity results from the fact that the boy is doubly removed from the real woman by being both an actor and a male, as if doubly rarefied. He can play this role, moreover, only as long as his youth allows it, since he will soon grow a beard and experience a lowering of voice. He resembles the famous courtesan when she suffers oppression by lecherous men and villainous masters, and like her embodies purity and transcendence when he refuses to participate cheerfully in social gatherings at which he is supposed to entertain guests. Through him the novel dramatizes a feminine position that is arrived at neither solely by means of costume or gesture nor by the biological determination of sex. The subject in this position is someone who undergoes a type of transcendence that takes quintessential form in the boys' revolutionary act of "leaving the profession" and burning their acting paraphernalia. They commit a symbolic social suicide that delivers the political message of the *dan* hero who, like the remarkable woman who leaves the world of common male mortals, expresses his repudiation of male masters. Their exit from the "*dan* corps" (*dandang,* 60.769), in short, is a symbolic death carried out from the position of a heroic, feminine subject.[23]

The Chastely Erotic in *Precious Mirror*

According to the aesthetic principles of *Precious Mirror,* actual sex or any graphic description of it will fail to capture the sublime quality of love between literatus and boy actress. The most exalted form of same-sex love is thus nonsexual, though the novel secretly suggests the existence of a kind of male-male relationship that is both romantic and erotic, as I will soon discuss. The author's preference is for innuendo and euphemism, the sexual drive being too direct and vulgar.[24] Hence the repeated delays the lovers experience in even meeting each other, and the foreclosure of any sex between them. The beauty of the boy actress is for the eye only; to love only women is to be merely "lustful" (*hao yin,* 12.148). When their faces unintentionally touch, Huifang blushes, while Chunhang almost loses control as an "extraordinary fragrance penetrates his nostrils and travels straight to his heart" (14.171).[25] Purer yet, Qinyan and Ziyu achieve their nonsexual consummation only after Qinyan has been freed and when they sleep in the same bed, using the same pillow, "with their clothes on." They forget that any "suspicion" might arise because of their intimacy, although Qinyan feels "awkward" (*jucu*) the next morning when a friend of theirs sees them "lying with heads drawn together, talking in tones that no one else could hear" (59.765–766).

Chastity is not so much a denial or repression as a going farther in the direction of the sublime quality of male-male love. To engage in such a relationship is a sign of ultimate attainment in the unattainable realm of *qing* love. Although men of equally high status can be sexual lovers elsewhere in Ming and Qing fiction, *Precious Mirror* chooses to portray such men only obliquely. It concentrates the explicit descriptions of sex on relationships between men of unequal status, in which pleasure is for the dominant man only. Huifang's blush when his face accidentally touches Chunhang's is as intense as needs be for sublime lovers; it is a sign of the innocence and virginity that is necessary to keep *dan* like him in a category of their own. As with the famous courtesan, the *dan's* fragile beauty is not something a patron can casually and directly enjoy.

Pornography and the World of Ugly People

Without exception, the pornographic sections of *Precious Mirror* focus on vulgar behavior among ugly, venal, and sometimes outright rapacious characters. The worst of them suffer grotesque and terminal injury to the penis (Xi Shiyi) or anus (Pan Qiguan and Ba Yingguan). The elite *dan* who maintain their virginity are in constant danger of abuse at the hands of men like Xi Shiyi, who tolerates no rejection. The description of this ugly world is nevertheless robust, vivid, and entertaining in a way that typifies pornography in the Ming and Qing. The graphic rawness of these scenes evokes an obverse sublime with comparable intensity. How can the author choose to write in such lurid detail of something he otherwise condemns? Or rather, how can he do so without affirming what he goes to such trouble to negate? He is like other fictionalists in the Ming and Qing who describe explicit sex but then conclude the story by having the participants undergo punishment and death. In general, a cardinal rule of Chinese fiction is that a normative ending should not be seen as canceling the wayward body of the story. Like others, Chen Sen in effect does two things at once in order to aim at a sort of radical pleasure that lies outside the homeostatic world of pleasure and pain. The chaste sublime is not true enough unless accompanied by its pulsating obverse. Love that transcends sex must occur alongside raw sex among vulgar and rapacious characters. He cannot portray the complete truth of the vision of love between men without evoking such a split and using it to express the intensity of an obscene but also irrepressible passion, hence his exploration of every mode in which he sees that passion occurring.

In *Precious Mirror,* ugliness includes both low "moral character" (*renpin*) and ugly physical features, as in Xi Shiyi, the crass opium merchant from Guangdong Province, who is dark-skinned and despotic in temper.[26] Naked bodies and sexual acts belong to a comically hideous world in which a vagina looks like a "beard stained with milk tea" (23.5ab), or the sound of a man and woman having sex is like "a dog slurping" (51.10a).[27] A man has "fox stink" (body odor, 40.498); using a wet piece of "wood mushroom" as a "cap" keeps the bad smell off the penis (23.16a); men who like anal sex "like to ride the night-soil wagon" and "like to clean out the outhouse" (27.328). The merchant Pan Qiguan tricks a boy into sex by getting him drunk, then stuffing the boy's anus with hair to make it itch and crave penetration (40.500–501, 8ab). Friends help the boy take revenge by stuffing Pan's anus with hair mixed with a chemical (40.507–508), which makes him go to ridiculous lengths to find someone willing to penetrate him and sooth the itch (47).[28] He finally solicits Tianxiang (Heavenly Fragrance), a female impersonator and prostitute who once had the same trick played on him. The grotesque reaches its height when Xi Shiyi contracts syphilis from Tianxiang, which makes Xi's penis swell painfully until it looks like a "rotten eggplant" (40.7b) and part of it falls off. He undergoes an operation in which a section of a dog's penis is grafted onto his (47), but he finally ruins himself permanently when he takes aphrodisiacs and has violent sex with his concubine followed by a boy whose anus he damages and who dies of the injury a year later (58).

In spite of the relentlessly obscene imagery, the author also hints at a realm that lies somewhere between callous dissipation and passionate chastity. Several passages tantalizingly point to a sexual love of a more everyday variety, that is, a nonmercenary love that includes romantic attachment. The main vehicle for portraying this relationship is the hint in passing, that is, the knowing look or the telling detail. Hua Guangsu and Feng Zipei appear to be engaged in an affair, the first indication of which, only understood after reading back, is the mere detail in chapter 6 of Feng's arriving late at a gathering, having just come from Hua's. The reader later learns that Feng is the son of a deceased official and that he relies on friends to get by after having wasted his family wealth (19). When two guests arrive at his apartment, he emerges "daintily and charmingly" (*niaonuo duozi,* 19.236) wearing an entire outfit of delicate material. One of the guests "hugs him tightly"; then all three hug each other around the waist and "play and tussle for a bit" (*sihun yizhen,* 236), a vague euphemism for playful, possibly sexual, physical contact.[29] More traces of the affair emerge when Hua's wife senses that Hua and Feng "might be up to something" (26.319) and when Feng arrives unexpectedly one day, causing Hua to become "distracted for a moment" (30.372). Watching Feng sing, Hua is "mesmerized" (30.375), while others admire Feng's femininity.

Feng blushes because he insists on one thing, that he not be taken as a *dan* or a *xianggong* (another term for the boy female impersonator, not necessarily an actor). In general, his failure to free himself from that image has to do with the fact that he emerges into the scene of sodomy in Beijing expecting that he can avoid the risks that the lower-class *xianggong* faces, including rape, Feng having once been raped by Xi Shiyi. The episodes involving Feng are the only ones in the book in which men of more or less equal status interact sexually. The scenes are a sort of whispering indication of another dimension of same-sex love that is less tied to the masks of status than the relations between patron and *dan*.

"We Are All *Dan*"

The true sign of *qing* love, as I have said, is shown when the partners at least hypothetically exchange with each other, that is, when they look alike and mingle both masculine and feminine. The more valuable direction of exchange is becoming feminine, which is more conducive to realizing the subjectivity of the other person than being masculine. The true knower of the *dan* thus understands him in the sense of *titie*, meaning to sympathize and empathize with, be considerate of.[30] If the understanding scholar had a motto, it would be "We are all *dan*," an alternate version of the motto "We are all women" that I coined in chapter 1 when discussing the male consort in relation to the remarkable woman.

Precious Mirror evokes equality and exchangeability between the *mingshi* and *dan* via scenes and statements that mingle status, gender, and identity, usually in the form of the transient moment or the overlapping image. Hua Guangsu is as good-looking as a *dan* (5.65). Qinyan thinks that Hua looks like Mei Ziyu (25.311). Ziyu looks like the *dan* Lu Sulan (10.122 and 15.189). Status values relax in gatherings at Xu Ziyun's, where the *dan* may visit whenever they like (5.61), where they occupy higher sitting positions (37.459), and where everyone addresses each other by literary style names (9.118).[31] Gender roles dissolve when friends arrive unexpectedly at the home of the opera devotee Shi Nanxiang, who greets them wearing his wife's padded jacket because, he says, he just awoke and had no time to put on proper clothes (Nanxiang puns with "affinity for men," 15.187). Wearing women's clothing or looking like a *dan* happens obliquely and by accident. It is not a matter of deliberate posturing. Ephemeral moments and gestures contrast with situations in which roles are fixed and in which the subordinated subject feels entrapped. Qinyan hates being a *dan* because he hates the people he captivates. To captivate them is to be locked into the structure of their desire, like Pu Songling's Weaving Girl when the man writes a "lewd poem" about her. Hence Qinyan's constant depression and illness, which his true lover echoes as they share their entrapment in a world in which they lead a fractured existence. Like Daiyu, they constantly weep and fall ill, and like the famous courtesan they are listless and spiritually absent in gatherings at which they are admired for features they do not want to have.

Women versus Boys

Evoking the difference between women and boys is *Precious Mirror*'s way of creating its own distinct version of the *qing* aesthetic of the feminine. The difference and even rivalry between the two describes the gap between the real of husband-and-wife marriage and the sublime of earthshaking same-sex love, which can never last. The real of the smart and capable gentry women competes with the more enchantingly feminine *xiaodan* who aren't real women. Chen Sen's gentry woman is a kind of wiser person who waits for the man to awaken from his obsession with opera. In the episodes about women that are periodically interspersed with the main episodes about men, the women behave as if they have already attained what the men still insist on not being satisfied with and therefore fantasizing about. It goes without saying that the women are exquisite, even the older married ones, whom the narrator makes a repeated point of complimenting (e.g., 6.69, 52.664–665). The women inhabit the long-established world of talented beauties who have parties and write poetry that their husbands publish and adore.[32] As the wives politely complain, however, their husbands spend too much time with male friends in the company of boy actresses. One woman asks her husband what the good of *dan* is (11.133). She hosts a party at which the women swear sisterhood and announce that Qionghua's (Ziyu's future wife) poetic brilliance proves the superiority of women over *dan* (57.741). The author could not make a better case for the excellence of women, except that they lack the extra element of sublime that only the *dan* possess.

In general, when women complain about the *dan*, they occupy the mode of orthodox morality. The best illustration of this can be seen by comparing *Precious Mirror* and *Dream of the Red Chamber*, with Mei Ziyu corresponding to Jia Baoyu, Qionghua to Baochai, and Qinyan to Lin Daiyu. Ziyu and Baoyu share the word jade in their names, which symbolizes their childlike purity (Ziyu is compared to a "virgin," 15.188). Both become ill and delirious when blocked in their attempts to realize their love. Qionghua and Baochai are both highly literate and vigorously intelligent, and they expect their husbands to take full part in the world of grown-up men.[33] The resemblance between Daiyu and Qinyan lies in their role as the sublime but moody *zhiji* lover, whose existence undermines the relationship dictated by the elders. They both die, except that Daiyu dies literally, while Qinyan symbolically kills his *dan* self and then becomes a free man. In general, the Baochai-like woman assumes the authority of orthodox moral discourse. When Hua Guangsu's wife offers him a concubine, which he refuses, she in effect tells him that he is supposed to satisfy himself with women, not men. Likewise, when Qinyan finally becomes a full-fledged young scholar, Qionghua lets Ziyu know that it is time to stop acting like a childish star-crossed lover. The novel ends neither as sadly as *Dream of the Red Chamber* nor as happily as the beauty-scholar romance or the sequel. This is its way of acknowledging the impossibility of actual same-sex marriage but nevertheless making as if same-sex marriage takes place after all. The novel accomplishes this contradictory goal by contriving two major instances of resemblance between *dan* and wife, that is, between Qinyan and Qionghua and between Huifang and Chunhang's wife, the latter two even sharing the same surname. In the end the heroes enter normally adjusted married life with women who, it turns out, look like their *dan* favorites and who meanwhile do not object to their husbands' continued friendship with the former *dan*. The prime instance of negating same-sex marriage but affirming it at the same time comes across in the logic of karma spelled out at the end of the novel. Qinyan was in fact a woman in his former life and as such the perfect match for Ziyu, but they have missed each other by a lifetime. The depth of their love is hard to explain otherwise, as marveled onlookers conclude (53.671).

The Salvation of Symbolic Death

It is easy to say that the resemblance between wives and *dan* is forced, and that it has to do with the overwhelming effect of the social norms of marriage and procreation.[34] The failed love between Daiyu and Baoyu in *Dream of the Red Chamber* had the effect of spawning the numerous sequels that tried to repair the damage. Would sequels that marry characters like Qinyan and Ziyu or that repudiate heterosexual marriage have made it into print if *Precious Mirror* had struck readers as powerfully as *Dream of the Red Chamber*? Or would the conditions of possibility "still," so to speak, prevent even the fantasy of such an ending? My general point throughout, however, has been to say that the *qing* aesthetic takes hold within a sequestered realm outside of which it had no easily detected social-political effect. It is within a polygynous and procreative outer core that an insulated and gender-fluid domain exists in which authors create worlds like the one in *Precious Mirror*. Chen Sen extends the already existing tropes of *qing* subjectivity to his own radical conclusions in his focus on the fundamental impossibility of the boy's existence as *dan*. This impossibility achieves perfect visibility under what *qing* circumstances? When the patron falls in love with the *dan*. The *mingshi* cannot love a slave without liberating him, in which case the two must by implication approach if not actually gain equal status outside marriage.

When Qinyan, now a liberated young literatus, leaves for the south to live with his adopted father, he and Ziyu exchange parting poems. Qinyan inscribes his poem on a fan that later ends up in the hands of Hua Guangsu's wife, who is puzzled because the poem resembles none of the usual parting poems between friends, husband and wife, or prostitute and patron (52.662–663). Hua Guangsu affirms her perception and explains who the lovers are. Like others, including Ziyu's wife, he is in awe of such an extraordinary love. It is extraordinary because it exceeds the bounds of worldly reality and because it can only be realized in transcendent forms. Whether Chunhang and Huifang or Ziyu and Qinyan, each is as ready to sacrifice himself as the other, in true *qing* fashion. Each cries for and defers to the other in ways that suggest neither can ultimately be superior to the other. Qinyan turns sacrifice into a supreme ordeal in which he enters a phase of living death, the best image of which is his refusal to smile for anyone, not only the vulgar Xi Shiyi, but also the refined Xu Ziyun and Hua Guangsu. Qinyan lives in Hua Guangsu's compound in order to avoid Xi Shiyi's predations, but passes the time there listlessly and tearfully, intending never to perform professionally again. It is this nonact of his that sews the entire novel together and that ties it to a long line of predecessors featuring similar forms of living death in the *nüxia, cainü, mingji,* and other cross-gendering declensions of passionate chastity.

Gong Zizhen's poetry, *Seductive Dreams,* and *Precious Mirror of Boy Actresses* all assume the backdrop of an era of decline, whether people rise above it or succumb to it. They further share their focus on the extravagant love relationship between a man and a courtesan, whether female or male. Let us pose at this point the question of the historical and political significance of the extravagant dramatization of *qing* in the mid-nineteenth century. The turbulent events of the time contribute to Gong Zizhen's frustrated departure from Beijing and to his readiness for passion. The same events only lurk at the edges of Chen Sen's fictional world in the form of reference to the opium trade and, as in *Seductive Dreams,* the pervasive depiction of opium smoking. Nevertheless, to anticipate the next chapter and its discussion of *Traces of the Flowery Moon* and Wang Tao's *Later Tales of Liaozhai,* is it not possible to see in *Precious Mirror*'s sustained focus upon the heroes and their sublime love a significance not unlike that of the loyalist lovers in the literature of the fall of the Ming? This is especially so if we place the novel alongside *Traces of the Flowery Moon,* which explicitly links the Taiping Rebellion with the sublime passion of literatus and courtesan. The contrast between Xi Shiyi and the noble heroes is enough in itself to enunciate a highly charged, even if unarticulated, political position. The novel's employment of the *qing* romantic ideology, as soft and sentimental as it may be, nevertheless signals a militant ethical stance in the face of broadly impinging danger. It is not difficult to see such heroes as bearers of a high cultural standard, especially in contrast to their eroded replicas in *Seductive*

Dreams and the opium-smoking villains and wastrels in both *Seductive Dreams* and *Precious Mirror of Boy Actresses*. For this reason we can begin to understand *1839 Miscellany, Seductive Dreams,* and *Precious Mirror* as part of an emergent late-Qing formation that draws inspiration from a similar formation in the late Ming and early Qing when Han identity was pitted against the foreign menace of the Manchus and when the *qing* aesthetic was likewise central to the enunciation of that position.

CHAPTER FOUR

The Love Story and
Civilizational Crisis

Sublime Passion and Cultural Renewal in
Traces of the Flowery Moon

Gong Zizhen's *1839 Miscellany,* Hanshang Mengren's *Seductive Dreams,* and Chen Sen's *Precious Mirror of Boy Actresses* precede by half a century the times in which Chinese intellectuals first defined China as a modern nation struggling to divest itself of an outmoded past. It is too early for ideas like *geming* in its sense of the complete "overthrow" of the traditional political system, or *wenming,* which instead of Chinese civilizational order, its original sense, will be redefined in terms of "modern" and "modernity." The literary and political discourse of the mid-nineteenth century still promotes the idea that the customary exercise of courage and virtue can repair China's crises.[1] In the 1858 *Traces of the Flowery Moon (Huayue hen),* by Wei Xiuren (1819–1874), the main practitioners of the kind of courage and virtue that it takes to bring about cultural renewal are pairs of exemplary lovers, whose romantic and erotic bonds embody the type of energy that will die if the dynasty dies or else will bring about China's grand-scale renewal.[2] Prior to the 1890s, *Traces of the Flowery Moon* is the novel that most explicitly equates the destiny of love and the destiny of China as a historically symbolic whole. The battle that takes place in this story between the armies of essential good and the enemy that threatens extinction is a battle between the native forces characterized by heroic love, on the one hand, and the demonic energy of the Taiping rebels and their heterodox religion, on the other. This chapter is about two *qing*-inspired authors who place the love story of the male consort of the remarkable woman in the context of the civilizational crisis of contemporary history. Both *Traces of the Flowery Moon* and Wang Tao's *Later Tales of Liaozhai* share the despair that literati male patrons feel alongside their prostitute-mistresses. The passion in *Traces of the Flowery Moon* is more earthshaking, while *Later Tales of Liaozhai* manages a modicum of optimism in tremulous times as long as the Chinese man can enjoy refuge with the Chinese courtesan.

Like *Precious Mirror of Boy Actresses,* passages of which Wei Xiuren copied directly, *Traces of the Flowery Moon* exalts *qing* soul mates in their protracted struggle against villainous forces.[3] But *Traces of the Flowery Moon* differs from *Precious Mirror of Boy Actresses* in its direct reference to historical reality. As I have said, the closest *Seductive Dreams* and *Precious Mirror* come to referring to historical reality are the pervasive descriptions of opium smoking, which can refer in only an implicit way to Western intrusion and issues surrounding the Opium War. In *Traces of the Flowery Moon,* on the other hand, a team of valiant love couples heads the defeat of the Taipings and the demise of their foreign-bred Christian cult. A brief but significant passage after the defeat describes the victorious Chinese government forcing the Europeans to reverse the unfair stipulations of their treaties. The central characters of the novel are a literatus and a courtesan who, before the defeat of the Taipings, endure a tortured love affair and die a love death as heroic loyalists, defeated by both corrupt brothel managers and the situation of China in a seemingly endless state of crisis. The author then follows with the swift victory of valiant love couples who bring about the successful regeneration of the Chinese empire. The contrasting love stories act as screens onto which the author projects the transition from dynastic cataclysm to healthy civilizational recovery.

The Taiping Rebellion is the most significant historical event in the lives of both Wei Xiuren and Wang Tao. Their self-conscious engagement of historical reality in their fiction allows us to make a key point about the symbolism of Chinese civilizational energy. The Taipings and their shadowy allies, the European Christians, represent a demonic force threatening the Chinese state. Who represents the sublime essence of Chinese civilizational energy? The genteel philanderer and his courtesan mistress. There is even a primal level at stake, especially when we consider the sexual elements involved. One of the love couples in the battle against the Taipings is a man and woman who are masters of Daoist sexual alchemy. Members of the Taipings, on the other hand, practice deviant sex and possess monstrous sexual capacity. An allegory thus emerges in which Chinese victory is linked with native sexual and romantic energy pitted against a demonic enemy characterized by base sexuality. In both Wei Xiuren and Wang Tao, the lover of the Chinese courtesan embodies the essence of Chinese civilizational excellence.

The Reading and Writing of *Traces of the Flowery Moon*

Wei Xiuren's story deeply inspired authors in the later Qing and early Republic, although it has since dropped from sight except in references by scholars.[4] Wei wrote his novel over the span of time in which Western powers were forcing the imperial government to make one humiliating concession after another and in which the Taiping Christian rebellion had taken over almost half of China, causing the deaths of at least twenty million people in its rise and fall between the 1850s and 1864. One of the novel's most often quoted lines became the name given to a genre of sentimental romance popular in the early Republican period called "Mandarin Duck and Butterfly" fiction.[5] The "foolish" (*chi*) man, Wei Chizhu, and the melancholic (*qiu* and *chou*) woman, Liu Qiuhen, represented the very type of lovers favored in this genre. Wei is the proud and noble but also utterly defeated talent (commonly called *luopo caizi*) who, having no role to play in the political world, finds his true soul mate in the equally noble but fallen woman of the brothel. Their common sense of loss and dejection drives their thorough repudiation of the objective conditions of life in times of turbulence and degeneration. The key gesture of their repudiation, as also seen in early-Republican fiction, is the self-willed failure of love in spite of the absence of obstacles such as parental opposition or meddling villains. In lacking such obstacles, the protagonists could have all along reversed the fatal direction of their affair, but instead act in ways that lead to failure and death.[6] They prefer the "traces" and "scars" (*hen*) of *qing* over actual fulfillment, where traces consist of things like poems and music, and gestures like drinking blood mixed with wine or returning a packet of love tokens sewn tightly shut. The ultimate trace is the missed opportunity to secure their relationship. *Precious Mirror* likewise preferred the aesthetic trace to the physical real in placing female impersonators above real women or the love poem on the fan above lovers actually getting together. But in Wei and Liu's case a more explicitly historical element also enters the picture. It is as if they are at the end of an era and, as David Wang writes, too late to achieve the grandeur of their illustrious predecessors at the catastrophic end of the Ming, their most proximate historical precedent. The novel compares Wei and Liu to the most famous loyalist lovers of the late Ming, the poet Qian Qianyi and the courtesan Liu Rushi (29.256). But now, in contrast, Wei and Liu "live in a world where grand narratives are in ruin, and they can only experience the traces of great emotion."[7]

I cite David Wang's observations in order to suggest a way to read the novel's aesthetic preferences not only in terms of the influence on later literature but also in terms of the rendition of China as a historically symbolic whole. In simplest terms, as I have said, the destiny of the sublime lovers parallels the destiny of China. As icons of high-cultural identity, the lovers live out their love in the only fitting way at this historical moment, a heroic love death. Wei Chizhu is the sensitive man who, frustrated by his failed career, seeks refuge among women in the secluded setting of a brothel. Consider, for example, the scene of a party in which Chizhu—whose name translates as "Foolish Pearl"—lies on a kang "lost in wonderment" (*daixiang*, 21.169) as he enjoys the luxurious presence of beautiful women and their young maids. The courtesan he most appreciates is a *qinü*, "extraordinary woman," who appreciates him above others, but the relationship with whom is unstable and impermanent. Their time together is nevertheless like an eternal present in a world out of control. Thus far, Gong Zizhen and Wei Chizhu sound roughly alike. But a crucial feature distinguishes Wei from Gong and recalls male characters in Pu Songling, Cao Xueqin, and Chen Sen: the man, whether writer or fictional persona, who borrows the trope of the remarkable woman to adopt for himself a position of feminine subjectivity. Femininity in this case does not designate feminine features such as passivity, daintiness, or frailty, though these may play a role. Instead, it refers to the extreme situation I have referred to before, that of someone who finds herself in a fundamentally impossible social position, like the courtesan Liu Qiuhen. She is a gentry woman who was sold and kidnapped into the brothel, where like Du Qinyan she refuses to play the role of the courtesan who is supposed to entertain powerful and wealthy patrons. Although Wei could redeem her, he postpones doing so as long as he is trapped where she is in the north because of the turmoil caused by the Taipings at his home in the south. She does not blame him for his failure to act. Their goal is the perfection of success-in-failure, which elevates them as beautiful souls against the backdrop of the ugliness of social decay and corruption. Their love death is a sign of the futility of resistance in what is thereby symbolized as a fatal situation. In terms of historical allegory, they experience a torturous love affair not just because all sublime lovers do so, but also because they live at a time when China as a civilizational whole has lost the ability to absorb and tame its diabolical enemies.

Some think that the author stopped writing his story at their death. Then, when Chinese imperial forces finally succeeded in defeating the Taipings a few years later, he resumed his story by having the robust lovers win an empirewide restoration.[8] Regardless of the accuracy of this sequence, in the last few chapters the author does in fact for the first time portray the raw monstrosity of the Taipings, which thereby casts a retrospective shadow over the rest of the book and crystallizes the battle between enemies as one between primal forces. The final chapters about the Taiping defeat, in other words, have the retroactive effect of turning the Taipings and their monstrous sexuality into a force before which Wei Chizhu and Liu Qiuhen had to die to defy. The author then represents victory over that force in the form of heroic couples who embody harmonious love and healthy sexual energy, a combination also observed by Li Wai-yee in poetry and drama of the late Ming.[9] The ending of the love story may be facile and fantastic, but precisely as such it provides an overarching meaning that places Wei and Liu's affair in a framework as large and fundamental as the very existence of Chinese civilization itself. In short, it is the function of fantasy as such to crystallize the image of competing cultural orders, that is, the disorder of encroaching enemies and the order of the enduring homeland.

Two tasks will now occupy the rest of my examination of *Traces of the Flowery Moon* by way of illustrating the issues I have laid out so far, that of portraying the excruciating pleasure in melancholy that defines the perfect formula of love, and then examining how the novel plugs this formula into the political and historical framework of the late-imperial state in crisis. In brief, Wei Xiuren's version of the hallowed *qing* love story centers on the scene of a man leading a rarefied and tenuous existence with a remarkable courtesan who in effect masterminds their love death. Merging romance into the account of the Taiping defeat, Wei Xiuren then engineers the regeneration of Chinese civilization over the martyred bodies of Wei Chizhu and Liu Qiuhen.

The Affair of Wei and Liu, Pleasure in Doom

Wei and Liu have a lavishly emotional affair, utterly removed from all signs of turmoil. Their passion carries from chapter to chapter with tears, melancholy, and poetry, all of which demonstrate that they are beautiful souls who cannot succeed in a world that fails to reward the brilliant Wei and that subjugates the talented Liu. Liu is a young courtesan known for her disdain of the profane company of the brothel. She was originally of a good family but, because of her father's death and her mother's remarriage, was sold off as a maid, then kidnapped and forced to become a courtesan. Wei is a literatus in his forties who has suffered a failed career. His wife is trapped at home in the south because of the Taiping turmoil and his favorite concubine has just died, while he has already abandoned another courtesan with whom he had an earlier affair. In true *qing* fashion, when Wei and Liu meet, they immediately do away with formalities by addressing each other as equals. They weep and laugh together. It is the first time others see her come alive. The awed onlookers notice Wei and Liu acting as if "they had known each other all along," in the words of a well-worn trope for truly destined lovers (*yi jian ru gu*, 14.107). Thus begins an affair in which the lovers take outrageous pleasure in melancholy, lavishly indulging in their impending doom. Qiuhen tells Chizhu that their "foolish infatuation" (*chiqing*) only enriches her brothel managers while depleting Chizhu's resources (36.310). Foolishness and impracticality are in fact the premises of their relationship. They refuse to engage in the practical means through which they could redeem Qiuhen from prostitution and then marry. Wei Chizhu only enters the affair after turning it into a preconstructed failure, with which Liu Qiuhen readily agrees. He tries to leave immediately, insisting that he must return south to see his mother and wife. Besides, he tells Qiuhen, he has already "betrayed" one courtesan; how can he betray another? She insists that he stay, while Wei Chizhu proceeds to compose a set of "poems to ordain their love" (*ding qing shi*), after which she declares her permanent devotion to him (18.145–146).

The repetition of ordeals and near misses provides the story with one climax after another. After a grotesque incident between her and her managers, Chizhu decides to leave, as Qiuhen makes herself up for one last time, determined never to wear makeup again (24).[10] She cuts her arm and drips the blood into liquor, which they take turns drinking (24.208). By the next chapter, they are seeing each other as often as before. Meanwhile, in outstanding examples of action taken, Chizhu's friends offer to redeem Liu Qiuhen for the second time, while others redeem the courtesan Du Caiqiu for the scholar Han Hesheng (29), the parallel high-romantic couple of the novel. But Wei Chizhu refuses to take action even when offered the lucky opportunity. Again, the beauty of their relationship lies in their shared resistance to the mean trivialities that could ensure their union. They seclude themselves in Wei's compound, where he devotes himself to music and poetry, devises strategies against the Taipings, and writes about the scourge of opium. He relishes the vanity of these efforts and enjoys hearing a monk tell him that it is dangerous to become too passionate in love (34.294).

The Perfect Formula of Love

The key to the drama of Wei and Liu's affair is that the wise courtesan knows better than the vacillating man how to seal their pact and bring a climax to their otherwise interminably indefinite affair. Chizhu finally decides to leave Qiuhen upon hearing of the death of his brother (38), after which the brothel managers forcibly remove Liu from Wei's compound. This occurs after Wei's friends once again urge him to put up the money for Liu's redemption. Wei and Liu are brutally separated (39), after which Wei declines and dies of tuberculosis (43). Liu Qiuhen has already sent him a packet filled with their love tokens and with a message written in blood. In sending him the packet "sewn shut with thousands of stitches," she performs the ritual that seals them in the subliminal acknowledgment of their pact of death (41.351). He is noticeably sadder after this. She returns to Taiyuan after the death of her managers, learns of Wei's death, and hangs herself at age twenty (44).

How do they arrive at such an ending, and what hand does Liu Qiuhen have in perfecting their noble match? It is a question of what each brings to the affair in terms of both personal history and their status as male or female subjects. Wei Chizhu is a polygynist with a wife and a concubine at home, a courtesan lover named Juanniang whom he left in sorrow years before, and now the courtesan Liu Qiuhen, with whom he unexpectedly enters the deepest relationship he has ever experienced. In terms of established models, he lacks the exemplary resolve of men who manage to have many women and never love any too deeply. Wei is instead a man of "deep feeling," *duoqing* in the parlance of the novel, who as such is a gentle and refined practitioner of his privileges as polygynist-philanderer. Remorseful for betraying Juanniang, he declares himself unqualified for future affairs. He insists that he is too old and too late for love; that all lovers, especially women, eventually become old and ugly anyway; and that even if lovers are happy in this life, they won't necessarily know each other in the next (41.347). In spite of his remorse and hesitation, however, just before he dies he dreams of returning to an island on which in a former life he was an immortal in charge of a group of loving women, including Qiuhen and Juanniang (43.364–365). It is a scene of polygynous salvation, something that he never proposes in waking life but that nevertheless creeps through in this brief but telling passage.

As for what Liu Qiuhen brings to the affair, we should view her as a kind of mastermind who directs the flow of their love. The ultimate result of her master-minding is to create by means of suicide the retroactive effect that each died on behalf of the other. The sense of her controlling hand first takes shape in her insistence that they stay together, and lastly in the gesture of sending him the meticulously sewn packet with their tokens of love and its message in blood. That she can act in such ways has to do with both her personal story and her status as prostitute-courtesan. As a prostitute-courtesan she shares a destiny with fellow women who have endured the same entrapment and who thereby know how to take measures to save themselves or express protest. Her experience provides her with a sense of command lacking in Wei Chizhu the blank polygynist, whose characteristic reaction is to hesitate and lament. Because of what we may call Liu's collective and gendered experience as a courtesan, she in fact knows better than he how to seal their pact of death and bring a valiant end to their relationship.

Still, since her commanding role is nothing unusual in Qing literature of the remarkable woman, what makes her story something other than an embellishment upon the same? Would not her role be neutralized, moreover, if Wei Chizhu were a nonvacillating, nonmelancholic polygynist? What if he simply recovered from his melancholia after rejoining his wife? Perhaps he would then take another concubine or meet another courtesan, consorting with other younger women the older he became. Here, however, is where we must return to the notion of narrative as historically and socially symbolic act. If we imagine Wei simply recovering from his melancholy, do we not forget that his despair is no ordinary one and that he can in fact never recover from it? Liu Qiuhen sees the same truth of despair and dies with him in the fulfillment of that despair, an act that makes little sense in a historical vacuum. What provides the unwritten conditions for such a self-willed failure can be illustrated in two parts, first by looking at the cross between the historical and the romantic in terms of the trope of the "fallen woman and the scholar in dire straits" (*meiren duolo, mingshi kanke*), then by examining the novel's turn from self-willed failure to romantic and libidinal victory.

Love and History, Borrowing the Trope of the Fallen Woman

To get at the link between gender and history in the novel, let us start with the image of Wei Chizhu, the vacillating lover and emulator of the remarkable fallen woman. Like both real and fictional predecessors, the author borrows the trope of the fallen woman by way of creating a position of feminine subjectivity for the man Wei Chizhu. The words "fallen woman and scholar in dire straits" are the novel's own naming of the trope in Chizhu's description of his and Liu's shared fates (10.99). What is interesting in *Traces of the Flowery Moon* is the particular overlap of historical and gendered meanings. The position of feminine subjectivity embodies both the crisis of the historical moment and the crisis of Wei and Liu, the gendered lovers. The historical moment combines the factors of China in dire disarray and a hero who thinks he knows what China needs in order to repair itself. The crisis of Wei Chizhu the polygynous man has to do with the fact that arrival at the position of feminine subjectivity makes it impossible for him to carry on not only as a political subject in the Chinese empire, but also as a conventionally mandated philanderer vis-à-vis the courtesan. The impossibility of carrying on as a polygynously gendered man recalls the situation in *Precious Mirror* in which the scholar who loves the boy actress must therefore liberate the boy. Both stories are laden with the *qing* discourse of radical subjectivity. In *Traces of the Flowery Moon,* the use of the term *zhiji,* "soul mate," and the dropping of status markers in addressing each other are the hallowed signs of that discourse. Other signs emerge in the form of references characters make to imbalances in the relation between literatus and courtesan or the chasm that exists between man and woman in terms of freedom to select romantic partners or the possibility of achieving fame.[11]

Chizhu reflects the weight of such statements by being a man who wins the love of a woman like Qiuhen. His main defining feature is the one he shares with other men of the *qing* aesthetic, namely, the refined man's lack of blatant lustfulness. When he exhibits a brief tinge of disrespect, Qiuhen immediately chastises him for treating her as if she were like the wanton courtesan Bitao (20.162). In a gathering of courtesans and patrons, Chizhu expounds upon the history of women and ranges through topics including hairdos and bound feet. His tone is erudite, but two men interrupt him with ribald remarks, one urging him to discuss breasts, another referring to an ugly sort of bound foot but then cutting himself short when Qiuhen lowers her head in disapproval (21.173–174). As for the sex between Chizhu and Qiuhen, the description is always adumbrative.[12] At times they simply chat and recite poetry in bed, then go to sleep (19.156–157), or they go to bed after a long day exhausted, still wearing their clothes (32.299).

How can these scenes of daily devotion end with the deaths of the two lovers? For Qiuhen to die is less of a surprise, given the life of a woman kidnapped into prostitution. For Chizhu to die is not just a matter of the contingency of illness. It is a matter of the man of political ambition who has love affairs with one woman after another but finally finds it impossible to continue doing so when as a "scholar in dire straits" he sees himself as a "fallen woman." He thus falls in love with a last remarkable woman in what then becomes an affair he will die for. Arriving at this ending is an example of arriving at the position of feminine subjectivity. He does so in part through his own experience of being rejected by male superiors and in part through the agency of Qiuhen through whom he experiences the impossibility of the woman's lot as a courtesan. Agency in this case refers to her articulate resistance to the injustices a courtesan must endure and to the masterminding by which she seals their final love death. Masterminding is exemplified by her determined indifference to the cruelty of her brothel managers and by her willing participation in, but also subtle manipulation of, Chizhu's indecisiveness. Whether refusing to comply with the demands of her brothel managers or refusing to urge Chizhu to redeem her, Qiuhen exemplifies the determination to remain unsullied by vulgar attempts to manipulate both her enemies and her allies. In short, she rejects the entire social order that assigns her a role she refuses to fulfill. To succeed in this effort she must conduct herself in a way that can only result in both social and then real death, a trajectory into which she draws Wei Chizhu as well.

The question to ask at this point is how to make the jump from sentimental love death to loyalist love death. The connection that existed in the late Ming between *qing* and the theme of loyalty faded in the Qing as the relevance of dynastic loyalism faded into the past. *Traces of the Flowery Moon* rejoins loyalism and the eulogy of remarkable women. Wei's and Liu's roles as loyalists emerge both because of their resonance with late-Ming figures and, as said above, from the perspective of the subsequent defeat of China's enemies. If the novel ended at their deaths, with the Taipings still rampaging, we would have lovers exiting into complete darkness. Late-Qing fans of the novel would probably still extol Wei and Liu, viewing them as romantic heroes and cultural icons like Liu Rushi and Qian Qianyi or Li Xiangjun and Hou Fangyu. But the novel goes on to elevate them into martyrlike heroes through the action of their positive doubles, Han Hesheng, Du Caiqiu, and others, who complete the original mission of Wei and Liu and achieve the glorious result of civilizational renewal.

The Regeneration of China

The simplest way to state the formula of the novel's retrospective conclusion is that the regeneration of Chinese civilizational order occurs over the dead bodies of the martyred lovers Wei and Liu. In this light, they form an integral part of portraying the way in which China marshals healthy sexual energy into a force that overcomes the obscene excesses of the Taipings, the rude intrusions of Westerners, and the social degeneration that made it easier for such enemies to succeed to begin with. Each of the main signs of degeneration has to do with energetic disorder: opium addiction, Taiping demonism, the effects of foreign intrusion, and the decadence and corruption of the brothel. To take the example of the brothel, in the beginning of the novel false connoisseurs favor the "wanton" (*dang*) Bitao over the refined Liu Qiuhen. Immediately after the deaths of Chizhu and Qiuhen, however, Bitao undergoes a dramatic reform in which she cures herself of opium addiction by learning the art of internal yoga from a Daoist master, after which no man can match her in bed (45). She meets a filial Taiping bandit with extraordinary sexual capacity whom she persuades to join the imperial forces, after which they ally with other warrior couples to defeat the Taipings (Qing fiction commonly portrays warrior men and women from opposite sides falling in love). The defeat of the Taipings thus succeeds because China rallies healthy sexual and romantic energy. In contrast, Taiping sexuality is monstrous. A woman of the ruling circle has male concubines (42); two Taiping nuns are male one half of the month and female the other half, during which they sexually vampirize men kidnapped from the imperial army (48); the Taipings prohibit women, under penalty of beheading, from binding their feet (bound feet were still a symbol of Han cultural identity at this time); they require women to do heavy labor (48.408); and in general "the Lord's Doctrine" of Christianity, called *tianzhujiao,* practices freakish and inhuman customs (49). Opium addiction and Western intrusion are other signs of energetic decline and degradation, as named in Wei's and Liu's writings about opium and in the poetic justice delivered when the brothel madam and her common-law husband die from a fire caused by an opium lamp.[13] As for Westerners, a Chinese general sinks twenty-seven of their ships, then concludes a treaty that restricts the number of ports they can use, prohibits missionary activity, and forbids merchants from bringing family members with them into China, all points of contention since before the first Opium War (47.395–399). The British representative kowtows to the Chinese, thus repairing an insult going back as far as the Macartney mission to China in 1793, when the British refused to kowtow. The disposal of China's enemies also takes the form of the ways in which the author names them. The characters for "Taiping" appear rarely, and for the first time only late in the book (49.412). Otherwise the author uses a term commonly used at the time,

Yellow Turbans (*huangjin*), the name of an army of rebels from the Eastern Han more than fifteen hundred years before (e.g., 41.349). The term for Westerners is likewise a traditional epithet, in this case the word for Japanese coastal marauders, *woyi* (47.395–397). *Huangjin* and *woyi* are terms that absorb and tame diabolical threat by reducing it to something that has been dealt with time and again, not as something new and unprecedented.

Wei and Liu, on the other hand, instead of absorbing the threat respond to it as if it were something unabsorbable. A remark by the historian Chen Yinke (1890–1969) in his eulogy for Wang Guowei (1877–1927) fits well here: "Considering the monumental and devastating changes that have affected China in unprecedented ways in modern times, when things have gone beyond recognition, is it any wonder that those who represent the essence of the cultural spirit will disappear along with it?"[14] Wei Chizhu's weakness and vacillation, which others in the novel remark upon, are the inarticulate markers of this same breakdown.[15] Wei and Liu go on outings, sleep, weep, and write poetry, all in detailed, slow-moving fashion, with no resolution. The most obvious sign of the difference between them and the victorious couples lies in the transition to the fast-moving, fantasy-filled narrative of victory over the Taipings. Bitao's transformation from lascivious courtesan to Daoist adept likewise takes place in the new and faster narrative mode. She and the other warrior couples rely on magic, while the enemies are more like demons than humans. As facile as such an ending may seem, it represents fantasy in one of its common functions, that is, as a kind of supernatural solution to problems, and in this case, as a self-preserving reimposition of the sense of belonging-in-the-world.

In only a few decades it would no longer be possible to portray heroic scholars and beauties like Han Hesheng and Du Caiqiu saving China. Characters like these, as I will presently show in Wang Tao's fiction, can only withdraw into heaven and watch the "dusty world" from afar. In the fiction of the 1890s and after, the brothel is the arena for testing what can and cannot make the adjustment to modernity. There the mortal male patron searches for the courtesan goddesses who will best suit him in what remains of the hallowed master love story but only finds the prostitute who knows how to "do business" (*zuo shengyi*), which means to "fleece" him mercilessly (*qiao*). Like *Precious Mirror of Boy Actresses*, *Traces of the Flowery Moon* starkly contrasts with the eighteenth- and nineteenth-century novels I have mentioned earlier that feature the *ernü* kind of *qing*, including some of the sequels to *Dream of the Red Chamber*, and works like *An Old Man's Radiant Words, Routing the Brigands* (*Dangkou zhi*), and *Tale of Filial Heroes* (*Ernü yingxiong zhuan*). In these, sexuality is more a matter of healthy reproduction and harmony in the family than of sublime passion. The *ernü* hero appears at the end of *Traces of the Flowery Moon* in the courtesan Bitao and her reformed rebel husband, thus demonstrating the novel's drastic change of modes as it turns into a narrative like *Radiant Words, Tale of Filial Heroes, tanci* rhyme-narratives, and Qing military romances in which male and female couples ally to pacify unruly enemies.[16] The ending even recalls the episode in *Radiant Words* in which a Chinese man compels Europe to convert to Confucianism (though Wei Xiuren probably did not read *Radiant Words,* which was not widely known until the 1880s). China as a whole becomes an *ernü* type of hero, spreading its yang-enhancing effects throughout the world, extinguishing all heterodox religions and practices, and reestablishing healthy civilizational energy. *Traces of the Flowery Moon* was remembered most, however, for its portrayal of heroic love in its most precarious state of doom.

Wang Tao's Inalienable Pursuit of Pleasure

Because of his help in translating the New Testament into Chinese and the Confucian classics into English, Wang Tao (1828–1897) was one of the best-known Chinese intellectuals among Westerners in late-Qing China. Those Westerners probably cared little about one of Wang Tao's fondest pursuits, writing stories in the literary language in the manner of Pu Songling, thus Wang's *Later Tales of Liaozhai.*[17] Like Pu Songling, Wang centers his attention on the man's brief romantic encounters with courtesans, female ghosts and immortals, warrior women, and now also women from Japan and Europe. In Wang Tao, the radical edge of *qing* subjectivity loses the element of self-dissolution and transmutes into longing for refuge. A new world has arrived as a result of the political and economic developments introduced by the Europeans and the devastation caused by the Taiping Rebellion. By way of weathering these changes, Wang Tao's hero forms liaisons with women in order to escape to a purer other world. In Wang Tao's imaginary, the "gate of the mysterious feminine" leads to the "fairy gorge," which the deserving male finds as his last resort, opening up to him wherever he turns.[18] In general, his heroes are not polygynists with wife and concubine at home, but wandering philanderers whose favorite women are fallen ones, like courtesans and ghosts, or heavenly ones, like immortals. With Wang Tao we move from *Traces of the Flowery Moon,* which dealt with Westerners as enemies, to *Later Tales of Liaozhai,* which presents the perspective of a man who knows foreigners, has been abroad, and has even had love affairs with foreign women. Wang Tao adds an alternate, less traumatic perspective to the connection between love story and civilizational crisis than what we saw in *Traces of the Flowery Moon.* He evokes neither dire doom nor hyperfantasized victory, acknowledging Westerners while still insisting on the Chinese man's inalienable pursuit of pleasure with Chinese prostitutes.

Wang Tao is best known as one of the earliest modern journalists in China, a promoter of Western learning and reform, and a linguistic and cultural consultant for foreigners in China including Walter Medhurst Sr. (1796–1857), James Legge (1815–1897), Joseph Edkins (1823–1905), and John Fryer (1839–1928). Although these foreigners considered him a first-rate helper, they may not have known that his early employment with them caused him bitterness, which he wrote about privately and to friends, portraying foreigners as being of an utterly different ilk and his own work for them as worthless. Baptized a Christian in 1854, he never mentioned that fact in his diaries and later spoke disparagingly of Christianity and missionaries and skeptically about the existence of an afterlife.[19] Beginning as early as the 1850s he wrote extensively about courtesans, seeing himself like them as selling himself for a living.[20] Any account of Wang Tao must take his 1862 encounter with the Taiping rebels as the most damaging misadventure of his life. After presenting plans to the Qing government for suppressing the Taipings, he used a false name to present the Taipings with detailed plans for conquering both the foreigners in Shanghai and the Qing government in Beijing. Although he denied having done this, evidence says otherwise.[21] He narrowly escaped arrest by fleeing in 1862 to Hong Kong, where, except for time spent in Europe and Japan, he stayed until his return to Shanghai in 1884. There he continued to promote the benefits of experimental science and the political institutions of America and Europe and wrote about admirable European figures both past and present, in general emphasizing the magnitude of the change that China had to undergo. Meanwhile he wrote fiction and essays while establishing himself as a prominent journalist and working closely with foreigners.[22]

To read his stories is to go into something like a private corner, even if he published them in the best-known Chinese newspaper in Shanghai, *Shenbao*. He strikes a key note in "Island of Immortals" (Xianren dao), where he declares that the fairy isles no longer exist now that Western ships come and go according to schedule, transporting settlers to every island in the sea (43).[23] China is a grand fairy isle, and the brothel is one of the supreme fairy isles within it. In *Later Tales* as in reality, the Taiping Rebellion drove prostitutes from surrounding regions to Shanghai, where from the early 1860s on they established themselves in the foreign concessions in districts that became famous for decades to come. As one of Wang Tao's remaining fairy isles, the brothel constitutes an essence of China within the grand outside of epochal change. The visitors and inhabitants of the brothel prize the practices of Daoist inner alchemy and the art of the bedchamber, and they are learned in ancient history, belles lettres, and the gems of Chinese fiction. In one story, by way of influencing her learning, Wang Tao gives a courtesan a copy of *An Old Man's Radiant Words,* recently published and widely read in Shanghai of the 1880s (which she refuses to read because of its obscene contents). In general, Wang Tao's heroes are downcast men who cannot live up to the Confucian superhero of *Radiant Words,* Wen Suchen, who combines polygynous order at home with conquest of social chaos abroad. But they share Wen's unfailing attractiveness to women and his ability to radiate restorative energy, as they demonstrate in the numerous stories in which they save fallen women and infuse female ghosts with the power to return to life.

The Taiping Rebellion is the most significant temporal marker in *Later Tales,* representing catastrophic loss and threatening the collapse of the dynasty. In its aftermath, Wang Tao's protagonists encounter female ghosts who experienced the Taiping disaster and died because of it. In "Yan Exian," a man who is a chaste master of Daoist internal alchemy uses a magic pill to revive a woman who died during a Taiping attack (981–992). In "Feng Peibo," female ghosts discuss the Taiping ruler's profligacy, reporting that some women indulged him, while others committed suicide rather than join his harem (616–627). The swiftness of the Taiping rise and fall completely ravaged China, leaving Wang Tao's characters with no option but to withdraw to the imaginary realms he creates in his *Liaozhai* sequel.

The absence in Wang Tao of the radical edge of *qing* subjectivity is evident in his recurrent portrayal of innately endowed male heroes. Saving the Taiping castoff is an example. In "Strange Scene from the Deeps" (Haidi qijing), the hero has a great vision for China the "nation" (*guojia*) to fashion itself in the new world of technology and "international relations" (*waijiao,* 931–942). When the Chinese ambassador to foreign countries haughtily rejects his advice, the protagonist travels on his own to Europe and Japan. Wherever he goes, "women of the Western countries" (*xiguo funü*) love him (as also happens in "Grand Voyage Abroad" [Haiwai zhuangyou]). After his affair with a Swiss woman, he returns to China with Chinese objects that she gave him that had once belonged to the French empress (933). A Western man wonders how he, a Chinese man, came to possess objects once owned by Western royalty, which the protagonist rebuts by asking, "If Chinese treasures can travel abroad, why can't precious things from the French royalty end up with me?" (936).

In spite of the aura that makes them equal or superior to Western men, all that Wang Tao's heroes ultimately possess is their refuge with fallen Chinese women. In "Le Zhongzhan" frustration with China's inferiority to foreigners drives the protagonist to drink, after which he forms a relationship with a female ghost, achieves enlightenment, and withdraws with her to Mount Emei (968–980). Sometimes the woman is the cold, superior figure of Pu Songling's stories, whose integrity derives from her chaste avoidance of marriage and motherhood.[24] But Wang Tao keeps even these women from becoming utterly unattainable. "Li Siniang" features a cold martial heroine who teaches a lesser heroine sexual methods for conquering monster enemies (472–484). Thus far the story sounds like those of Pu Songling in which women remain dominant throughout (like "Chang E"). But Wang Tao then introduces a man who orders the martial heroine to marry, and he has the lesser heroine die after a victorious sexual battle.

In "Xu Shuangfu" (247–258), a slight exception to this rule, the story is as if to say that a man can succeed only if he is a woman reborn as a man, and that an ideal married couple is made up of two women. The implication could also be that the woman is the core human subject of whom the man is a temporary offshoot. The story climaxes with what looks like a conventional marriage and a brilliant man's successful career. But the man is in fact the reincarnation of a female adept in esoteric arts, the most important of which she learns from an elder nun, whom the man's wife resembles. The seemingly conventional marriage is in effect between two remarkable women, the female adept and the nun, free of the influence of dominant men. The special relationship between an elder nun and a younger woman is an old motif found, for example, in the frequently anthologized Tang tale "Nie Yinniang," by Pei Xing (825–880). Although stories containing this motif commonly slide the focus from female centrality back to male, the liaison of nun and disciple is a striking case of female self-determination.[25] Wang Tao's *qing* inheritance shows itself here, hence his overall message that men are in a state of crisis the only escape from which is refuge with Pu Songling–like women.

Nevertheless, "Xu Shuangfu" is an almost accidental exception to Wang Tao's generally more male-centered version of refuge with women, which can be phrased as follows. The man must find some way to make an honorable imprint of his failure, and that way is through his relationship with remarkable women. They await him wherever he goes during the period of China's devastation and decline, and with them the downcast man finds refuge in what amounts to withdrawal into an alternate and self-sustaining world of romantic bliss. Meanwhile, he carries out the grand mission of reporting on the fates of the women who, like the man, have important things to show and say about their times. Wang Tao has an eye for their individual personalities and experiences, about which his biographies treat case after case: one who runs a girl's school; a courtesan who, dressed as a Manchu, takes a walk in a Shanghai garden with a Western woman; a woman from a disbanded acting troupe in 1885 who says she would rather be the concubine of a talented scholar than the wife of a commoner; another from the same group who after marriage never wants to see her lute again; or a courtesan who marries but at age forty is suddenly abandoned after a fight with her husband.[26] The overall effect is something like Cao Xueqin's devotion to the endless details of life in the garden, admiring the women and sorrowing over their miserable fates. In "Talented Women of Japan" (Dongying cainü, 1316–1329), Wang Tao writes admiringly of Japanese prostitutes but nevertheless concludes that, compared to Chinese women, they have no sense of loyalty and true love. The man can entrust his most important keys to a Japanese courtesan, which he cannot do with a Chinese woman. The Japanese woman is very unself-conscious about nudity. Nevertheless, she is heartless even after many years of togetherness, whereas—he continues in a statement that sews the entire collection together—affairs between the Chinese man and woman are the site of the deepest human feelings (1322). Earlier I said that Wang Tao softens the radical edge of *qing* subjectivity. This can be rephrased by saying that, in adhering to the pastime of visiting courtesans, he turns the pastime into a trope of cultural containment, that is, Chinese cultural containment. Through prostitutes and ghost stories he finds refuge from what is in effect a homeless outside, the one he spends his time in as journalist or cross-cultural interpreter. *Qing* in the framework of solace in the brothel becomes an alternate repository of Chinese cultural essence.

Wang Tao may admire the ideal of neutral universality harbored in the "positivism" of the Western scientific method. He even extends the meaning of the Chinese *dao* to the level of a neutral universal when he says that the Chinese *dao* is everyone's *dao,* with no exclusive claim to a particular chosen people.[27] At the same time, the retreat to the private corner is a way of weathering the un-Chinese way of life that he has adopted since the fall of 1849, when he began working for foreigners. Let us say that his experience of scientific and neutral universality is liberating but also unnerving because of China's inferior position in relation to foreign powers. He may promote the concept of the neutral *dao* that belongs to everyone, but he also suffers as the subject who, like the courtesan, is in the position of selling himself to a social superior. He has no hope of occupying the privileged position of the missionary or Western scholar. His friendship with courtesans and his love for Pu Songling–like tales is the sign of this same sense of dislocation. At the same time, he escapes hopelessness by turning these pastimes into inalienable pursuits of pleasure. His love of Chinese prostitutes is a mark of cultural identity, an inviolable zone to which he repairs until the age of decline will, he hopes, pass.

CHAPTER FIVE

Passive Polygyny
in Two Kinds
of Man-child

The Clever Boy in the Body of a Man in *Courtesan Chambers*

Pu Songling's stories and the sequels to *Dream of the Red Chamber* have familiar-ized us with the formulae by which male authors construct a man among a group of women who join him unjealously as wives or concubines. The chief elements of passive polygyny are the simulation of the female arrangement of the marriage and some form of male subservience to and adoration of women. In applying these formulae, the 1878 novel *Courtesan Chambers* (*Qinglou meng*), by Yu Da (?–1884), provides the most dreamily suffused rendition of the man's polygynous affairs of all *qing*-inspired novels of the Qing dynasty.[1] From the beginning it enters a care-free dream zone in which a couple of male soul mates roam from one gorgeous courtesan to the next. Instead of tortured love affairs in the tradition of *Dream of the Red Chamber, Courtesan Chambers* features the man's uninhibited adulation of women, to whose coddling, prodding, and scolding he extravagantly subjects himself. The hero is like a knowing child in the body of an adult man who is a refined expert of the brothel. He moves around with a clever, knowing eye that permits him to enjoy the women's collectively indulgent regard, as if all agree that he is the most adorable man they could meet. In this regard, he is like the brazen knave whom we saw in the sequel *Silken Chambers Revisited* (*Qilou chongmeng*) and the master of the brothel in *Nine-times Cuckold* (*Jiuwei gui*) of chapter 8. Men like these show little sign of becoming the last polygynists of novels like *Traces of the Flowery Moon* or *Shanghai Dust*.

This chapter provides two contrasting portraits of the polygynous man-child who subjects himself to women's coddling and coaxing. In *Courtesan Chambers* he is a clever and self-confident philanderer whose subjection to women is a game by which he proves his expertise in sex and romance and that ends in a mar-riage to multiple women followed by ascension into polygynous immortality. In *Tale of Filial Heroes* (*Ernü yingxiong zhuan*), which like *Courtesan Chambers* also appeared in 1878, he is from start to finish a pure and unadulterated boy-polygynist whose subjection to women throws the man's ability to master both himself and women entirely into doubt. Compared to Chen Sen and Wei Xiuren, the author Yu Da makes only token attempts to imbue polygyny with the *qing* ethics of equality, a trace of which exists in his insistence that his concubines wear the same type of clothing as his wife. *Tale of Filial Heroes* features the *ernü* kind of *qing*, as announced in its title and prologue, in which lovers are filial and innately correct and in which the women smartly arrange and govern the polygynous marriage. The philandering lover of courtesans is completely absent. Instead the man marries two wives only (though his wives later give him a concubine), who, as predicted in the discussion of two-wife polygyny above, rise above jealousy and take agency into their own hands. The two novels are alike in that love in both lacks the kernel of inherent impasse that pervades *Dream of the Red Chamber, Precious Mirror of Boy Actresses,* and *Traces of the Flowery Moon.* There are no temperamental jousts in which one lover feels insulted or misunderstood, no extreme sacrifice for the other or much in the way of obstacles preventing union. Similarly, neither novel engages the historical realities of the period, though they can be read in the same historically symbolic way as *Traces of the Flowery Moon* and *Later Tales of Liaozhai.* I will save the historical reading for the final chapter but prepare for that discussion by focusing on the character Jin Yixiang's knowing eye in *Courtesan Chambers,* a key feature of the late-Qing master philanderer, and the battle of modes of enjoyment in *Tale of Filial Heroes,* which continues the discussion from the last chapter of the way literary fantasy arrays the forces of Chinese civilization against its detractors both within and without.

Affectations of *Qing* Sensibility

Yu Da, who also wrote poetry, anecdotal fiction (*biji*), a study of antiques, and a collection of illustrations of beautiful courtesans, was a close friend of Zou Tao, a reform thinker and the author of the commentary on *Courtesan Chambers* (Yu Da in turn wrote commentaries on two of Zou Tao's collections of *biji* fiction).[2] Zou Tao wrote the 1904 novel *Shanghai Dust* (*Haishang chentian ying*), the subject of chapter 7, which was heavily influenced by *Traces of the Flowery Moon* and which explicitly involves the lover of courtesans in the historical and political issues of the time. In *Courtesan Chambers,* both narrator and commentator avoid those issues as they collude in their enjoyment of the man's dalliance with courtesans. Both relish situations in which the man becomes the women's subservient but artful fool, especially when she is merciless in making him cower. Their collusion is the sign of the knowing eye that pervades each episode of the book but that disguises itself under an atmosphere of dreamy suffusion. That atmosphere should be read as an affectation of high *qing* sensibility. The story moves with unparticularistic transition from one scene and one woman to the next. When a courtesan emerges from her chambers, she treads slowly like a drifting cloud, with an air of unassuming loftiness. She plays music that moves the man to weep. They spend days together for a month; then he finally has to leave, at which point they shed many tears (9.58–60). Yu Da follows Cao Xueqin's mode of describing daily uneventful gatherings, poetry recitations, and occasions of eating and drinking.[3] The historical realities of the time make only the barest appearance, as in the opium one of the heroines swallows in an attempt to commit suicide (otherwise no one uses opium in the book) and the woman who was forced to become a prostitute because of war, perhaps a reference to the Taiping Rebellion (9.58).

A brief summary of the plot demonstrates the novel's central tone of *qing* sensibility. The hero Jin Yixiang has affairs with one woman after another, culminating when he gathers thirty-six of them in chapter 29, after which he turns melancholic as many of the women marry other men or die one by one. Although harmoniously married to a wife and four concubines, members of the original group of thirty-six, Jin Yixiang is constantly "full of sadness" (*menmen*, 49.334). He does his best to attend to women who are sick or dying or to arrange good marriages for them. Rushing to the side of a dying courtesan, for example, he trips and falls, but gets up and "has no thought of whether he hurt himself or not" (46.316). Since he is a man who simply will not "treat women poorly" (*qingdai meiren*, 31.213), he insists that his concubines dress in the same type of clothing as his main wife. He is outraged to discover a former lover with an ugly man (44). He can't stand it when one of his wives suffers the pains of childbirth (46 and 50). These realities push him beyond what he can endure, so he withdraws to become a monk (60), then returns in the last chapter (64) to retrieve his wives and retreat to their original existence as immortals.[4]

Although as I have said the novel lacks the kernel of inherent impasse that pervaded novels like *Precious Mirror of Boy Actresses* or *Traces of the Flowery Moon,* Yu Da makes frequent gestures toward the type of impasse that foiled the lovers in those works. For example, before their marriage, the prostitute and future main wife, Niu Aiqing (whose name puns with "love"), falls ill with an affliction of the eyes, giving Yixiang the opportunity to demonstrate devotion by administering the cure of licking her eyes over a three-day period (16; as the prostitute Fenglin did to her patron Jia Ming in *Seductive Dreams*). After an argument with her madam, Aiqing tries to commit suicide by swallowing raw opium. Yixiang saves her by using his tongue to draw out the bits of opium still left in her mouth (20). In getting married, their main ordeal is to obtain permission from Yixiang's father and to raise the money to redeem her from the brothel (Aiqing redeems herself with gold from her own savings). Once married, impasse turns tame in that his first major problem is to get into one wife's room before she shuts him out in deference to another wife. Soon after, however, trouble returns as Yixiang falls gravely ill and dies (33). Before his death, in grand gestures of passion, two of his concubines declare that they will follow him to death, but he urges them not to because, as he tells them melodramatically, he has already ruined their lives enough by leaving them widowed (33.228). The climactic moment of his death dissolves, however, when it turns out that an error was made in having him die, and the King of Hell orders him resurrected (35).

The general rule in *Courtesan Chambers* is that nothing should shatter the frame of the wanton dream. In chapter 37, an innocent remark becomes the cause of a concubine's histrionic display of jealousy. The concubine Suyu thinks she hears Aiqing and Yixiang talking behind her back and demands to know what they have said. She accuses Yixiang of breaking the rule against comparing one woman with another and then pretends towering rage as she rides on top of him like the classic shrewish wife who pummels and berates the miscreant husband. The more he denies guilt, the more upset she becomes, until he begs her to stop. She knew all along that there was nothing behind their remarks, but when he kneels in submission she leaves him there until at long last she takes his hand to let him stand up. Zou Tao delights in the scene of Suyu pushing Yixiang down, saying, "She rides him like a horse!" After Yixiang kneels and begs her to stop, a favorite gesture of the polygynous connoisseur, Zou Tao writes, "Suyu has him in the palm of her hand!" In short, both narrator and commentator love it when the man is at the mercy of one of his women who puts on a show of temper (37.250–252).

The Philanderer's Knowing Eye

The nods that pass between Yu Da, the author-narrator, and Zou Tao, the commentator, or between two characters in the narrative convey the novel's sense of controlled irony, which in sexual terms is all about affirming Yixiang's particular brand of boyish expertise in the brothel. The narrator and commentator savor the endlessly varied particulars of that expertise. In his commentary at the beginning of chapter 6, Zou Tao writes, "Jin Yixiang simply has the nature of a child. He is a true romantic lover (*duoqing*). Look at him pretending to be drunk so that he can stay the night with Yuesu [a courtesan]. He puts himself where he wants to be, whether Yuesu approves of it or not" (6.33). Jin Yixiang is not just a child but a knowing child who toys with the rules that he himself makes up. In this scene of brothel repartee, Yixiang teases Yuesu by saying that because he is too drunk, she will surely forbid him to leave the brothel that night. She answers sardonically, "You are really a laugh. No one is keeping you. You know very well how to lift anchor and set sail. But if in fact we were to keep you, I'm afraid all we could offer at the moment is a night with the old serving lady." Yixiang naturally realizes that her response is a teasing way of "saying no, but really meaning yes" (*xinxu koufei*). His repartee is, "I don't mind sleeping with the old lady—as long as it doesn't embarrass you too much, that is (*zhi yao meimei guoyidequ jiu shile*)." Yixiang thus proves his proper cleverness, as Yuesu shows by smiling "and giving him a pointed look" (*ba Yixiang kanle yi kan*). "You are a foolish lad with a clever tongue," she says; "I've got to hand it to you, you have me outwitted." They undress and get into bed, where they talk for awhile before "going to sleep. As the poem has it, 'Their love went beyond what money could buy. A treasure of a night, it lasted forever'" (6.36–37).

Zou Tao praises the delicacy of the episode, declaring that although the book is more "licentious" (*yindang*) than others, the author is skillful enough to let no traces of the licentiousness escape, so that "readers who aren't perceptive enough will miss it." Readers in the know, however, will "get the point" (*hui yi*, 6.33). In Yu Da's form of refined licentiousness, the key is suffusing the story with eroticism without being explicit, hence passages like the one above in which no sexual act is described. Refinement also includes childishness. Yixiang is like a boy in a man's body, falling into a woman's lap as if he's about to nurse like a baby, or beholding women in a group and "hallucinating as if in a daze" (7.50). He is ready to dissolve into tears at the slightest teasing rebuff, to which he angrily pouts that he will "go off and become a monk!"(13.91). When he gets cheeky, Wanqing pushes him away, which makes him "become even more childish by falling into her lap," to which Aiqing says, "You're not a child nursing at the breast, so what are you doing in a person's lap?" This excites him all the more: "'I was just about to suck on her breast,' as he begins to undo the buttons of Wanqing's clothing." "Absolutely splendid!" exclaims Zou Tao (*miao, miao, miao*, 16.115–116). Such scenes of "fooling around" (*hunao*), as the narrator calls it, remind Zou Tao of the "narrative techniques" (*bifa*) of *Dream of the Red Chamber* (16.116), which he does not specify but which summon to mind scenes like Baoyu's throwing himself on the fragrant and creamy neck of the maid Yuanyang or tickling the helpless Lin Daiyu.

Looking at His Own Corpse

The polygynous dream reaches the peak of fantasy when the ghost of Yixiang observes his wife and concubines carefully preparing his corpse for burial (35.240–241). He thus fulfills a wish he once had that he would lie dead before a group of beauties who would grieve over him as they sent him off to the afterlife. The transparency between life and afterlife is the same here as in the sequels to *Dream of the Red Chamber*, in which characters traveled easily between the two. Looking at women mourning his own death and then reentering his corpse and suddenly sitting up in his coffin describes the perfect circle of the polygynist fantasy. He follows this, his first death, by his second death many chapters later, which occurs after the melancholic Yixiang "has enjoyed all there is to enjoy in the rooms of wives and concubines" (*qiqie fangwei zhi le yi lingluejinle*, 58.395). Claiming total enjoyment and then proceeding into melancholy and death is the obverse of savoring the scene of mourners at one's own funeral and then proceeding to reenter one's corpse. It is a case of claiming control over life and death, enjoyment and its reversal, and thereby merging with the cosmic law of the cycles of pleasure and pain, living and dying. Accordingly, at the end of the novel, after abandoning his wives and achieving enlightenment about the impermanence of pleasure, he resumes his status as an immortal in heaven, where all his women finally join him.

Looking at his own corpse is another version of the knowing eye, which in essence has to do with Yixiang's being able to look openly and admiringly at one woman after another with no need to hide his feelings or intentions, and thereby gaining their accommodating response. Women eye him back with only a little bit of looking askance. Yu Da relishes constructing such scenes, as can be seen when the courtesan Yuesu tells Yixiang that she plans to introduce him to Wanqing, who, Yuesu assures him, will "send his soul flying" (*xiao hun*, 6.35). But the day after their introduction, Wanqing realizes that Yixiang slept with Yuesu the night before. Looking askance at him, Wanqing "smiles knowingly" (*xiao er buyan*) and, when he asks her why, "continues to smile knowingly" (*rengjiu xiao er buyan*). He immediately "gets what she means" (*hui yi*), saying, "I understand" (*wo zhidaole*, 6.39). Yu Da likes what is unspoken and between the lines, which is what in Zou Tao's eyes makes the novel so licentious. In this case, the unspoken meaning has to do with the fact that, although Wanqing is in line to sleep with Yixiang, he should know that she will not follow so easily after Yuesu. She resists him for the time being, and it takes seven chapters before they finally spend their first night together (13).

A similar knowing eye appears in Zou Tao's *Shanghai Dust* and Zhang Chun-fan's *Nine-times Cuckold* (*Jiuwei gui*), but in critically divergent ways. In Zou Tao, the sentimental young man has no choice but to face the fact that he cannot love more than one woman at the same time. In the brazen *Nine-times Cuckold*, on the other hand, the knowing eye persists but now becomes that of the mature, self-confident, and nonmelancholic polygynist who serves as a model of the successful modern man. A strong admirer of Wei Xiuren's *Traces of the Flowery Moon*, Zou Tao reveres the image of *qing* lovers set against the backdrop of civilizational crisis. Zhang Chunfan likewise admires *Traces of the Flowery Moon*, but he resolves civilizational crisis by creating a polygynist-philanderer who is the hero of a new China. Yu Da avoids the overt politicization of the *qing* lovers as dynastic loyalists.

The courtesan's chambers remain a safe and insulated retreat in which the man's love of women is the mark of the philanderer's inalienable pursuit of pleasure. As in Wang Tao's *Later Tales of Liaozhai,* in between the lines we can read the same story of sublime *qing* lovers who enjoy their last times together on earth before the end of time as they know it. But the grand display of brothel connoisseurship, with its carefully perfected scenes of passive polygyny, makes *Courtesan Chambers* read more like a prelude to *Nine-times Cuckold* than to either *Shanghai Dust,* with its ending in love death, or *Flowers of Shanghai* in the next chapter, in which the Shanghai prostitute turns the tables and frustrates all masters of the brothel.

The Passive Polygynist and His Protective Co-wives in the *Tale of Filial Heroes*

Male subjection to female will appeared in sequels to *Dream of the Red Chamber,* where the notion of female agency stood for the scenario in which polygyny appeared to be at the will of the co-wives. The sequels divided into two general types, one emphasizing erotic love that was robust and problem free, the other involving characters who engaged in nonromantic pursuits. With its suffused eroticism, *Courtesan Chambers* takes after the sequels in which subservience to women is merely an appearance of passivity that hides an ambitious polygynous drive. *Tale of Filial Heroes,* by the Manchu author Wen Kang (mid-nineteenth century), opts for a chaste polygyny in which male passivity is the sign of naïve purity.[5] In this novel, the two wives and one concubine exhibit a shared sense of command and self-assurance. They love the man's other women as much as the man does if not more. They go so far as to take charge of the moral and material management of the entire household. The key to the arrangement of strong co-wives and coddled husband is the happy acceptance of general male ineptitude in everything but scholarship and examination knowledge. Women assume the superior role while remaining under the nominal authority of the Confucian patriarch, the husband's father. Under such conditions, the marriage of the benignly useless man to two wives and a concubine is an arrangement that guarantees social and familial stability.[6]

The young man of this polygynous scenario, An Ji, recalls the blank male hero like Baoyu, but minus "lust of the mind." His polygyny is passive and will-less, where will-less refers to his lack of explicit intention to marry more than one woman. The true manager is the main co-wife, He Yufeng, a metaphorical queen-goddess Nüwa, the mythical woman who restored cosmic order by patching the heavens after a battle between male enemies.[7] Men in general live in light-headed freedom from worry. An Ji in particular is coaxed and coddled by mainly female figures under whose watch he shields himself as much as possible from the harsh outside world. He is like a child who lives with the assurance that the mother or mother figures—wives in this case—can always keep the world whole. The main risks for him are that he might not know how to set limits on pleasure and that he might become engulfed in female indulgence at the expense of his ability to adjust to reality. But his strong co-wives protect him from himself, even while upholding the polygynous regime.

Since the last chapter, my question has been how to read the polygynist-philanderer against the backdrop of turbulence and decline in the last century of the Qing. In terms of *Tale of Filial Heroes,* the best way to answer is to look at the novel in a group with other works from the beginning to the end of the dynasty. It is a matter in all these of battling modes of enjoyment, a concept I will return to more fully in the conclusion, but for now suffice it to say is a handy way of describing Wen Kang's battle against his foes in the form of the *Dream of the Red Chamber* and, further below, *Precious Mirror of Boy Actresses.* Mode of enjoyment has to be understood in a special sense, having to do with a character's or a group's preferences and habits of sexual and marital custom, eating and hygiene, and also including music, clothing, and other areas of art, pleasure, and physical well-being. Alignments within and between novels vary, since *Tale of Filial Heroes* shares some modes of enjoyment with a novel like *An Old Man's Radiant Words* but in other cases resembles works like *Dream of the Red Chamber* or *Traces of the Flowery Moon.* That is, instead of the heroic polygynist of *An Old Man's Radiant Words* and some of the sequels, Wen Kang favors the chaste and girllike man, handing the heroic role to the woman. In this choice the novel roughly resembles *Traces of the Flowery Moon* and the later *Shanghai Dust* (1904). In those, however, the theme of female superiority is the telltale sign of crisis in male leadership, and the polygynist fantasy undergoes dissolution as the authors stage sublime love deaths in which man and woman are like icons of high culture in the face of civilizational calamity. *Tale of Filial Heroes* engages in a grand disavowal of disorder, which it replaces with the fantasy of successful polygyny nominally headed by a man who is a smart exam candidate and honest official. In other words, as in *Radiant Words* and other polygynous erotic romances, healthy polygyny is the mark of order both domestically and in society at large. Nevertheless, unlike *Radiant Words, Tale of Filial Heroes* modifies the theme of healthy polygyny by elevating the remarkable woman but turning her into a strange double. Whereas she was once the one soul mate of the one man, now she helps the man in his polygyny, assumes the role of dominant spouse, and promotes the values of Confucian patriarchy.

The key to Wen Kang's model of passive polygyny lies in the way men and women occupy separate planes of existence—another term for separate modes of enjoyment. In short, women get the pleasure of ruling and managing, while men get the pleasure of living a life centered on play. Although Wen Kang assumes the inevitability of male weakness, he virtually celebrates that weakness by creating a young male hero who to the very end of the novel is as if fatally inept and helpless without the company of wives, elders, and servants. But weakness is beneficial because it is cause for the permanent prospect of masterful wives and concubines cuddling and coddling the man to keep him benignly weak and therefore firmly in the position of nominal head of the family. To put this in terms of Wen Kang's most prominent literary predecessor, he has refined Jia Baoyu to the point of putting him securely in the hands of good mothering women while at the same time, as I have said, removing all traces of Baoyu's "lust of the mind." Wen Kang's understanding of "lust of the mind" has to do with not only the insidiousness of lustful thoughts but also Baoyu's sense of conflicted love for numerous remarkable women, only one of whom can be his sublime soul mate. Like the Baoyu of the sequels, Wen Kang's counter-Baoyu—in his counter-mode-of-enjoyment—experiences no such internal conflict, nor do his potential co-wives experience any anxiety of self-esteem.

The Domestication of the Swordswoman

Both Wen Kang and the commentator Dong Xun in fact take the novel's main object of criticism to be *Dream of the Red Chamber,* which Wen Kang vilifies throughout. He resembles the earlier Xia Jingqu, author of *An Old Man's Radiant Words,* in deradicalizing *qing* by installing it in characters who are scrupulously observant of Confucian orthodoxy. As we know, Wen's defining term is *ernü yingxiong,* "child-like heroes," where *ernü* stands for primordial purity, like that of the first humans on earth.[8] As in *Radiant Words,* the *ernü* kind of *qing* amounts to a vehicle of wholesome energy that sweeps away all forms of corruption and social ill, whether by valiant action or simply out-staring the problems and treating them as trivial and easy to repair. At home, *qing* is filial and familial, that is, always with an eye to the good of the family. When *qing* manifests itself in the sphere of righteous heroism and duty to one's rulers, then it is expressed with an eye to the good of the empire. In all this, the remarkable woman is superior to the man in maintaining the eye for the good of both family and empire. Wen Kang paints a world in which men must remain pure and naïve all their lives so that practical, talented women can keep at bay the chaos that men would otherwise create. The result is that at the didactic level the novel makes the same statement as that of normative patriarchy, but at the level of narrative enactment, the subject who carries out the contents of that didactic message is no longer the patriarchal man but the heroic co-wife.

It is precisely the split between the didactic statement and the subject who performs the contents of that statement that signals the core unconscious assumption of the novel, which is that the world led by men is in a state of crisis, as is the state of manhood as a whole.[9] "Unconscious" means unstated, disavowed, and distorted. What is unstated are the contemporary social and political realities of China in a state of massive corruption, imperial weakness, and foreign intrusion. What is disavowed is that male weakness is the sign of a general crisis of leadership. Distortion comes in the form of the fantasy of a world saved and led by strong women. The unconscious of *Tale of Filial Heroes* also emerges in the form of juxtaposition with other literature of the late Qing, especially novels like *Traces of the Flowery Moon* and *Shanghai Dust,* which explicitly relate the love affair to national crisis, or poetry like the line Zhou Shi (d. 1911) wrote: "No more sign of life in the vast Central Plains, only heroines remain valiant and bold"[10]—hence Wen Kang's prime concern that the man not turn into a wastrel and hence the man's need for multiple nonwanton wives, who will keep his heart from "fattening" (*fei*) and growing wild (30.658).[11] From birth to death, whether at home or at a distant post, women care for him in his daily life. They tuck him in bed at night, but also criticize him when he transgresses. The supreme example of the unwanton wife is Thirteenth Sister (Shisan mei), the swordswoman whom An Ji's father An Xuehai succeeds in taming by persuading her to give up the sword in order to become his son's main co-wife. In taming her, however, the learned patriarch domesticates her only nominally, while actually granting her jurisdiction over the entire household and its rural estates.

The domestication of the swordswoman is in fact central to the man's supposed submission to female control. Understanding this submission involves discovering what *Tale of Filial Heroes* does that is new and unusual in terms of its predecessors and how it was received in later times. *Tale of Filial Heroes* has troubled twentieth-century readers because of the swordswoman's agreement to domesticate herself by becoming co-wife to the young hero An Ji.[12] It is as if the cold swordswoman of Pu Songling's "Nüxia" and other similar tales from centuries back decided to get married after completing her mission of revenge instead of disappearing forever. In the first part of the novel, the steely heroine intends in good tradition to withdraw from the world and remain forever unmarried once she avenges her father's enemy. Like the heroines in Pu Songling's tales, marriage means nothing to Thirteenth Sister but insult and imprisonment, her mission of vengeance spurred to begin with by the fact that her father was murdered in response to his refusal to marry her to a young wastrel. The stunning scene in chapter 7 in which she rescues An Ji as bandit monks are about to eviscerate him has her coolly delivering the killing blows (including the strike that slices off the face of a garrulous woman working for the cannibalistic monks, 7.139). But several chapters later An Ji's father and her co-wife-to-be Zhang Jinfeng persuade her that she must relinquish her swordly attire and join the filial family so that she may assume her predestined role as a virtuous wifely woman.

The trouble with the transformation from the self of Thirteenth Sister, her hero's epithet in the first half of the novel, back to the self of He Yufeng, her original name, is that the story of martial heroes and heroines is not supposed to transform into the story of daily married life, training for the imperial exams, and then the future of offspring and career. The transition from the riveting narration of heroic deeds to the placidity of domestic life creates anticlimax. Wen Kang nevertheless defies narrative custom by joyfully portraying that transition, which he accomplishes by retaining the gender inversion he began with after all. In other words, He Yufeng's domestication is not complete. An Ji's utter lack of wits and nerve in critical situations, as I have said, prevails throughout the novel, allowing He Yufeng to continue playing the dominant role as guardian of the moral and physical stability of the household. She remains cool and decisive even after her supposed conversion, always ready for valiant action after all, "even in peace never forgetting the possibility of danger," as the idiom puts it (*an buwang wei*, 30.670). She is such a figure because of the experience of risking her life to stand up for justice. Women like her emerge when men have declined to a point that they no longer know how to assume the role of the bearer of mandate, that is, the one who maintains the eye for the good of family and empire. Even the Confucian patriarch is one in name only, as An Xuehai, who is happiest in the role of modest and periodically laughable pedant, repeatedly demonstrates.[13]

Boyish and Girlish All His Life

An Ji is likewise nominal in his role as polygynist, which in this case means that he is a passive and will-less one. Wen Kang addresses the most sensitive issue of polygyny, jealousy, in a detailed discussion in which he transcends the problem by stating that women are jealous only if they are weak and lacking in talent. In An Ji's polygyny the problem of jealousy is irrelevant because outstanding women like He Yufeng are unjealous to begin with. The narrator notes the "somewhat unfair" rule that a woman must remain loyal to one husband but a man is permitted to have wives and concubines (27.576). How can this be so? He declares that it is so simply because "it is the most logical and proper way for human beings to behave" (*rensheng zhi zhili*, 27.576). Nevertheless, he realizes, the number of women who are unjealous is infinitesimally small. He divides women into two groups, those who "can eat vinegar" and those who cannot. At the "divine" end stands the woman who, whether because she fails to have a son or her son dies early, actively initiates the installation of a concubine, whom she loves and treasures more than the man does. She constitutes the "divine grade" (*shenpin*) of unjealousy. In general, the two highest levels of unjealous women include those who are confident in their looks and abilities and those who place the interests of the family over their own. At the other extreme is the vinegary woman who is incapable of managing her husband except by subverting him, and who at her worst would rather the family line go extinct than have her husband take a concubine. The discourse on jealousy is a prime example of a male-constructed justification of polygyny.

An Ji is the unjealous woman's perfect counterpart. Zhang Jinfeng must persuade him to take He Yufeng as co-wife, beginning her argument with a line we have seen elsewhere by professing her own "love" (*ai*) for He (23.486).[14] At first shocked by her proposal, An Ji claims that adding another person would "divide our love for each other" (*fenle niwo de en'ai*, 23.489). Even after he finally agrees, several chapters later his parents and wives have to insist all over again that he realize the logic of taking the maid Changjie as concubine. Will-less polygyny has to do with remaining boyish and girlish all his life, hence virtually by accident achieving the idyllic state of marriage to multiple wives, a state to which even the Jade Emperor aspires, as a narrative aside tells us.[15] In An Ji, being boyish and girlish includes slightly spoiled childlike traits such as "extending his arm for his clothes to be put on and opening his mouth when he is about to be fed" (*yi lai shen shou, fan lai zhang kou*, 30.670). This is an idiomatic expression the narrator uses to characterize An Ji as someone who even in adulthood needs women and elders to take care of him (thus, when he is about to be assigned to a distant post to which his pregnant wives cannot accompany him, his family promotes the maid Changjie to concubine so that she can accompany him and provide for his intimate daily necessities). He will eventually take over the father's rule, but all along he needs women to enforce that rule. As for the father An Xuehai himself, he is a monogamous Confucian patriarch, an honest and impractical scholar who passes the highest imperial exams late in life and a father and husband whose greatest pleasures include things like discussing an abstruse topic with his son or exploring an ancient historical site (38 and 40).

Model Men and Modes of Enjoyment

Another emblematically model man is Old Deng, or Deng the Ninth (Deng Jiu-gong), who rounds out the novel's portrayal of genuine male counterparts to He Yufeng and Zhang Jinfeng. Having once been a wastrel himself, Deng finally acquires the discipline to become a bodyguard and teacher of martial arts.[16] He is a model of hearty vitality and lack of civilized pretentiousness. If we use David Wang's logic of the continuity between the *Tale of Filial Heroes* and the early-modern fantasy of nationalist heroism, then Deng prepares the way for various twentieth-century dismissals of the Chinese man's decadence and depravity. It is not farfetched to see in him a precursor of the hearty underling of a Communist general like Zhu De, and thus a representative of a time when men, as it were, take over again.[17] Like Thirteenth Sister, Deng has the innate ability to stare aside whatever is rotten and decadent. How he does so appears in the remarkable scene that Wen Kang imports from *Precious Mirror of Boy Actresses,* a novel that to Wen Kang vies in depravity with *Dream of the Red Chamber.* He borrows only the vulgar characters, thus ignoring Chen Sen's idealization of sublime homoerotic love among Jia Baoyu–like men. Wen Kang treats sex between men as something so unimaginable that one can only make vague reference to it. Old Deng watches a group of "opera fanatics" engaging in outlandish behavior in the cramped audience of a Beijing theater (32.711–715). A plump man with protruding teeth joins a skinny, nearsighted hunchback, both accompanied by a dirty and unruly band of boys dressed as women, described as "a most mother-forsaken band of boy actresses who made up a queer and screwball troop of irregulars" (*qichang baduan qiuqiu dandan de . . . taniangde yidaqun xiaodan,* 32.712–713).[18] A group of rich young men appears, one of whom says something to a boy who reacts by skewing the man's hat and slapping him on the back of the head. To Deng's surprise, "This didn't annoy the man at all! I began to wonder who was paying whom for what!" (32.714). Finally, three actors gather around two men, one with an inflamed face and the other with a syphilitic nose. When Deng asks his friend why actors would sit with such scurrilous-looking men, the friend, in a gesture of wordless innuendo, merely "motions with his hands and sticks out his tongue" (where sticking out the tongue in this case indicates something too bizarre and embarrassing to put into words, 32.715). The critical weight of this scene is that frivolous and abhorrent things should not exist, and therefore the author will refer to them only obliquely. Deng relates the scene in the theater in robustly vulgar language, then ends with a description of his favorite kind of opera about court cases and the adventures of righteous heroes (32.715). It is again a matter of battling modes of enjoyment, with vigorous Deng on one side and grotesque opera fanatics on the other.

Another telling example of mode of enjoyment takes the form of a grotesque alternate to An Ji, his tutor, a man of loathsomely filthy habits and outlandish manners who visits the An household to congratulate An Ji on passing the exams. The tutor is revolting to the women, especially the maids who have to clean up the tobacco and chewed remnants of food that he spits on the floor. "Sometimes he has leftover food in his mouth that he never bothers to swallow, which he pries out with the ivory mouthpiece of his pipe. He examines what he picks out and then puts it back to chew and swallow" (37.878–879). An Xuehai insists that habits like these are the sign of a superior man of learning, one who transcends the petty concerns of common cleanliness and appearance (37.883).[19] If we consider their relation to bodily needs, then the tutor and An Ji in fact occupy a common realm. Relishing filth and blithely spitting on the floor parallel "extending his arm for his clothes to be put on and opening his mouth when he is about to be fed." They are habits of boy-men who occupy a plane of existence in which they have no need to see themselves as others see them. Who sees them? The women and others who feed them or sweep up after them. In short, both in varying ways assume that others will attend to their bodily needs. Their refusal to grow into mature adults distantly resembles the celebration of the adolescent "mind lust" of *Dream of the Red Chamber*. But the difference is that in *Dream of the Red Chamber* the avoidance of adult roles was the sign of a radical unplugging from social-symbolic mandate. Male inferiority to women was a motif of feminine subjectivity. *Tale of Filial Heroes* takes the same motif but contentedly subjectifies the man as weak and inept. As a mode of enjoyment, male weakness becomes something that An Ji thrives on better than his conflicted counterpart, Jia Baoyu, and that for Wen Kang represents a successful model for a man who will not turn into a wastrel.

Keeping the Heart from Fattening

In other words, An Ji is superior to Jia Baoyu because An Ji is better at being a passive, will-less polygynist. In a parallel sense, An Ji's father is better at being a passive patriarch than Baoyu's, for he has learned how to tolerate and even benefit from the women's indulgence of his son. Indulgence now takes the form of having women place the necessary limits on pleasure, thereby avoiding the situation in which the son becomes overwhelmed and engulfed in feminine coaxing and cuddling. Polygyny becomes a method of replacing paternal rule with the rule of wives who divide the man between themselves and thereby indulge and control him at the same time.

The question at this point is where to locate male agency. Is the woman truly in charge? If so, what is she in charge of? The key to passive polygyny, two-wife polygyny in particular, is that the polygynist achieves his goal by appearing to hand the realization of his goal over to the woman. Her command of the polygynous family is a form of female agency. But it is only an apparent command or a semiagency in that it realizes the man's goal of collecting multiple women. We could also explain the relationship by saying that, needing the women's protection, the man requires that they trade agency over themselves on their own behalf for agency over themselves on his behalf. The woman begins the novel fully in charge of herself but ends by exchanging her charge over herself for her charge over the man. The ultimate designer of such an arrangement is the author Wen Kang, who in creating An Ji and his co-wives constructs a mechanism by which the weak-fathered and blithely inept son achieves the goal of remaining nominally dominant without succumbing to an excess of coddling. Recall the scene in chapter 30 in which An Ji almost explodes at his wives for forbidding him polygynous pleasures but then thanks them for their disapproval. If they failed, then An Ji would be engulfed in an excess of pleasure and would suffer the fate of all brazen wastrels and spoiled boys who are the central cause of anxiety in *Tale of Filial Heroes*. Hence, being obedient to the women is also a case of making their polygynous bond with him a matter of moral discipline, and his potential for bad behavior makes it absolutely necessary for him to have multiple wives.

Two final asides have to do with my use of the word "filial" in the English title and with the novel's elements of Manchu ethnicity.

Translating *ernü* as "filial" is by way of emphasizing the author's anxiety about filiality. Seeking refuge in passive polygyny is a sign of anxiety at the degeneration of the filial bond, which the wives regenerate by maintaining better than the men the eye for the good of family and society. The author stems the tide of male weakness by making a virtue of it and at the same time staging an exchange of gender roles whereby women become the enforcers of male discipline. It is a case of remolding polygyny by means of a correction from within, where the normally inner woman corrects and partly takes over the normally outside man.[20]

Another element lurks in the background of the portrayal of strong and commanding women, namely, Wen Kang's Manchu ethnicity. The preface pretends that the novel was written in the Yongzheng reign period (1763–1835), a gesture that may reflect the author's nostalgia for better times since which his family and many other Manchu bannermen suffered serious decline. Wen Kang's portrayal of Manchu practices is a prime example of nostalgia. The Manchu women in particular—with their unbound feet, their Manchu rituals of greeting, and their Manchu clothing and hairstyle—evoke the image of nativism and the prominent roles women played both inside and outside the family in Manchu society. Before the Qing, the Manchus (like other nomads and seminomads since at least the Northern Wei) practiced a form of polygyny with plural wives of roughly equal status, that is, in which the distinction between wife and concubine did not apply. In general, Manchu women (like Mongol women and women of other nomadic groups) enjoyed more liberty to mingle with men and share in strategic decision making.[21]

Explaining the author's peculiar form of passive polygyny in terms of Manchu ethnicity, however useful, would be insufficient in itself. My argument is that *Tale of Filial Heroes* and its modes of enjoyment are readable only if set alongside previous literature like *Dream of the Red Chamber* and its sequels, especially *Revisiting the Silken Chambers* (*Qilou chongmeng*), *Return to Dream of the Red Chamber* (*Honglou fumeng*), and *The Illusion of Dream of the Red Chamber* (*Honglou huanmeng*), as well as contemporary and later novels like *Courtesan Chambers* and *Shanghai Dust,* all of which variously feature women assisting (and in some cases limiting) the polygynist-philanderer's hold on self-satisfaction. Even female-authored *tanci* portray cross-dressing heroines who return to female dress in polygynous marriages in which they become household managers.[22] The most common link between these narratives of the last century of the Qing dynasty is the correlation between healthy polygyny and mastery over chaotic reality. In the case of *Tale of Filial Heroes,* the correlation depends on ensuring that the man not become a wastrel, which can only happen when women of the "divine grade" agree unjealously to create a morally and sexually proper polygyny. This is the ideal realization of the *ernü* kind of *qing.* In *Courtesan Chambers,* no He Yufeng is necessary because the man's self-mastery is not in doubt. In either case, it is a matter of passive polygyny in which women are assumed to be naturally willing to co-marry the same man. He in turn is naturally assumed to be the deserving recipient, not the acquiring taker, of their love and care, while the marriage in general is supposed to be the supreme expression of civilized order. Finally, the polygynist is boyish, whether knowingly so, as in *Courtesan Chambers,* or unself-consciously so, as in *Tale of Filial Heroes.* It is no longer "we are all women," but "we all love the man-child."

CHAPTER SIX

Fleecing the Customer in Shanghai Brothels of the 1890s

The Passing of a Master

Two models of master figures stand behind the man who would become a polygamist or philanderer in late-Qing fiction. One is the dry Confucian father who discourages excess and disparages romance (like Jia Baoyu's father Jia Zheng); the other is the potent polygamist and brothel master who confidently enjoys his many women (like the hero of the erotic romance). A third master enters the picture with the intrusion of Western nations in nineteenth-century China: the well-armed, technologically advanced European monogamist. In fiction, when does his presence register itself in a way that signals paradigmatic change—in particular, change in the form of the end of the polygamist fantasy? Wang Tao is the first one to register a shift when he notes the definitive arrival of the Western ships that link all the "fairy isles." But he still declares allegiance to the native mode of enjoyment of the affair with the Chinese prostitute and thus still takes comfort in the role of the master philanderer. Something like the end of the polygamist fantasy makes its first fictional appearance in the 1892 novel *Flowers of Shanghai* (*Haishanghua liezhuan*), by Han Bangqing (1856–1894).[1] The end occurs not in a literal sense, however, since there is nothing like an outright dismissal of the institution of polygamy or prostitution, and the custom of monogamy among Westerners is never a topic. But unlike the authors of *Courtesan Chambers* or *Tale of Filial Heroes,* Han Bangqing refuses to write on behalf of the lucky man who steadily ascends into polygamous fulfillment. Instead, he stages the emergence of a new kind of remarkable woman in a categorically new kind of setting: the prostitute of the foreign-ruled concessions of Shanghai. It is in this setting that the role of the traditional Chinese master, whether Confucian father or potent polygamist, drastically weakens and where the vigorous and entrepreneurial prostitute profits from that man's foolish and outmoded fantasies. Along with her emerges a new kind of man, neither brilliant, nor virtuous, nor valiant, like old-mode heroes. He simply adapts himself to the fast-paced present and learns to be neither nostalgic about the pre-Shanghai past nor bitterly victimized by the glittering but unstable present.

This and the next three chapters each treat a single novel in order to examine three separate presentations of the sexuality of polygamy and prostitution in the last two decades of the Qing: the 1892 *Flowers of Shanghai* and the prostitute-businesswoman's fleecing of the brothel patron, the mid-1890s *Shanghai Dust* and the pathos of the last Chinese polygynist, and the 1906–1910 *Nine-times Cuckold* and its proposal for a modern Chinese polygynist. All three novels and a few more I include take place in the Shanghai brothel, which becomes a metaphorical staging ground for portraying the destiny of the polygynist-philanderer and his female counterparts in China in a period of paradigmatic change. The pathos of the polygynist's claim to pleasure figures centrally in each case. The main question can be phrased as follows: Will that claim as it has been known until then come to an end, and if it does, how will it do so and who will be the new man and woman, and if it does not, what will the new and self-consciously modern polygynist-philanderer and his female counterparts be like?

Flowers of Shanghai is remarkable among late-Qing novels in that all at once it embodies at least three levels of radical change: the status of its author, its physical setting, and the presentation of a new kind of man and especially woman, which is my focus in this chapter. In terms of authorship, Han Bangqing was a literatus and a first-level exam candidate (*xiucai*) who abandoned the pursuit of office for the life of professional writer, an occupation that only came about with the formation of the second of the above three levels, the foreign concessions of Shanghai. The novelty of this development pervades the literature of the 1890s, especially when it comes to exposing the naïveté of the Chinese man and woman who first arrive in the city.

As for the presentation of a new kind of man and woman, this will be the subject of the sections below discussing the status of love and "doing business" in Shanghai, the prostitute's emotional control of the man, and the image of the brothel facilitator Hong Shanqing. To orient that discussion, it first pays to align the novel with its literary and cultural past, in particular the tradition of literati sympathy with women, which Han Bangqing initially appears to undermine. He begins the novel with the timeworn vilification of prostitutes as vicious and manipulative "yakshas" (1.1). Yet he then implicitly sets that viewpoint aside as one belonging to the stymied male. Han's true focus is on the reality of the life of the prostitute, that is, the good reasons she has to promote her own interests: for example, to begin with, the fact that she is a prostitute because she was sold to the brothel by unscrupulous relatives after the early death of her parents; or the little-known fact that she customarily regurgitates liquor after an evening of drinking with men who expect her to swallow numerous cups of wine (50); or the necessity for the intricate contractual arrangements insisted upon by a prostitute when she buys herself out from her crafty madam (49). These details constitute the reality of the prostitute's life, which in *Flowers of Shanghai* always gains precedent over the man's reality, which in contrast is a fantasy—that of the self-delusion that goes into making his mark in the brothels of Shanghai. One passage in particular sums up Han's general way of favoring the woman's reality over the man's, the confidential statement made by one of three sworn sisters that "being a woman means having problems that can't be put into words" (52.443). Like the author of *Dream of the Red Chamber*, Han Bangqing takes on the task of putting those problems into words, as it were, behind the backs of foolish men.

If the new woman is the Shanghai prostitute, then the new man is the one who no longer seeks or pretends to be the master philanderer. If we recall, the cardinal rule of *Courtesan Chambers* was that, for the talented polygamist and philanderer, subservience to women should be no more than a superficial passivity hiding what is in fact a sophisticated sense of mastery over women. Han Bangqing exposes the bluff of such mastery by demonstrating that it is the talented prostitute who is always in control. In a mundane sense, as in brothels elsewhere, her dominance comes down to compelling her customer to continue spending money in the brothel. But her true secret—diabolical in the eyes of the resentful man, yet perfectly natural to the Shanghai businesswoman—is that the most successful prostitute is the one who constantly stays beyond the man's grasp yet keeps him wanting to achieve that grasp. If the patron knew this truth, he would either stop visiting the brothel altogether or would continue to visit, knowing all along that it was just a game. One of the few men who knows this truth is the brothel facilitator Hong Shanqing, about whom more will be said below. For other men, the glamorous prostitute makes a living by becoming a woman whom men cannot bear to leave, and she succeeds in doing so by taking advantage of the fact that the man's desire to achieve success in the new city of Shanghai depends upon his success with her.

There is in this scene both a sense of eternal return and a sense of radical change. The return of the same has to do with the scene of the brothel, which for centuries has been a sexual and romantic space apart from the ritually defined home of marriage and family. Likewise, the recurrent situation has been the man's fascination with a prostitute followed by his final undoing when he spends all he has; or else, from the woman's perspective, the prostitute's devotion to a customer who promises his love but leaves and never returns. In Shanghai, however, the brothel is doubly a space apart, both from the domestic space of the family and now also from the old Chinese city that the brothels abandoned when they moved to the foreign concessions in the 1860s. *Flowers of Shanghai* stands out because of the way in which it crystallizes its moment of historical transition in which one master begins to pass away as another inevitably arrives. The in-between moment, moreover, exposes the arbitrariness of all masters, the past one especially, and hence the dramatic effect of the novel's round after round of polygynist-philanderers failing to conquer savvy Shanghai prostitutes. Han Bangqing makes the unprecedented nature of his era clear by starting at the bridge where "China" meets the "West" (1.2), that is, the bridge dividing the Chinese part of town from the foreign districts. The time frame, moreover, is "ever since Shanghai began doing business with foreigners" (1.1). Prostitutes and playboys have poured into Shanghai, freshly unsprung and ready to throw everything aside in an untrodden place in which everyone can be larger than life in ways they have never known before. Those who succeed, as Han Bangqing portrays it, are, as I have said, neither brilliant, virtuous, nor valiant. They adjust to the fast-paced life of Shanghai and neither long for the pre-Shanghai past nor resent the rising star of the present, the trend-setting Shanghai prostitute.

Late-Qing Shanghai

Before continuing, let me first provide a brief but essential summary of the novel and a short discussion of the author and the Shanghai of his times, which others have already examined at length.[2] The novel's central strand, to which many others are attached, has to do with Zhao Puzhai, his sister Zhao Erbao, and their uncle Hong Shanqing. Zhao Puzhai travels from the hinterland to Shanghai hoping that his uncle will find him work, but he ends in dire poverty until his mother and sister arrive in Shanghai to rescue him. The sister represents the female version of the naïve outsider who succumbs to the lures of Shanghai. First one man turns her into a kept woman and forces her to take up prostitution; then another man promises to marry her but disappears, leaving her severely in debt and utterly trapped in Shanghai. Other key characters include the older patron Wang Liansheng, who tries but fails to abandon the prostitute Shen Xiaohong, even after she physically attacks his new mistress and cheats him by seeing another man; the patron Luo Zifu and the prostitute Huang Cuifeng, the most formidable woman in the novel, who succeeds in keeping a secret lover while earning enough money from Luo to buy herself out of prostitution; and the young Zhu Shuren and the virgin prostitute Zhou Shuangyu, who swear eternal love and plan to have her become his main wife in spite of the fact that such an outcome is impossible between an elite young man and a prostitute. That she can conceive of such a marriage, even if she doesn't achieve it, is a sign of a new level of independence that the Shanghai environment evokes in women like her.

As for the uniqueness of the author and his work, the first twenty-eight chapters of *Flowers of Shanghai* appeared over eight weeks in 1892 in a biweekly magazine founded by the author, such serialization being a relatively new mode of publication.[3] He was one of many professional writers from the foreign concessions of Shanghai who through their association with newspapers or the work of translation pursued a livelihood outside the traditional system that prepared them for service in the imperial bureaucracy. Han Bangqing predated by only half a decade or so the explosion of the professional writing of fiction by authors such as Li Boyuan, Wu Jianren, and Zhang Chunfan. His source of income is unclear but at least in part came from his contributions to the Shanghai newspaper *Shenbao*. He kept company with other literati who joined to write poetry and enjoy the company of prostitutes. Like the character Hong Shanqing, he was an opium smoker and reportedly lived with his mistress-prostitute in her chambers.[4] Writing about prostitution in Shanghai was a thriving industry, *Flowers of Shanghai* being the first of many novels in this vein, which also included biographies, essays, and city guidebooks. Han's novel was not popular at the time and had to rely on such twentieth-century writers as Lu Xun, Hu Shih, and Zhang Ailing to promote it (an English translation finally appeared in 2005).[5] The popularity of *Nine-times Cuckold* more than ten years later suggests that readers preferred a more sensational hero who, as we will see in chapter 8, was both a master of the brothel and a supposed adept in international relations.

The features that made the Shanghai of late-Qing literature so singular include such things as the use of the Western calendar, that is, the seven-day week with Sunday as a day of rest (an arrangement that the rest of China, except for other concessions, did not adopt until later). Time in general was lived in a radically different way from the agricultural hinterland in that prostitutes and clients commonly went to bed just before dawn and woke up after noon. Shanghai was governed by Western law, which provided a newfound security to do business and gave prostitutes freedom from Chinese authority.[6] Western-style buildings, wide city streets, trash removal, steamships, and eventually electricity, photography, and telephones all joined to provide men and women with novel and appealing forms of entertainment and opportunities for moving about in unprecedented ways and at all hours of the day and night. Men and women mingled in teahouses and coffeehouses, in theaters, restaurants, and public parks, and drove in open carriages, a favorite activity of women in *Flowers of Shanghai*. Most of these features decorate the background of the novel, which barely portrays even Westerners except for an occasional policeman or overheard footsteps in a foreigner's firm. What is important in this picture is not the introduction of specific Western customs and ideas or Chinese reactions to them but the subliminal sense of change that is crystallized in the figures of the formidable Shanghai prostitute and her male clientele in the foreign concessions of Shanghai.

The Status of Love and "Doing Business"

The central question of this chapter can be rephrased as follows: Given the tradition of the sublime relationship between beauty and scholar, or courtesan and literatus, what is the status of love in the Shanghai brothel? *Flowers of Shanghai* answers in a way that bars all illusions of love in the new world of the foreign concessions. Given that everything is a matter of doing business and that everyone nowadays is a possible cheat, even someone "from your own home village," then the rule is that the deeper the feelings, the worse the outcome.[7] The prostitute Lin Shufang dies slowly of tuberculosis while her young lover Tao Yufu cares for her until her death. Like Zhou Shuangyu mentioned above, Lin holds an impossible desire to marry her patron as his main wife, something a family like his could never imagine but something that the young Shanghai prostitute boldly, if naïvely, now envisions. When she dies, he grieves uncontrollably, making an embarrassing public display. Onlookers observe that client and prostitute should not take each other too seriously and that prostitutes and customers never mean it when they commit themselves in love. In general, love is not a gift that anyone is presumed to have, although it sometimes breaks out anyway.

A sense of radical change lurks behind every generalization about Shanghai in a writer like Han Bangqing. Money's legendary capacity to turn things into their opposites has made a drastic leap. What is repulsive becomes attractive; what is low becomes high; what is lofty and priceless is rendered passé. An ugly and older but nevertheless famous prostitute, Tu Mingzhu, earns more money than good-looking younger ones. A nouveau-riche, half-educated man like Chen Xiaoyun can become a customer of a high-class brothel just by showing he knows how to spend money. The foregrounding of money is most apparent in the prostitute's constant reference to "doing business" (*zuo shengyi*), a phrase that could never occur in *Traces of the Flowery Moon* or *Courtesan Chambers*.[8] The disappearance of the educated courtesan is another sign of money's leveling effects, especially as captured in the opium-addicted poet Wen Junyu, who complains that, except for herself, there are only vulgar prostitutes left in Shanghai (56.482). A patron puts on glasses to discuss poetry with her and, in the tradition of Yuan Mei (1716–1797) and other famous literati who gathered female writers around them in earlier years of the Qing, later insists that she is his "female disciple," not someone he has indecent feelings about. But immediately after, he strikes a deal with an older, illiterate prostitute whom he soon marries, thus concluding a practical bargain between relative equals, both past their prime and otherwise unable to find marriage partners (59.510–511, 60.512–513). Words that label the new versus the old appear in the conversation of two merchants on their way to the home of the famous literatus Qi Yunsou (about whom more below). The merchants are confident that Qi's "cultured sophistication" can hardly hold its own against their "true business sense" (*siwen qiangdiao* versus *shengyi bense,* 47.402).

The Elite Prostitute and Her Control of the Man

Jumping Troughs

Flowers of Shanghai is a study in the essential moments of the prostitute-patron relationship, especially in terms of the woman's exercise of control over the man. Han Bangqing excels at crystallizing the psychic formations and mental turns that govern when and how a patron decides that a certain prostitute is worth his commitment, what types of deals are struck between prostitute and patron, and above all what constitutes the truly successful prostitute, that is, in the words frequently used by characters in the novel, the one most "capable" (*you benshi*) and able "to make good for herself" (*zheng qi*).

As one patron says, the man who "does" the first-class prostitute does so for the sake of the "better reputation" he gains by associating with her (15.127). Her aura amounts to the ability to hold and gain ground with a specific man, with the managers of her brothel, and with the wider audience of onlookers in the brothel community. Aura has to do with her ability to control and channel (*guan*) the man's feelings and activities by steering him away from other prostitutes and compelling him to commit to her. *Flowers of Shanghai* portrays men pursuing and even enjoying being controlled by her, as if she constitutes a foundation upon which they seek to find firm footing. To get assurance of that footing, the man looks for signs of it in the form of objects (jewelry, clothing, furniture) and favors (promises, clearing of debts) the woman gains from him, often seemingly against his will. An epitomizing moment occurs when she erupts in furious outbursts, including mock outbursts, when all he begs for is that she not be upset with him. It is at times like these that he is most delivered into her hands and that the novel best captures the man's mock and not-so-mock abjection.

One of the most sensitive situations in the brothel community is the man's attempt to switch from one prostitute to another (called "jumping troughs," *tiao cao*), something that would seem perfectly natural to the man as roving customer. When the patron Wang Liansheng tries to switch from Shen Xiaohong to Zhang Huizhen, Shen pummels Zhang in a public park in front of Wang and numerous others. Wang never succeeds in severing himself from Shen, even after he marries Zhang, who marvels at Shen's "ability" (*benshi*) to keep Wang being "good" to her (12.98), even covering his body with scratches that she inflicts on him and that Zhang can plainly see (33.279). The prostitute's talent is something others discuss and admire from a distance. The highest compliment comes when someone says that a woman "looks like she will go her whole life as a prostitute and never marry" (17.144 or 18.155–156), the common wisdom being that when a prostitute marries, she loses independence because she must kowtow to the man's mother and main wife or because she risks the possibility that the man will spend all her savings and force her back into prostitution. The prostitute's ultimate goal, in reality available to very few, is to amass enough money to buy freedom from her managers and live self-sufficiently for the rest of her life.[9] If the hero in *Courtesan Chambers* enjoyed being coddled, prodded, and cajoled, he still knew how to remain the center of attention. In *Flowers of Shanghai,* the woman turns the tables by subjecting the man to a thorough form of subservience in which she becomes a woman he can never succeed in either marrying or abandoning. Her turning of the tables can be summarized in the following series of vignettes.

Treating the Patron as Her Son

Everyone in *Flowers of Shanghai* fills out what the author portrays as a kind of complete scene of prostitution in Shanghai. The mediator and facilitator Hong Shanqing comes nearest to representing the focal viewpoint of the novel, whose perspective is the one from which all players are measured as they perform their antics while he roves through Shanghai in a constant series of rendezvous and mediations. All along he maintains an amiable relationship, like a companionate husband and wife, with his mistress Zhou Shuangzhu, who meanwhile earns her own income as she goes on calls (referred to as *chu ju*), which consist of banquets, parties, and other gatherings that men pay prostitutes to attend. Hong Shanqing settles conflicts, assists transactions, and in general makes his living (besides working at his ginseng store) from the wealthier men who trust him thoroughly. His goal is to keep the love fantasy on course by insuring that it remains profitable yet entertaining and that no one becomes too emotionally involved.[10]

Subservience to the prostitute is a prominent mode of behavior among men in *Flowers of Shanghai,* as in the case of Wu Xuexiang and her patron Ge Zhongying, whom Wu reins in through a masterful use of temper. Cross at him for staying too long with a neighboring prostitute and her patron, Wu tells Ge that he can only go where she allows him to go, for "you are my son," she suddenly declares (6.42). She is so proud, moreover, because her son sports in brothels, thus "giving her great face," she adds sarcastically. In fact, she continues, if she had her own son, she would "beat him to death" if he went to brothels. "She is crazy today," Ge says to a maid standing nearby, after which he and Wu "playfully tussle for a bit" (*guihun yizhen,* 6.43). He then readies to leave by himself, but to his surprise she insists on going with him, and he cannot persuade her otherwise. Playful subservience thus transforms into real subservience. She controls him more than his wife does, he exclaims.

Wu's insistence on controlling the man's movements underscores a critical feature of the Shanghai courtesan, her newfound mobility resulting from her residence in the foreign concessions. Self-promotion goes hand in hand with the freedom that women now enjoy to move about and be seen in public without being subject to traditional restrictions. Ge Zhongying and Wu Xuexiang exemplify this change shortly after when they go shopping in a Western store. Although they are a prostitute and patron on an excursion, they are harbingers of middle-class consumers on a shopping trip in modern downtown Shanghai. She is pregnant with his child, and they will soon marry.[11]

The Man Who Is Afraid of His Wife

Philanderers afraid of their jealous wives is a stock situation in Ming and Qing fiction. What can Han Bangqing do that is new except confirm the notion that fear of the wife undergoes revaluation when the man and woman cross the bridge between China and the foreign concessions? Yao Jichun's wife storms into the first-class prostitute Wei Xiaxian's brothel, where Yao is visiting, only to have Wei tell her that as soon as a man passes through her door, he is no longer anyone's husband. "If you have what it takes (*benshi*), then *you* control your husband," shouts Wei, reducing the wife to tears. Otherwise, "we run this brothel as a business; whoever enters is our customer" (23.196–197). Yao's fear of his wife is the butt of the prostitute's sarcasm when he visits Wei several days later and she asks him how long his jailer has been keeping him (27.229). Wei Xiaxian confirms the notion that when a man enters a Shanghai brothel, he undergoes a drastic transformation. A revaluation suddenly takes place that turns him into his "opposite": formerly a husband, now a customer; free to spend money, but subject to what the woman declares is a cost. Both Ge Zhongying and Yao Jichun exemplify the man who "fears his wife" (*ju nei, pa po*), as featured in scores of novels, stories, plays, and jokes throughout the Ming and Qing. The elite prostitute of Shanghai understands that psychology and knows how to turn fear of the wife into greater fear of the prostitute.

Stolen from the Family

As two young people who fall in love, Zhu Shuren and Zhou Shuangyu exemplify the kind of relationship that the brothel facilitator Hong Shanqing tries to prevent. Zhou Shuangyu, a newly bought prostitute (*taoren*), is a woman of nerve and talent who, as mentioned above, immediately forms the impossible desire to become the main wife of a patron she falls in love with, Zhu Shuren, a virgin like her. Zhu is the naïf who falls in love with his first prostitute, then promises to marry her. While his elder brother secretly arranges a marriage for him with someone else, the two lovers swear a suicide pact. When she discovers the betrothal, she challenges him to drink a suicide potion with her (63). He resists, but she is furious: she will be his main wife or she will die. The outcome is a deal arranged by Hong Shanqing to redeem Shuangyu from prostitution and to pay a settlement to the family of the woman to whom Shuren was betrothed (in the end Zhu marries neither woman). Shuangyu yells at Shuren as he cowers behind Hong Shanqing: "For ten thousand dollars you bought your life. You got off cheap!" (64.547).[12]

A parallel young couple is Tao Yufu and the prostitute Lin Shufang, who fall in love and swear eternal loyalty as she dies of tuberculosis. Women like Zhou and Lin steal young men from their families by turning the relationship between prostitute and customer into a personal arrangement no longer controlled by the patriline. In the process of accomplishing this theft, they stipulate the conditions under which they must be treated and thereby call a new man into being. Lin blames Tao for staying away too long and not caring for her well enough. He admits that he has been "bad" and has "harmed" her (18.148), and thereafter cares for her day and night until she dies. A man like Tao hardly knows what has come over him. He agrees that he is worthless and that he owes the woman everything. He invites himself into this situation by way of becoming a full-fledged person, perfectly loyal to the woman who invokes his new self.

The Formidable Prostitute

Two other men, Luo Zifu and Wang Liansheng, have yet more formidable mistresses, Huang Cuifeng and Shen Xiaohong, who manage to keep the men loyal without marriage, suicide pact, or love death, all along keeping their own secret lovers, as if they were polygamists themselves. Huang Cuifeng is the superior businesswoman in that her lover is a paying patron like Luo Zifu, while Shen's lover is an actor and thus low class like herself, that is, someone she relates to personally and without taking payments. Huang is an example of a prostitute who dictates her conditions to others, even if it means a metaphorical duel to the death. She began the process of liberating herself from her madam when as a child she won her first battle of nerves by threatening suicide, a technique she passes on to others. To a prostitute who has been beaten by her madam, Huang says that she should have let herself be beaten more, then eaten raw opium to pretend suicide. "If you are afraid of pain, then you should have been the wife or daughter of a Mandarin. What are you doing as a prostitute!" (37.316). When Huang buys herself out from her madam, she refuses all parting gifts from her, and has every word of the contract minutely reviewed. She symbolizes her transition to independence by dressing in mourning for her long-deceased parents (whose death brought about her entry into prostitution) and at last making an offering to them in her new home, even ordering her patron Luo Zifu to bow as well. She has renewed herself as a free woman now ready to do business independently.

Luo Zifu provides an excellent example of the mental turn that occurs when a man decides to patronize a famous prostitute like Huang Cuifeng. It is as if he becomes her subject and thus subjects himself to what a prostitute does to a man: she "fleeces" him (*qiao*). Before becoming her patron, Luo is outraged by her insolence, which insults what he feels is his patron's privilege to command her presence and compliance (6). But his outrage turns to subservience when he hears about her temper from another man who tells him the famous story about her defiance of her madam, one of the most notorious in Shanghai. In receiving him as patron, Huang immediately demands that he leave a chest of important documents at her brothel. As for money, she says that she will take it from him when she pleases. But if it pleases her for him to "give her a brick," then a brick will be better than money (8.61–62). "You are truly a rare one," he reacts in awe, as if congratulating himself on winning such a remarkable woman. When they discuss her business, she declares that she will "do" only him, and that he will do only her. "So you can fleece just *me* then!" he responds in mock resentment. "If I only stay with you, then if I don't fleece you, who else will I fleece?" she asks (9.74). All along she secretly sees a favorite, the suave and self-certain Qian Zigang, who likewise helps redeem her from her madam.

If Huang Cuifeng exemplifies a woman who succeeds in cheating her customer, then Shen Xiaohong is an example of one who miscalculates and ruins her business. Her relationship with Wang, the most complex in the novel, provides an extended portrayal of the male customer's inability to tear himself away from a woman who aggressively hangs on to him, even after betraying him. His attachment to her comes down to a simple factor: he cannot stand her to be angry or displeased with him and will do anything to calm her down. In fear of her anger, he avoids telling her that he has taken a new prostitute. When Shen finds out, she reacts with rage, even faking suicide, at which point he does precisely what the formula calls for: he demonstrates in sincere, well-acted-out fashion that he is still loyal to her alone (10–11). He continues to see the other prostitute, as if trying to pry himself from Shen and prove his talent at jumping troughs. Later, when he accuses Shen of "having an affair with an actor" (*pin xizi*), a notorious thing for a prostitute to do, he finally feels righteous enough to break with her and marry the other woman. In a final twist, he begins "doing" her again when he discovers his new wife having an affair with his nephew, but Wang soon departs for an official post in another province, an utterly failed philanderer, defeated by two Shanghai prostitutes in a row.

Hong Shanqing and the Self-dissolving Fantasy

Brothel Facilitator

The remarkable aspect of Shen Xiaohong's story is that she is never labelled a lascivious woman. What the novel mainly foregrounds in the blame laid upon Shen is her miscalculation, not the idea that she is unbridled and lascivious and therefore destructive of men. The role of Hong Shanqing is key to this lack of indulgence in the theme of the lascivious yaksha. His goal is to maintain a low and manageable level of fantasy between customer and prostitute. He intervenes to remind Wang of his obligation to pay Shen's bills, for example, regardless of Shen's behavior, for business is more important than emotional entanglements. As the facilitator of brothel affairs, he is a kind of overseer of the love fantasy. If the fantasy grows too unwieldy, he attempts to divert or rechannel it, which is in essence to expose it as something artificial and contingent. When necessary, he exposes people to their entrapment in the fantasy, which amounts to exposing them to the fantasy of the glittering but deceptive world of Shanghai.

A brief moment crystallizes his role as exposer of illusion when one morning, in bed with his mistress, he dreams that he is on a hunt with the imperial princess, but someone awakens him because of an urgent matter (17.145). The dream is as near as the author comes to a self-conscious exposure of the male fantasy. It is as if he curls himself up inside the sleeping Hong Shanqing, who does his fantasizing in dreamland only, then wakens to attend to the fools in the real world of Shanghai. In this case, the fool is Hong's nephew, Zhao Puzhai, who has gotten himself beaten up in one of the low-class brothels in the French Concession. Hong's dreamland is the blatantly false Nanke Commandery (Nanke jun), an allusion to the old story of a man who goes to sleep and dreams of marrying a princess and serving in high office, where he achieves wealth and glory, but then experiences utter failure, after which he wakens and realizes the vanity of life.[13] In the classical tale the result of the dream is enlightenment. In Hong Shanqing, the theme of the vanity of life is old hat but nonetheless still practical. It turns into a self-dissolving fantasy, as if Hong knows there is no imperial princess and that even if there were one she would never go out with the likes of him.

It is Hong's job, the one he returns to after he is awakened, that colors the dream as a self-dissolving fantasy. As facilitator and go-between for brothel transactions, he negotiates both commercial and emotional minutiae, keeping the business fair and respectable and preventing relationships from becoming explosive or otherwise unmanageable. In the disastrous affair between the virgin prostitute Zhou Shuangyu and the young Zhu Shuren, Hong might have averted the disaster had he succeeded with another plan, introducing Wang Liansheng to Zhou Shuangyu. In other words, Hong was ready to restart the clock by putting Zhou Shuangyu together with Wang instead of with Zhu Shuren and taking Wang away from both Zhang Huizhen and Shen Xiaohong (57.490). The notion of creating a new couple crystallizes Hong's role as the overseer of the love fantasy, where restarting the clock performs the function of blanking out previous overblown fantasies. Hong's mistress is his frequent comrade in his role of analyst and observer of the players in this drama. In idle moments before bed, for example, they issue various truths about the affairs of the brothel. Hong's mistress advises Zhou Shuangyu: "As a prostitute, a woman can only do so much, even if she has talent and can make good for herself. Keep this in mind now and make the best of what you've got" (17.142). The mistress later tells Shuangyu that Zhu Shuren did her wrong by not telling her of his betrothal. But "you're too young and naïve. How could you believe the promises of a customer? Even if Shuren had not gotten engaged, he'd never be able to take you as wife!" (63.543). Another prostitute asks Hong Shanqing in mock wonderment (so as deliberately to pester Zhou Shuangyu, who is within earshot), why so many prostitutes want to become main wives of respectable men. She lists the examples: Lin Shufang, Zhao Erbao, and now Zhou Shuangyu (62.537). Like the immortal or the swordswoman in Pu Songling, a prostitute should know that marriage is an institution in which she will always have to compete with other women and in which only respectable women can be main wives.

The Grand Master of Love

Hong Shanqing has what can be considered a high-cultural double in the form of the elderly literatus Qi Yunsou, whose estate contains a large garden to which he invites friends and their prostitute-mistresses to spend days at a time in pleasure and entertainment. Qi presides as someone who has arrived at final authority, as is evident in the respect others pay him and in the liberties he is allowed to take, such as coming and going as he pleases, napping whenever he wants, and directing the topics of conversation. He is known as the Grand Master of Love (Fengliu guangda jiaozhu) because he is considered a man of feeling who deeply understands the love affairs of men and prostitutes. Whereas Hong Shanqing tends to be consulted in practical and financial matters, Qi is referred to in matters of emotional entanglement. Yet Han Bangqing portrays Qi as someone blithely unself-conscious in his role of authority. The underside emerges through the words of three women who serve him and who swear a secret pact of sisterhood. They talk of how "horrid" Qi's half-opened eyes look when he naps (51.437). As benevolent as he may be, they say, the Master (*daren*) can never know what is truly in their hearts (53.454).

As the eldest man in the novel, Qi fits the mold of the traditional master polygamist who confidently enjoys his women, whom he expects to be unjealous, hence his lesson on jealousy to the thirteen-year-old, still self-assertive Qiguan (51.438). When he discovers the pact of sisterhood between her and two others, it gives him a chance to play the Grand Master of Love again by then declaring (to the original three women's frustration) that all the women he has invited to the garden should swear sisterhood in a great ceremony, for which he commissions a written record containing biographies of each woman. He epitomizes the man of sentiment who sympathizes with the fallen or abused prostitute, whose secret pact he appropriates for himself in a gesture of extolling her. Meanwhile he regards her as someone whom one should not love too deeply, as illustrated when he presides over the funeral for the dead prostitute, Lin Shufang. When her loyal lover Tao Yufu overflows with grief, Qi "frowns and says, 'This is truly going too far!'" (47.397). Tao's brother had earlier expressed the same viewpoint when he said that men do not follow their mates in death and that even wives must be mourned within proper ritual limits (42.357).

The New Shanghai Citizen

If Qi is Hong Shanqing's old-fashioned, high-cultural double, then Hong Shanqing represents a clean break who adheres more closely to the realities of the life of the prostitute-businesswoman. Qi's estate is like Wang Tao's fairy islands, a world apart from gritty Shanghai, run by an old man who signals the last days of the self-contained pleasures of the literatus-philanderer. Hong Shanqing's difference from Qi is registered from the very start by the fact that he is constantly in motion as he performs his nebulous job as brothel facilitator. His quintessential moment is to be walking from one engagement to another and to be sidetracked by running into someone presenting him with a new matter. A similarly epitomizing moment takes place when the soon-to-be-married Ge Zhongying and Wu Xuexiang shop in a foreign store where they see all kinds of objects they have never seen before (6.43–44). "Their eyes are blurred and their minds go numb" (*mu xuan shen jing*) as they look at the movable wind-up toys—people, animals, boats, and carriages, miniature figures of the new world of international Shanghai. One becomes a new person by this act of shopping: a citizen of the city of Shanghai. Hong Shanqing's niece Zhao Erbao is similarly fascinated with the novelties of the city's restaurants, theaters, and fashion, but she fails to learn the ropes and thinks her newly enjoyed romantic liberties will lead to a life of married security. Instead she falls into the cycle of selling and reselling herself, her resistance to which finally incites an unruly customer to wreck her chambers as the novel draws to a close (64).

Hong Shanqing exemplifies yet one further, crucial sense of those times, the lack of paranoia at the loss of footing experienced by the former male hero, however that hero is labeled—polygynist, philanderer, wastrel. In other words, he never expresses a nostalgic desire to withdraw from Shanghai and go back to the village. He escapes fascination with Shanghai's attractions and thus avoids being duped, yet he is also free of the overconfidence of never being duped. The over-confidence of never being duped is an example of overcompensation in the face of overwhelming change, and reveals an ultimate sense of resentment that Hong Shanqing likewise fails to express. The certitude of never being duped—which we will see exemplified in the novel *Nine-times Cuckold*—is like an imaginary place-holder for the absent or weakened masters of traditional China, while resentment is resentment at the fact that those masters have been undermined and weakened in the new environment to which people have been forced to adapt. In other words, the self-certain subject in the brothel of the Shanghai concessions, like Qi Yunsou or like Zhang Qiugu in *Nine-times Cuckold*, represents the remnants of a father who is in fact already lost. Hong Shanqing, on the other hand, is closer to the new subject, the prostitute-businesswoman, who takes her chances and sometimes gets a good deal, but sometimes miscalculates. When unexpected things happen, Hong Shanqing can only wonder to himself how unstable and unpredictable things have become (35.296). He can attempt to repair the situation, but otherwise he can only shake his head as he moves on to his next rendezvous.

In the foreign concessions of Shanghai where the traditional hero is no longer viable, Hong Shanqing is in effect a replacement, not a latter-day reincarnation. Looking back from the May Fourth period, he may not constitute an admirable figure in that he lacks an overtly political vision and still engages in supposedly decadent behavior such as smoking opium and consorting with prostitutes. But he has already made the definitive step away from the positions of either sentimental nostalgia or reactionary reconstruction vis-à-vis the traditional past. His position becomes the clearest when viewed in terms of his relations with the prostitute-yak-sha. He neither venerates women in the mode of the passive polygynist and man of feeling nor is he on a vengeful mission to spread the word about the deceitful prostitute, as if to vindicate victimized men and reform decadent women. He has a grasp on the currently emerging love fantasy, in other words, and gets that way by allying himself with the icon of the modernizing Chinese city, the Shanghai prostitute.

CHAPTER SEVEN

Cultural Destiny and Polygynous Love in Zou Tao's *Shanghai Dust*

The Pathos of the Polygynist's Claim to Pleasure

A missed chance to marry a remarkable Shanghai prostitute was Zou Tao's (1850–1931) inspiration for writing the novel *Shanghai Dust* (*Haishang chentian ying*).[1] Zou Tao was a close friend to Yu Da, as we have seen, and in addition was a disciple of Wang Tao. His novel, however, takes after *Traces of the Flowery Moon* far more than after *Courtesan Chambers* and *Later Tales of Liaozhai*. Mostly written in the mid-1890s but not published until 1904, it begins with the premise that China has been cruel to women by forcing them to bind their feet and tolerate polygyny (which goes by the term *yiqi shuqie*, "having a wife and concubines," 1.13). Like *Dream of the Red Chamber* and *Traces of the Flowery Moon*, *Shanghai Dust* features the scene of failed love and the man who is a victim of split loyalties, immobilized by his linkages to more than one woman. What makes *Shanghai Dust* more than an embellishment upon earlier models is the significance of this male figure as a kind of last Chinese polygynist. He and his plural female lovers together embody high-cultural identity threatened with extinction, this time with no regeneration in sight.

The last chapter said that two masters stand behind the man who would be a polygynist, the Confucian father and the potent polygynist, with a third master, the Western conqueror, now entering the scene and signaling fundamental change. Han Bangqing registers the shift and proposes a new man and woman in the form of the brothel facilitator and the Shanghai prostitute. The overseer of the love fantasy stands ready to advise patrons of the brothel about their transformation into citizens of Shanghai. The sense of transformation implies a framework in which China as a symbolic whole finds itself opposed to an alien order in the form of the combined forces of Europe, America, and Japan. While this opposition is implicit in Han Bangqing, it is repeatedly and explicitly foregrounded in Zou Tao. Like writers in many other contexts since the first Opium War, Zou Tao presents the situation of a weak and defiled China against aggressive outsiders. But a turning point was reached after China's disastrous and humiliating defeat by Japan in 1895. The imperial form of government still lasted for more than a decade, but in the eyes of many, including Zou Tao, China as it had been known for millennia had become definitively obsolete. If his novel can be taken as a historical marker of this turning point, then it is as if the pathos of the polygynous claim to pleasure now intensifies. The first articulations of China as a modern nationalist whole began to emerge in the next few years, but Zou Tao already conveys the sense of definitive change that Han Bangqing pronounced more subtly in *Flowers of Shanghai*. The change has the effect of raising the level of urgency to depart from the obsolete past in order to assume a newly globalized sense of self-positioning. Zou Tao's novel, however, is distinctive not because of its forward-looking attempt to resolve crisis. Instead, it engages in an act of sentimental retrospect that crystallizes the past into something that is over or about to be over and that designates the love death of the prostitute and her lover as the culminating act.

Two overlapping tasks will occupy me in this chapter by way of examining the grand narrative of polygynous love. Through detailing the way *Shanghai Dust* plots the parallel love affairs of its two main male characters, the first task is to demonstrate the novel's strategy of passive polygyny, especially in terms of the recurrent theme of the exaltation of women and the way that theme treads a thin line between the polygynist's self-dissolution before women, on the one hand, and his elevation as a man who wins many women's love, on the other. Both enjoyment of this love and the failure to enjoy it represent sublime and beautiful states of being in the manner of the *qing* aesthetic. The second task is to return to the theme of the resonance between the polygynous love story and cultural destiny that began to emerge in *Traces of the Flowery Moon* and that *Shanghai Dust* carries to fruition three and a half decades later. The central feature of this shared love story is the melancholy and pathos of the failed polygynist and his superior female companions in a historical moment of social fragmentation. The unachieved love in such relationships is that of a man who in an implicit sense would like to be the perfect polygynist. The proven method of attaining this goal is the strategy of passive polygyny in which women are structured as willing agents of the polygynous marriage. The successful polygynist exercises this strategy brazenly, while the failed one fails with refined pathos. The resonance between such failure and the historical moment has to do with the way in which the man and his female lovers embody Chinese cultural essence threatened with extinction. They can do so because the polygynous literatus and his talented female lovers have long constituted a repository of political and cultural values and practices, thus the fascination with which Zou Tao portrays them once again in a time when they are now crossed with the knowledge and experience of a strong and invasive foreign culture.

In sum, the love story in *Shanghai Dust* acquires the quality of a culminating narrative because of the history of the relationship between literatus, concubine, and courtesan and in general because of the structure of feeling that it inherits from previous polygynous love stories. *Shanghai Dust* openly signals the inheritance of this tradition by citing three other recent inheritors: *Dream of the Red Chamber, Precious Mirror of Boy Actresses,* and especially *Traces of the Flowery Moon,* the latter two from the previous half-century and books that Zou Tao's characters read with great reverence. But as I want to reemphasize, continuity with the great past is only part of what makes this narrative significant. Again, it is the historical moment as characterized by the confrontation with alien forces that produces the particularly grandiose effect. The novel's emphasis on Western learning and its descriptions of Europe and the United States are new elements in a work of Chinese fiction that dramatically distinguish it from its predecessors. It is precisely this open juxtaposition in a lengthy literary format that creates the sense of a culminating narrative.

The Translocation of *Dream of the Red Chamber* into Shanghai

Early in the book the reader encounters the statement that China is cruel to women by failing to educate them and forcing them to bind their feet and tolerate polygyny. One of the main goals of the group of goddesses who are about to descend to earth to begin the story is to set up a women's school for the sake of "equality between men and women" (*nannü bingzhong,* 1.13). The novel thus begins with an overtly reformist, egalitarian statement. But although the novel refers to American democracy and the French Revolution, it never develops their ideas or ideals. Instead, it concerns itself with the fictional pathos of fallen women and the philandering men who love and admire these women. As specialists in refined lust for women, the men recall Jia Baoyu of *Dream of the Red Chamber,* who bestows upon all of the men their most critical problem, namely, "how to reside with more than one woman at once," or *tongjufa,* as *Shanghai Dust* puts it. *Tongjufa* is the nearest equivalent to polygyny in the special sense *Shanghai Dust* inherits from its literary and cultural past, that is, passive polygyny. Now, however, Zou Tao places this classic love story under the pressure of the themes of Chinese cruelty to women and inequality between the sexes. He parades the blithe attempts of men to "reside with more than one woman at once," but like his predecessors in *Dream of the Red Chamber* and *Traces of the Flowery Moon,* he undermines those attempts and thereby denies the men their polygynous utopia. His replay of old scenarios contains something that is already budding in *Traces of the Flowery*

Moon and now comes to fruition in *Shanghai Dust,* that is, the correlation of failed polygyny and lost or threatened cultural identity.

Before defining the particular elements of the strategy of *tongjufa,* let us summarize the contents of *Shanghai Dust* in terms of its translocation of *Dream of the Red Chamber* into the world of modern Shanghai. The novel accomplishes a seemingly safe relocation at first, but eventually drives the relocated world to a dead end. The safe arrival consists of the family of the young hero Gu Lansheng moving from an old-style home in Yangzhou to a modern house in Shanghai (6.76–77, 81). There Gu continues his study of foreign languages and Western knowledge, all along expressing disdain for ancient Chinese learning. As a boy, Gu Lansheng concludes a love pact with a young woman, Yang Shuangqiong, a Daiyu-like figure in her sensitivity to his dalliance with other girls, her tendency to illness, and the masculine features of her room (such as her fondness for scientific experiments, 3.33, 19.299). The other main male hero is the slightly older and established Han Qiuhe, who speaks English, travels the world, and knows modern technology, Western history, and Western principles of government. He falls in love with a courtesan, Su Yunlan, whose brothel in Shanghai will become the site of a girls' school to carry out the program of equality between men and women.[2] The novel's situation in the newly international world has its dark side in the form of the ineptitude of China's rulers (women like Shuangqiong know more about science than China's leaders, 19.299), Japan's superiority to China, and the fact that the United States passes laws discriminating against Chinese immigrants (2.30). Some of the male heroes take part in losing battles with foreign nations, while Han Qiuhe dies at the hands of "Boxer bandits" (58.1008).[3] His melancholy after his long journey through Europe and Russia is due to his failure to advance China's causes internationally. Lamenting the lack of a soul mate (16.236), he compares himself to the famous Wei Chizhu of *Traces of the Flowery Moon* (16.241). With its reverent evocation of *Traces of the Flowery Moon,* Zou Tao's novel plays on the same nexus of sublime love against the backdrop of social dislocation, in *Traces of the Flowery Moon* caused by the Taiping Rebellion, in *Shanghai Dust* by China's national weakness and decline.

Becoming the Instrument of Female Will

Passive polygyny, or the construction of female agency in polygyny, is apparent if we compare the two main male characters to Jia Baoyu and then Wei Chizhu. Han and Gu are alternate versions of Jia Baoyu, one an adult, the other still a child. Han is a melancholic and tortured soul, who like Jia Baoyu has suffered major loss in love. In *Shanghai Dust* he gains a second chance, only to lose once again. Gu Lansheng is the adolescent and sometimes still infantile version of Jia Baoyu, characterized as a precious but also precocious naïf. He is Baoyu in his aspect as prepolygynist, that is, a boy whose family has maids and courtesans accompany and supervise him before marriage. Whereas Han Qiuhe overdoes Jia Baoyu's melancholy, Gu Lansheng overdoes Baoyu's coddled sensitivity. Han Qiuhe tends toward temperate love, valuing reserved respect (*jing*) over open love (*ai*, 30.501), and fears "falling deeply in love" (*zhong qing*, 30.493). Gu Lansheng, on the other hand, loves daily intimacy with girls, especially sensitive courtesans and maids, who in his mind embody the highest state of humanity.

It is their way of gaining intimacy with sensitive young women that joins Gu and Han in their strategy of *tongjufa*. In essential form, it is a strategy in which the man achieves bodily intimacy with women by subjecting himself to their needs and thereby gaining their trust, followed by their participation in and even arrangement of his simultaneous involvement with many of them. As we have seen already, a central feature of this man is his certainty that he serves the interests and enjoyment of the women. Such certainty may be brazen, as in *Revisiting the Silken Chambers* or *Courtesan Chambers,* but in *Shanghai Dust* it is artful and indirect. Instead of certainty there is doubt and disillusion, hence the image of the failed polygynist. Let us first look at the evidence of the man's subjection to the women's will, that is, the situation of the man making himself a passive instrument of female will. Becoming the instrument of female will is a further way of elaborating upon the man's art of subservience to the woman that we saw in various forms in previous chapters.

Two features stand out as touchstones linking the polygynous strategies of Han and Gu: their displays of nonsexual intimacy and their attempts to reconcile their attachments to more than one woman. A brief synopsis of their affairs is necessary in order to clarify these points. Han's nonsexual intimacy with Su Yunlan begins when, gravely ill, she issues an appeal for a cure in the form of flesh from a man's chest (as a monk advised her to do, 11.149). Her husband scoffs at the proposal, but Han gladly offers himself, and she is cured. On becoming a prostitute because her husband can no longer support her, she reencounters Han Qiuhe, and they become close. But the story gets complicated when Jin Cuiwu, Qiuhe's former courtesan lover, now a nun (who had previously left him when she took a Western merchant as her client) joins him and Su Yunlan in Shanghai, politely yielding to Su. Now begins the story of the attempt at *tongjufa*. Tortured by his split loyalties, he fumbles when Jin Cuiwu asks him whom he loves more (39.656). He replies that he loves Su Yunlan because Jin Cuiwu is now a nun, but still, "Probably I have affinities with both of you" (39.656). Soon after, Su Yunlan proposes a deeper stage of love, after which he and Su become sexually intimate, as then do he and Jin Cuiwu. The love triangle soon ends (an almost two-wife polygyny), all three separate, and Han dies.

Gu Lansheng's contrasting story of polygynous love begins with the fact that he is the young son of a Japanese concubine, coddled by his grandmother and maids. He likes girls so much that he will personally empty their chamber pots (6.75). He admires Baoyu's belief that men are dirty and young women are pure (26.425). Before moving to Shanghai, he and Yang Shuangqiong exchange love tokens and vow to marry. Arriving in Shanghai, he meets courtesans with whom he begins his episodes of nonsexual intimacy: Pei Rang, whom he helps as she vomits (9.118–119) and makes sure that her chamber pot stays clean (9.122), and Xiashang, who sews for him (like Qingwen in *Dream of the Red Chamber*) and asks him to buy her sanitary napkins, newly introduced from abroad (10.133). When Pei Rang sees the signs of his intimacy with Xiashang, she merely "takes note of it" (33.543–544), but Yang Shuangqiong is angry when she sees Gu holding hands with Pei Rang (32.520), placing food in her mouth (33.537), and handing her toilet paper (36.599).

The above scenes of Gu Lansheng's promiscuity intersperse with scenes of Han Qiuhe losing his mind as he is caught between Su Yunlan and Jin Cuiwu (32). Lansheng is oblivious of hurting Shuangqiong until she breaks with him. He makes up with her after a crucial conversation with Su Yunlan, who tells him that he has to adopt the "method of cohabitation," *tongjufa*, that Jia Baoyu supposedly established with Baochai and Daiyu. That is, Gu Lansheng has to "gradually" persuade Yang Shuangqiong to accept his relationships with other women (36.600). Lansheng then apologizes to Shuangqiong, promises that he will no longer be intimate with Pei Rang, and declares that his feelings for Shuangqiong are deeper than for anyone else. She softens but says that he must observe limits and cannot be intimate with every woman who is "nice" (*hao*) to him (36.603). He then epitomizes the refined and subservient polygynist by replying that he will gladly do whatever she "directs"—*zhishi*—him to do. Then in a gesture of missed chance and failed love, she tries to say she would like them to marry, but cannot finish her sentence (36.604), echoing Su Yunlan, who likewise fails to finish sentences at least three times when she is about to utter her wish to be married to Han Qiuhe.[4] Soon Shuangqiong and Lansheng are separated when elders, including Han Qiuhe, attempt to arrange their marriage to other people. Shuangqiong dies (51), and Lansheng goes mad at the loss (55).

Soaking in Her Fluids

Men making themselves instruments of female will must also be read in light of Ming and Qing fictional predecessors. In particular, Lansheng's intimacy with female bodily functions has a thorough history in Ming and Qing fiction, starting with the famous case of the oil peddler in a late-Ming story. He saves money for the sake of one night with a beautiful courtesan, only to find her drunk from a previous outing and uninterested in him. In the middle of the night she awakens because she has to vomit, thus supplying him with the opportunity to proffer as receptacle his robe, which he had specially purchased for the long-awaited tryst. To her apologies the next day he responds that he has been fortunate to be "stained" (*zhan*) with her "leavings" (*yuli*).⁵ Such patience and lack of aggressiveness eventually win her love and enable him to buy her out of prostitution and marry her. Although this is a story of monogamous love, it supplies us with two key elements of male self-instrumentalization: soaking in the woman's fluids and abstaining from sexual aggression. The same two elements are evident in *Dream of the Red Chamber* and its sequels. In *Dream of the Red Chamber,* Jia Baoyu enjoys washing in water already used by the girls, bathing with maids, tussling with them or his female cousins, combing their hair, or buttoning and unbuttoning their clothing. Although he has sex with his maid Xiren, he is portrayed doing so only once. Jia Baoyu loves the mode of floating among multiple female partners, but not in a sexually aggressive fashion, thus establishing what by the next century becomes a quintessential polygynous scenario.

It takes the author of *Revisiting the Silken Chambers,* the 1797 sequel to *Dream of the Red Chamber,* to carry those acts of adolescent intimacy to their comically brazen extremes. In doing so, the sequel provides us with an interpretive tool for reading Gu Lansheng's ablution intimacies and Han Qiuhe's sacrifice of flesh and sharing of himself with Su Yunlan and Jin Cuiwu. As we saw above, the young Jia Baoyu of *Revisiting the Silken Chambers* plays with girls in bed or while bathing, teaches a girl how to kiss, or has girls watch animals copulating; he concerns himself with women's illnesses and menstruation, about which he educates them as they experience it for the first time. The singular feature of this version of Jia Baoyu is his brazen presumption that he knows more about the woman than she does. His familiarity with female bodily functions models itself on the original Jia Baoyu's precociousness, which the new Baoyu takes to the perverse extreme of hypernormalizing nonsexual intimacy by way of making it a certain step to sexual intimacy. The unabashed repetitiveness of these nonsexual acts demonstrates a virtually preemptive mastery. He makes of himself an instrument that by repeatedly being available at the most intimate right moment thereby guarantees that one woman after another accepts and desires his availability.

The normalization of nonsexual intimacy that we see in this daily mingling was also defined as the attempt to create the illusion of erasing customary boundaries between men and women, a common feature of such scenarios. Such erasure is a seemingly egalitarian move, but like the gesture of self-instrumentalization it also contains a perverse potential. It was likewise another sequel to *Dream of the Red Chamber* that took the erasure of sexual boundaries to similarly blithe extremes. As we saw above, in *Return to Dream of the Red Chamber* (*Honglou fumeng*), the 1799 sequel, the reborn Baoyu is all "sentiment" and no "lust," such that when he consorts with his wives and maids, "he is not even aware that he is male and they are female," and women "forget that he is a man" (26.287 and 13.139–140). The sequel turns Baoyu into a benevolent polygynist whose wives forget that he and they are of unequal status and instead accept him as one of them. The key to such an arrangement lies in the acceptance that the polygynist succeeds in receiving from his female others. In general, the polygynist's utmost wish is to create a predictable mechanism by which he can achieve the goal of gaining multiple willing partners.

With these demonstrations in mind, let us summarize the polygamous intimacies of Gu Lansheng and Han Qiuhe. The polygynist's self-certainty appears in Gu Lansheng's obliviousness to Yang Shuangqiong's jealousy as he openly holds Pei Rang's hand. The unconscious goal of such certainty is the lack or removal of jealousy and rivalry. In telling him to refrain from being familiar with any woman who is nice to him, Yang injects him with a dose of self-consciousness. But he reacts to that restraint with a prime gesture of polygynous self-instrumentalization by replying that he will be happy to have her "direct" him, thus making as if he were a passive object or instrument of her will. Gu Lansheng is an example of a man engaging in symbolically old gestures of polygyny while having entered the symbolically new world of Shanghai and modern learning. Where does "tradition" end and "modernity" begin, we might ask? In his more grown-up counterpart, Han Qiuhe, we see an important elaboration upon the Jia Baoyu–type male that appears in *Traces of the Flowery Moon*. Both *Traces of the Flowery Moon* and *Shanghai Dust* take Jia Baoyu into an adult phase in which he no longer does foolish things like lick women's lip rouge or see to the emptying of their chamber pots. Han Qiuhe is an alter–Wei Chizhu, that is, a man who is married, has failed to find a useful political role, and finds himself brokenhearted over a former lost love at the same time that he forms a deep liaison with a new love, both women being courtesans. Like Wei Chizhu, Han is so caught between the two women that he cannot but allow the failure of the former affair to continue into the present. Like Baoyu, he fails with one woman, Daiyu, and must therefore also fail with another, Baochai. My question then is, how and to what extent does Han Qiuhe after all constitute a more mature version of Gu Lansheng?

Self-negating devotion to the woman is what these two men share in their alternate forms of nonsexual intimacy. I have read Gu Lansheng's actions as moves by which he serves women in order to be sure of surrounding himself with them. He believes in the "strategy of cohabitation," something that a woman (Su Yunlan) advises him about. Like the new variation upon Jia Baoyu exemplified in Wei Chizhu, Han Qiuhe can be said to have abandoned Gu Lansheng's childlike knavishness. He no longer engages in the supposedly innocent promiscuity in which he is oblivious to the feelings of his female lovers. Nevertheless, he does for a while succeed in "cohabiting" with both Su Yunlan and Jin Cuiwu, an interlude that illustrates an abbreviated version of polygyny through female arrangement. When Su Yunlan proposes that they strive for a greater level of intimacy, he asks what she means, but she tests him by avoiding saying anything concrete. He makes several guesses—for example, that he should be like a minister to his lord or a child to a parent (39.660). She replies, "Even closer than that." Should he clean her chamber pot, he wonders. That is an "ordinary" form of intimacy, she answers, then whispers in his ear and shortly after summons him to her bed. Then comes the construction of his sexual intimacy with Jin Cuiwu, which begins when she notices an erotic album signed by Su and Han (42.710) and accidentally encounters Han Qiuhe bathing another woman (43.740), at which point he invites Jin to become his bedmate, and she joins him shortly after. In contrast to Gu Lansheng, Han Qiuhe is less blithe, while the women appear to join him as if by their own considered decision. He can propose cleaning a woman's chamber pot, though he does not actually do so. Han can be bathing with one woman while another, Jin Cuiwu, walks in. Like other couples before them, he and Su Yunlan enjoy the use of an erotic album, which he leaves in a place where it by chance, as it were, arouses the other woman. Han Qiuhe—or the author Zou Tao through him—thus engineers Jin Cuiwu's arousal and willingness to join Su Yunlan as sexual partner to the same man.

History and the End of Polygyny

Let me conclude by now addressing the second theme of this chapter, the resonance between the polygynous love story and cultural destiny at a time of radical social upheaval. Han Qiuhe is like Wei Chizhu in being an agonized lover who represents a high-cultural way of life threatened with extinction. In the context of the Western ideology of equality between the sexes, the polygynous gestures of such men should be considered atavistic and self-consciously impossible. Instead, in *Shanghai Dust* they become rarefied in a way that turns the men and their female partners into objects of sentimental admiration. In terms of literary inheritance, the polygynous love story of *Dream of the Red Chamber* has transformed into a privileged refuge in a time of historical crisis. Literary inheritance in this instance does not necessarily pass self-consciously from one text to another. Jia Baoyu's refusal of social mandate—marriage to Xue Baochai—does self-consciously pass into the sequels to *Dream of the Red Chamber*, which repair his conflicted monogamies by turning them into polygynies welcomed and even arranged by the women, especially Lin Daiyu and Xue Baochai. The authors of *Traces of the*

Flowery Moon and *Shanghai Dust* did not necessarily read the sequels, and they avoided the sequels' brazen extremes, but they nevertheless drew on the same polygynous fantasy, especially *Shanghai Dust*. The result is that Jia Baoyu going from woman to woman in his and their daily ups and downs turns not into a polygynous utopia, but a kind of last moment of sublime pathos before dissolution in the face of epochal change.

To make the link between love and cultural destiny in the late Qing clearer, let us again look at *Traces of the Flowery Moon*. Wei Chizhu and Liu Qiuhen died a love death while the dynasty was in the midst of war with the Taiping rebels. If the novel had ended there, as I have said, love death and dynastic catastrophe would be the culminating act. But after some years of delay, Wei Xiuren finished his novel with an ending in which an army of triumphant lovers defeat the evil Taipings. The story of Bitao was particularly useful in illustrating how the victors harnessed sexual and romantic energy for the sake of cultural regeneration. Put in symbolic terms, the defeat of the Taipings amounted to a victory of Han Chinese men and women who marshaled heroic forms of romantic and libidinal energy against a wanton and subhuman enemy that was motivated by a set of religious practices from an alien culture. As for Han Qiuhe in *Shanghai Dust*, given his travels abroad and his frustrations over China's desperate situation, he is the same bearer of the Chinese cultural standard. His act of severing a piece of flesh for the sake of a soul mate should be read in the same light. It is an act of grand passion, however distant it may seem from fighting for the empire, and however maudlin it may appear. (Yu Dafu, 1896–1945, for one, found the novel extremely "maudlin."[6]) Loyalty to a soul mate resonates in a larger sense with loyalty and dedication to a higher cause, not simply to individual romantic happiness. It is thus not stretching things to liken Han's act to loyalty to a ruler, a fallen dynasty, or an endangered social order and way of life, just as we see in the love affair of the earlier models Wei and Liu in *Traces of the Flowery Moon*.

Why, however, does *Shanghai Dust* mingle the story of loyal love with the story of the polygynist-philanderer caught between his love of multiple women? This question summarizes the quest of this book, which is to remember how polygamy, concubinage, and prostitution constituted the dominant scene of sexual relations in China on the verge of modernity. Loyalty to China the political and civilizational whole in sexual terms included loyalty to polygamy, concubinage and prostitution. *Shanghai Dust* inherits the sentimental tradition of the *qing* aesthetic in its portrayal of sublime love between man and famous courtesan in a traumatic historical moment. Its fictional cousins are works like *Liaozhai zhiyi, Dream of the Red Chamber, Precious Mirror of Boy Actresses, Traces of the Flowery Moon,* and Wang Tao's *Later Tales of Liaozhai*. In this lineup it is necessary to see Zou Tao's portrayal of sublime polygynous love in light of nineteenth-century attempts to resolve the beautifully failed love affair of *Dream of the Red Chamber*. The brothel is the supreme place not only to resolve this problem but to elevate it to the level of high-cultural drama. In a time when it has been declared that China is cruel to women, that there should be "equality between the sexes," and that Western law and science make the West superior to China, it is also the case that Chinese women are smarter and more adept than China's male rulers. The men who realize these truths find refuge in the brothel, which is the purest remnant of Chinese high culture still surviving in the midst of chaotic and "dusty" Shanghai. *Shanghai Dust* sharply contrasts with other literature about courtesans in the late Qing—for example, *Flowers of Shanghai, Shanghai Splendor* (*Haishang fanhua meng*), *Nine-times Cuckold,* among many others, as well as popular guidebooks about Shanghai brothels. In these the brothel is not a refuge but a kind of newly tooled engine for a bustling and savvy Shanghai. The brothel retains only a shadow of its former sublime self, naming courtesans after Lin Daiyu, for example, but mainly in order to lure customers whom it can fleece more efficiently. Only a few men still believe they will find a goddess in a courtesan, while the women who still take themselves as the soul mates of goddess-seeking men can hardly make a living. *Shanghai Dust,* on the other hand, still attaches an ethereal aura to the brothel. There, divested of all forms of aggressive lust, the polygynous hero stained with female fluids awaits invitations to join various goddesses in perfect fulfillment.

CHAPTER EIGHT

The Polygynous Politics of the Modern Chinese Man in *Nine-times Cuckold*

Polygyny as a Structure of Feeling

When cultural reformists of the early 1900s declared fiction the ideal format for portraying models of China's new men and women, they did not have in mind the extremely popular *Nine-times Cuckold* (*Jiuwei gui*, 1906–1910), by Zhang Chunfan (?–1935). As in numerous other novels of the time, the focus was on men and prostitutes, as if to say that they constituted one of the chief arenas for witnessing what the new Chinese man and woman would look like. Since *Nine-times Cuckold* was a publishing success for decades to come, it must have struck a deep chord.[1] Its fame is evidence of the continuing influence of polygyny as a social and cultural formation, in spite of the resistance of reformist politics. The 192-chapter novel twists reformism to its own purposes by portraying a polygynist-philanderer who fully answers the call of the times by insisting on the legitimacy of his form of sexual and romantic pleasure. The egalitarian man and woman sung of elsewhere at the time are absent. The hero's polygynous politics is both a correction of an old and faltering regime and a defiant demonstration against egalitarianism, which he implies can only worsen the already wanton and untamable Shanghai prostitute.

Since Qing fiction long linked successful polygyny with the reestablishment of mastery over chaotic reality, it is not surprising that *Nine-times Cuckold* identifies the success of the polygynist-philanderer as a nodal point in the transition to the new modern man in the form of its hero Zhang Qiugu (whose name is homophonous with "modeling after the ancient"). Nevertheless, by the early 1900s the blatant promotion of the philandering man should amount to a literary scandal. As already pronounced in fiction, essay, school textbooks, journalism, and public speeches, the true reformist mottoes of the day were monogamous marriage and equality between the sexes. Although legal measures to abolish polygamy were still decades away, abolitionism was in the air in the form of new models of women and men who married monogamously or, even more rebelliously in the case of new women, did not marry at all.[2] Zhang Qiugu's self-confidence was scandalous because it carried no sense of obligation to the new-style women establishing themselves at the very same time. Zhang Chunfan serialized his novel during the same years in which the first cohort of girls and women of good family took relatively unsequestered life for granted. These were the years in which the Qing government first sanctioned schools for girls (1907), in which women had their first opportunity to study abroad under government sponsorship in Japan (1905) and the United States (1907), in which women gave public speeches and worked for newspapers promoting their very formation as new women, and in which biographies, translations, textbooks, and journalistic and fictional accounts all apprised readers of the possibility of female independence.[3] The correspondingly new man, both real and ideal, not only no longer took concubines, but actually admired and in some cases extolled the newly independent women who went to women's schools, studied abroad, worked for newspapers, became doctors, and entered politics as reformists, anarchists, and even assassins—all famous prototypes of the new woman in the early 1900s.[4]

Of what relevance then is a novel like *Nine-times Cuckold,* which is not only devoid of these new women and men, but promotes what they would see as their domineeringly retrograde other? My point is that the shameless prostitute of *Flowers of Shanghai, Shanghai Splendor, Nine-tailed Fox (Jiuwei hu),* and *Nine-times Cuckold,* among many others, coexisted with the new independent woman just as polygyny, concubinage, and prostitution were inextricably bound with the egalitarian formation that emerged at the same time. If we were to take the egalitarian man and woman as the representatives of new China to the exclusion of the polygynist-philanderer and the concubine-prostitute, we would be dismissing what continued to be productive forces in the formation of the supposedly liberated types. Productive in this sense refers to a structure of feeling that continued to form and influence the categories and roles of sexual behavior, including destructive and self-destructive behavior. It means the continuing effect of Zhang Qiugu the master philanderer's belief that women are always seducing men unless men acquire the skills of the master philanderer. The hierarchic principles of polygyny and concubinage, in other words, still dominated the late Qing in spite of the egalitarian ethic trying to prove them wrong. Although more study has to be done in order to better understand the gradual disintegration of polygyny after the end of imperial China, to acknowledge its dominance is to affirm the relevance of the roles of main wife, concubine, and prostitute—especially the wanton and savvy one from Shanghai—to the late-Qing discourse of modern femininity. Similarly, the scandalous and retrograde polygynist-philanderer still exerted an affective influence alongside the man struggling with egalitarianism. In short, any observation of the progress of egalitarianism and the independence of women must inevitably take into account the process of remolding that the new man and woman had to undergo given the effects of the polygynous formation. *Nine-times Cuckold* demonstrates the stubborn appeal of the brazen polygynist, brandishing the notion that even he can turn into a modern Chinese man. If in fact the Chinese man doesn't make the switch to being a modern polygynist, the novel asserts, he will turn into his pathetic underside in the form of the dispirited man who loses in the Shanghai brothels because of the overwhelming power of the wanton prostitute. Han Bangqing's *Flowers of Shanghai* and Li Boyuan's 1899 *Tracks of the Snowgoose* (*Haitian hongxue ji*), both far less commercially successful, portrayed this man's profound failure, against which a novel like *Nine-times Cuckold* was so popular.

Whoring Aptitude and the Reformist Man

The unmelancholy man is the one who has a special aptitude for whoring, which *Nine-times Cuckold* proceeds to define at luxurious length, and who understands the psychology of the modern metropolitan prostitute, who according to Zhang Qiugu has sadly turned into an incorrigibly wanton woman. I will deal first with how we must precisely define the man's aptitude and then, equally precisely, with how that man understands the psychology of the wanton woman, the word psychology having actually entered late-Qing parlance and even appearing in the novel itself (22.169).[5]

The novel's general proposition is that Shanghai is where the best of Chinese men learn how to deal with the world as it has now become. The actual statement of this proposition, also found in Li Boyuan's *Tracks of the Snowgoose*, is that Shanghai's "world of whoring" (*piaojie*) is the equivalent to both the political "world of officialdom" (*jinri de guanchang*, 16.123) and the world in which the Chinese man must master "the tactics of foreign diplomacy" (*waijiao shouduan*).[6] Zhang's key word for capturing the qualities the man must have is *gongjia*, "skill and aptitude" (9.70). Such a man is a true "love genius" (*fengliu caizi*), a traditional label that now connotes a sense of maturity that distinguishes him from those still behaving in old-fashioned, grotesque, and boorish ways. He is a man with savoir faire, warm and understanding, with a wry sense of humor, who is never mean or unreasonable. He understands what the modern Shanghai woman wants, which means he has outgrown the old-fashioned man who expects the woman to understand him like a mother who naturally cleans up after his mess and caters to his slightest upset. Nor is he like the old-fashioned man who caves in to the slightest upset of the petulant and overdemanding woman whom the man can never satisfy. If the savvy prostitute's ultimate weapon is her persistent dissatisfaction with the man at all possible times, then the reformed man sees through her tricks and pronounces his freedom. He replaces the out-of-favor patron who fails to realize that others are laughing at him, even when they do so to his face.

Zhang Qiugu thus declares the end of the male consort of the domineering woman. He subtly parallels that end with the end of the man who, like the one in another popular novel of the time, *Flower in a Sea of Karma* (*Niehai hua*, 1905–1907), fails to tame unruly foreign powers.[7] In contrast to *Flower in a Sea of Karma,* however, Zhang Chunfan switches the battleground from that between imperial officials and foreigners to that between patron and prostitute. Victory is won not with weapons and diplomacy, but with the polygynous man's masculine self-possession. Thus it is that we should view Zhang Qiugu's supremacy over women and all other men. It is a supremacy that so overwhelms the woman that when she draws close to him, she loses her sense of self-possession, feeling "as if she had nowhere to put herself" (*haoxiang yige shenti meiyou fangchu yiban,* 27.205).[8] A man who can accomplish this is a model for the China that needs to recover its true source of national strength.

The political message of the novel is thus a sexually political one that asserts two things: China needs men like Zhang Qiugu; and for there to be men like him, the first move must be to contain the unruly Shanghai prostitute. Accomplishing this goal relies on reasserting the notion that the woman needs to be strictly enclosed, even when she has achieved the unprecedented freedom to be seen in public. The sense of enclosure is apparent in the relation between Shanghai and the hinterland, especially cities like Suzhou, one of several in the lower Yangzi region legendarily known for providing men with beautiful prostitutes and concubines. Prostitutes in *Nine-times Cuckold* and other novels since the 1890s in fact speak primarily in Suzhou dialect, which at the time was perceived as enhancing a woman's charm. The prostitute who finally proves virtuous is Chen Wenxian, whose wishes Zhang fulfills by marrying her and installing her in his Changshu home (not far from Suzhou) with his not-so-good-looking but loyal main wife. At this point Chen converts to speaking Mandarin, abandoning the seductive language she spoke as a prostitute.[9] Zhang then returns from Changshu to Shanghai to resume his life of engaging beauty after beauty, each affair amounting to the containment of another woman. The state of being that Zhang's aptitude finally represents is one of permanently floating from one woman to the next, maintaining a condition of geniuslike readiness to enjoy himself at all times. Such readiness proves that he can prevail in the world as it has become at present (he becomes an official at the end of the novel, suggesting that he eventually has more to offer than being a master of the brothels). If he were transferred to *Flower in a Sea of Karma,* his containment of the wanton Shanghai prostitute would take the form of taming the wanton Fu Caiyun, whose affairs with multiple lovers was a female travesty of polygyny (I will return to her shortly).

Polygyny as structure of feeling thus centers on the man's larger-than-life insistence on enjoying himself in his state of permanent fluidity and readiness for romantic involvement. When Lu Xun calls this character a "genius plus hooligan" (*caizi jia liumang*) or when Hu Shi sums up *Nine-times Cuckold* by calling it a mere "guidebook to the brothels" (*piaojie zhinan*), they put their fingers on what they view as this man's shamelessness.[10] But in dismissing the novel, they also emphasize the contrary message, namely, that Zhang's brazenness overflows in such a way as to constitute a countermanifesto to the program of the civilized, egalitarian new man. When *Nine-times Cuckold* equates the "world of whoring" with the "world of officialdom" and "foreign relations," it needs to be seen in light of the portrait of the Shanghai prostitute as recorded since at least 1892 in *Flowers of Shanghai*. The Shanghai prostitute has now become an ultimate decider of a man's worth in the new world represented by the great modern city. *Nine-times Cuckold* confirms this message, but instead of opting for the view that women have evolved beyond men, now supplies the reading public with an example of a man who finally overwhelms all savvy women and supersedes all foolish men. The novel's political message in brothel form, then, is that, while other men buy time with a prostitute who hardly if ever lets them in bed with her, Zhang Qiugu relies on innate genius to attract any woman he wants, spending a modest but not too little sum of money and in general always expanding upon his "canon of whoring" (*piaojing*).[11] The main theme of that canon should always have been obvious, but in an age of turmoil it now needs urgent reiteration, namely, that the most masterful man is still the one who enjoys the most women.

The author nevertheless softens these brazen-sounding claims with a layer of *qing* decorum that makes Zhang Qiugu infinitely appealing and forgivable, hence, for example, his ability to enjoy ephemeral moments with women, even missed moments, as expressed in the allusion to a Tang poet evoking the "regret of missing the peach-blossom face" (*renmian taohua zhi hen*, from Cui Hu's (?–831) poem about a woman he once met and returned to look for but didn't find, 22.164). Zhang's lightness of being amounts to a principle dictating limited duration with any one woman, a whole night or at most several weeks being as long as ephemeral eternity should last. In terms of descriptive detail, the ephemeral outweighs by far any reference to actual sexual activity, which finally occurs in the highly adumbrative passage in chapter 179 when Zhang sums up his version of the ancient philosophy of "Peng Zu's art of riding women." The man should be like a general who has to make a deep foray into enemy territory. The woman is like an immovable fastness, calm and easygoing, while the man is nervous and unsure. The man must have twice as much "power of attack" (*gongzhanli*) in order to win. But if he lacks that or if the woman is especially fierce, then he must use "special forces" (*qibing*), which amount to "teasing" (*tiaodou*) the woman until she burns with ardor and begs for battle (179.1164–1166). Zhang proves his mastery by attracting the most formidable prostitutes in Shanghai, the most formidable of all being the legendary Sai Jinhua, with whom he spends a stupendous night, after which he delivers the above discourse on the art of riding women.

As a historical person, Sai Jinhua was one of the most focal signifiers of the symbolic overlap between whoring and politics in the late Qing and early Republic. She already starred in *Flower in a Sea of Karma* in the form of Fu Caiyun, the prostitute-concubine who excelled her *zhuangyuan* (first in the imperial examinations) husband in mastering foreign languages and customs, thus becoming another symbol of the Chinese man's endemic failure to understand China's need to adapt. The legend of her intervention in affairs of state (especially her supposed romantic involvement with an influential German general) had it that she did more for China than the efforts of all its inept men. Appearing shortly after *Flower in a Sea of Karma, Nine-times Cuckold* engages in a provocation of the earlier novel's portrayal of Sai Jinhua by portraying her when she is past her prime, long after her legendary splash in the national and international realm. Now one of Zhang's most famous conquests, she appears in retrospect to have been a short-lived aberration.[12]

In general, the same man who reinvents whoring aptitude is the one who exposes the foolishness of not only the old-fashioned Chinese man but the new student radicals who belong to the "new party" (*xindang*), which allies with foreigners to overthrow the Manchus (7.56). Zhang detests the pretenders of the party who return from study abroad in Western clothing spouting revolution, independence, and freedom. They criticize Chinese men for wasting their time with prostitutes instead of solving national problems, treating women like toys, and forcing women to bind their feet. When one of them pulls a gun on Zhang Qiugu, he simply invokes the foreign laws of Shanghai, which prohibit the brandishing of firearms, after which the student scurries off in shame (70.507–511). The same rational coolness emerges in another exemplary scene, when a rickshaw coolie callously knocks down an old man on the street. Zhang's friends see the coolie as an illustration of how the Chinese people mistreat their own "compatriots" (*tongbao*), like the imperial ministers who give in to foreign powers. Such actions, the friends say, prove the inherent "slavishness" (*nuli xingzhi*) of the Chinese people and their lack of a "sense of national citizenship" (*guomin sixiang*), a theme that also appears on the first page of *Flower in a Sea of Karma*. No wonder that foreigners compare the Chinese to the blacks of Africa. How will our country ever "reform its political system and strengthen itself," they ask in the language of the day (*bianfa ziqiang,* 43.313–315)? Zhang replies that they have drawn too wild a comparison in applying the notion of "sense of citizenship" to "a man who has the consciousness of a beast" (*jue wu yishide chusheng,* 43.315–316). Ruckus in the street is a violation of the laws of the Shanghai concessions, which he will invoke if they continue. In short, a reliable legal system is more efficient than grand theories of revolution. Spouting nationalism and revolution is like the student pulling a gun to challenge someone who is merely pointing out that he is a fool. These scenes confirm the master of the brothel as an enlightened and rational master of politics and international relations, superior to the failed diplomat-polygynist of *Flower in a Sea of Karma*.

The Psychology of the "Incorrigibly Wanton" Prostitute

If knowing how to enjoy himself is Zhang's way of proving the truth of his polygynous aptitude, then that truth contains a clear statement about the state of being of the prostitute, his centrally defined Chinese woman. Getting worse even as the novel progresses, she has turned into a brazen and shameless wastrel and parasite whom it is Zhang's duty to expose and, if possible, transform into what she should be, the perfect partner of the moment. The difficulty of that task has to do with the fact, as Zhang Qiugu constantly asserts, that she is always deceptive, hence his tenet that since a prostitute can never be trusted, she can never be married. As for the meaning of marriage, Zhang Qiugu begins the novel as a man dissatisfied with his average-looking wife by arranged marriage and thus a man in need of sojourns in brothels to find other women. The man unhappy with his arranged marriage is in fact a steady motif in the reformist era of the early 1900s and for many decades to come. The motif symbolizes the difficult transition from arranged marriage to so-called free marriage. The implicit point of *Nine-times Cuckold* is that a wife by arranged marriage is hardly a call for independence in the form of free marriage, that is, free monogamous marriage. Instead, the inherently unsatisfying arranged marriage is merely the reestablished excuse for the reformed man to continue the rule of the polygynist philanderer who has always left home to form liaisons with other women.

Brilliance in male and female psychology constitutes the core of Zhang Qiugu's reformism. The word "psychology" (*xinlixue*), a neologism of the time, appears in *Nine-times Cuckold* when Zhang states that the prostitute Lin Daiyu fails with men because she fails to understand that science well enough (22.169). Being a detective of the human heart like the "new scientists" (*xinfa gezhijia*) of psychology allows Zhang Qiugu to outwit an indomitable prostitute like Lin Daiyu, one of four famous prostitutes called the "four Shanghai door gods" (*Shanghai sida jingang*).[13] The prime feature of a woman like her is that she is *fangdang guanle* (2.13), "incorrigibly wanton," so used to being wanton that she knows no other way of being. This is the same knowledge conveyed in *Flowers of Shanghai* a decade earlier and in *Seductive Dreams* of 1830s Yangzhou, before the era of grand Shanghai. She is rude to customers, has her own lovers, and cares only about profit. It used to be that the prostitute "catered to" and "flattered" the patron (*bajie, fengcheng,* 9.68). Now she selects him; he doesn't select her. She accumulates debts, spending her money however she pleases, because she knows that there is always a fool she can marry who will pay off her debts, after which she can leave him and return to her adventures in Shanghai (a process that in Shanghai dialect goes by the name "taking a bath," *huyu*).[14] If he wants to prevail over such a woman, the man must always counter "falsity with falsity," never be completely serious, and "wait quietly for her to exhaust herself" (*wo yi bi lao,* 9.70), a reference to the fourth of the "thirty-six strategies" of war.[15]

Mastering the psychology of women and other men means seeing through the woman's machinations and the man's self-blinding fantasies. Han Bangqing portrays the same mastery in the brothel facilitator Hong Shanqing, but without the self-certainty of Zhang Qiugu. In *Nine-times Cuckold,* reading other people's minds takes the form we saw in *Courtesan Chambers* of the movements of the knowing eye, of which Zhang's eye is the keenest. The knowing eye takes quintessential form in the glance that is cast between him and another understanding party. Sometimes he loses control of his eyes, such as when he is "captivated" by the beauty of a woman. Then he "looks on in frozen wonder," as if awestruck (*daidaide kanzhe,* 1.3). But staring helplessly at one woman also serves an intentional purpose, which is both to call that woman's attention to himself and to be seen doing so by a second woman. He thus makes the two women he stares at in the first pages of the book compete for his attention. When he has one of them sit down beside him, she "lowers her head knowingly with a smile," while the other woman "stares at him, but though Qiugu notices her stare he ignores it." When one of the women pulls on him to keep him from going, he says, "Why do you insist on plying me with your tricks of doing business?" (1.8–9). In another scene, he exchanges an understanding glance with a woman who is overcome with appreciation at his understanding of women. Zhang detects Chen Wenxian, his soon-to-be concubine, noticing the exchange of glances, which elicits Chen's admiration as well (16.127). In general, the look that Zhang directs is one that controls and prohibits jealousy, which he knows is the "thing that the prostitute most fears being accused of" (*guanren zui fanjide shi shuo ta chi cu,* 44.319). The "taboo" (*ji*) against jealousy gives Zhang the license to be open with one woman about the other woman he just visited or is about to visit. The lucidity that he generates through his knowing eyes dispels the aura of the dominant prostitute and replaces it with his own.

The Woman Too Free and the Man Too Afraid of His Wife

The shameless lack of self-doubt is what led Lu Xun to call characters like Zhang a "genius plus hooligan," a type that Lu Xun said flooded the movies of his times with stars for whom "slickness and cheekiness" (*youtou huanao*) denoted proud ways of being.[16] This is the man for whom "living in Shanghai and knowing all its ways" (*zhuguanle Shanghai*) meant knowing how to flirt with Shanghai prostitutes. Lu Xun thereby sums up the entire last two decades of Qing literature about prostitutes in Shanghai, at the same time affirming the enduring popularity of the master of the brothels into the 1920s and 1930s. That hero has two foils, the forward-looking egalitarian monogamist like Lu Xun, and the backward brothel fool. *Nine-times Cuckold* portrays only the fool. But the master of the brothel needs the backward fool in order to have someone he can constantly outdo. Many of the novel's most interesting and sensational portraits are of this weaker man, commonly called the "plagued fool" (*wensheng*), that is, the gullible brothel patron, who also includes the "learned idiot" (*shudaizi*), that is, the successful exam candidate and imperial official like Fu Caiyun's learned but idiotic husband Jin Wenqing in *Flower in a Sea of Karma*. The ultimate fool, as the title of the novel signals, is the man whose wife and concubines cuckold him while he is away in Shanghai trying to succeed with prostitutes. Hence the character Kang Jisheng, former provincial governor, whose five concubines, two daughters-in-law, and two unmarried daughters, nine wanton women in all, combine to make Kang the most cuckolded man in Shanghai.

Polygynous aptitude amounts to never becoming infatuated (*milian*, 16. 126) with one woman, infatuation being the main defect of the plagued fool. In displaying the patron's worst traits, "penny pinching," "pawing the woman whenever he can," and "making an obnoxious nuisance of himself," the fool naturally invites the woman's mockery and abuse.[17] Zhang most detests the ungenerous and miserly patron who aspires to spend as little as possible on the prostitute, thinking that she is always cheating him or imagining that she will like him for himself rather than his money. The fool wants to believe that he is dealing with a "real" woman, that is, a woman who really likes and needs him, often called a *renjiaren*, "another person's woman," an emblematic term with profound meaning in the Shanghai world of prostitutes and patrons. *Renjiaren*, a good woman of decent family, supposedly likes the man for who he is, and is untainted and less mercenary because she is supposedly not a true prostitute. In some cases, she is an exciting catch because she is someone else's wife, though the term is also used with unmarried women.[18] In reality she is a lure who concocts stories about her desperate straits, such as an abusive husband or severe indebtedness. In the eyes of the plagued fool she represents an escape from the complex and high-cost world of the fashionable prostitutes with whom he is a clumsy failure. Even if he patronizes a true prostitute, the fool wants to believe she likes him as if he were "one of the family" (*zijiaren*), as Jin Hanliang, the opium-addicted, adopted son of a cuckold, insists. Only others notice that the prostitute he visits treats him with brazen contempt (40.291; Zhang finally explodes and tells Jin that she is cheating him, but Jin resents him for it). His foolishness includes other typical gaffs, such as visiting prostitutes too early in the day; asking to take a ride in the prostitute's sedan chair, not knowing that a patron never rides in such a vehicle; and returning from his ride to ask how much he should pay, not knowing that payment should take place more discretely (13–15).

Zhang Chunfan's learned idiot is hard not to see as a mirror of the foolish hero of *Flower in a Sea of Karma*, Jin Wenqing, who in turn stands for the stereotypical imperial official who doesn't even know the proper geographical coordinates of China on the world map. The older Hanlin scholar, Wang Boshen, is someone who "flaunts his seniority" (*yi lao mai lao*, 69.498) by always insisting on having the last pedantic word. As a learned idiot, he spends his life doing what it takes to achieve the highest examination status, curbing sexual pleasure until finally after age fifty he decides that he may have missed something by never visiting a Shanghai brothel. In spite of spending a large sum on his favorite prostitute, Wang caves in to her anger, assuming that a bad temper is part of what he is paying for. Disgusted by Wang's ineptness and hypocrisy, Zhang Qiugu "stuffs his mouth" (*saile tade kou'er*) by saying to his face that the "learning of the brothels" gives a man more skills than a lifetime of reading "dead books" (69.498–500). Satirizing the learned idiot is an old motif in Ming and Qing fiction, but "stuffing the mouth" of a high-placed elder, the type who is supposed to have the last word, is the sign of the new stage of radical dismissal in novels like *Shanghai Dust*, *Nine-times Cuckold*, and *Flower in a Sea of Karma*. Zeng Pu, the author of *Flower in a Sea of Karma*, likewise treats the *zhuangyuan* Jin Wenqing as if he were so beyond hope that his mouth finally had to be stuffed. At the same time, dismissing the scholar-official who represents centuries of accepted tradition stops short of revolutionary radicalism. In both *Flower in a Sea of Karma* and *Nine-times Cuckold*, the supersession of the old-style scholar-official takes place because of his tediousness and stupidity, but doesn't necessitate violent overthrow.[19] Zhang Qiugu's reform is a case of sexual revitalization by which the originally good polygynist-philanderer restores his mandate by valiantly proving that he can never be cuckolded.

The seamless effect of such self-confidence is apparent in the fact that *Nine-times Cuckold* never treats the plagued fool from the inside, as if his feelings represented a significant, epochal sort of melancholy. Li Boyuan's 1899 *Tracks of the Snowgoose* takes this approach, suffusing itself with an atmosphere of male disaffection from beginning to end. The patron Yan Huasheng is full of frustration because he can never achieve "results" (*jieguo*) (6.33) in the brothel. Fang Bosun, a Zhang Qiugu–like man of the world, steals a woman Yan has just begun to court, thereby sending Yan into a permanent state of embarrassment and creating a sensational item in the gossip columns. As a dignified patron, Yan can't display jealousy or try to prevent Fang from stealing his prostitute (a move that in the parlance of the time is called "cutting from the edge," *jian bian*, 3.15). Everyone including Yan himself can see what is going on, but in this case exchanging knowing looks as the cuckolding process begins is all that can be done (3.14, 16). Other fools include a man who is ecstatic when a prostitute agrees to marry him. If a famous courtesan (*mingji*) loves him, that must mean that he is a "famous scholar" (*mingshi*) after all, he concludes (13.74–75). The patron Jiang Youchun has a jealous wife and a loving concubine whose discord makes it impossible for him to stay at home. He befriends the fashionable Gao Xianglan, who likes to spend all night telling him about her life. Her "methods of diplomacy" (*waijiao shouduan*, 16.92) are so sophisticated that she doesn't need to "do business" or "go out on call." If a man wrongs her, she embarrasses him by getting a scandalous story written about him in the newspaper. If she doesn't like a rival prostitute, she has her driver squeeze the other woman's carriage off the road (20). He is full of respect for Gao Xiang-lan, who he sees is more than just a heartless Shanghai prostitute. In *Tracks of the Snowgoose*, the prostitute is the master of psychology. She would like to escape the brothel but can't, however, since as she says she can only do so by "leaning on the arm of a man" (*kao nanren yizhang paizi*, 18.105). The final scene of the novel has Jiang and Gao lying together talking all night without becoming lovers. She is too wanton and free; he is too afraid of his wife. These two present a crystallizing portrait of man and woman out of synch in the late-Qing moment of transition.

Conclusion

The Postpolygynous Future

Goddess Nüwa Repairs Heaven

The man's ruin because of his affair with a wanton woman is an ancient motif in times of dynastic decline. The vilification of the Shanghai prostitute in works like *Nine-times Cuckold* is a sign of the same motif, as is Zhang Qiugu's victory over wanton women, which is a metaphor of dynastic renewal. He is a sexual adept and master of the brothel, as if to say that these features represent a fundamental inheritance of the modern, internationally adept Chinese man. Who are his modern female counterparts? If we conjure an image of such a woman based on the new standards established in the early 1900s, then she is absent from *Nine-times Cuckold* since she cannot be the main wife, concubine, or prostitute anymore. The man whom the modern woman marries, if she marries at all, has to be the sexually chastened monogamist who forswears polygamy and prostitution.

A form of modern liberated women can be found in a novel like the 1905 *The Stone of Goddess Nüwa* (*Nüwa shi*), which promotes the grand notion that "if women change, so will the whole nation" and which in grand fashion then shows how the prostitute-heroines of the story will change and what they will do to save the world. First they will stop binding their feet, and then they will assassinate male leaders and force polygynists to liberate their concubines.[1] Such acts indicate that in order to be politically active in the new China, women must subvert the regime in which sex is inherently the polygynist-philanderer's sex. According to the old logic, a woman in public is either an improperly exposed main wife or concubine or else a prostitute. By way of transcending this sexual structure, the prostitute-heroines in *The Stone of Goddess Nüwa* utterly disavow marriage and sexual intercourse, and will conceive children only by newly invented scientific methods. They still in fact do what women resisting the polygamous sexual regime have always done, that is, divorce themselves from sexual activity with men.

This book has shown that the polygynist-philanderer and his main wives,

137

concubines, and prostitutes were the dominant characters in the portrait of sexuality that China presented to itself and the world at the verge of modernity. At that time, the decline of the Qing dynasty also meant the decline of the polygynist-philanderer, for China as a social and symbolic whole was so deeply formed by this sexual practice that when one was in decline, so was the other. This statement does not mean that a plan was already forming to abolish polygyny or that polygynists necessarily thought their days were coming to an end. China did legally end polygyny in the 1930s (that remnants of it continued to exist for decades, and that forms of it continue to exist today, is a story for another study). Why and how China did so is still a question that needs careful examination, as is how men and women remolded themselves in order to become postpolygynist subjects. Suffice to say for now that the rationale for the abolition of polygyny was similar to that for ending such things as footbinding and the sequestration of women, namely, that in the face of what came to be defined as modernity, these customs were to be defined as relics of the past. So were the practices of patronizing boy female impersonators and associating with "famous courtesans."[2] A key factor in these changes—though again one that needs careful examination—had to do with the fact that the Judeo-Christian West was monogamous and antihomosexualist and that it succeeded in imposing the standards of monogamy and antihomosexuality upon China and other non-Western cultures. The late-Qing sources studied in this book bear no imprint of the imposition of monogamy from the West. But they do bear marks of paradigmatic changes that I want to examine in this conclusion both by looking back in overview and by taking a forward glance at what the weight of the polygynous past must have had on its future. In ending at a point that I call the verge of modernity, this book emphasizes both the continuity and the break between the verge and what comes after in terms of polygynous sexuality, including the status of the *qing* aesthetic. Simply put, what changes, what stays the same, and what goes underground but still exerts residual and shadowy influence?

I first answer the question about continuity and break in terms of what female-authored texts did or did not share with male-authored texts, which have been the main sources thus far. In particular, how did female authors live with and portray polygyny, and is the notion of passive polygyny relevant in their literature as well? This question belongs to the proposition introduced at the beginning of this book that polygyny always had to be justified, was never a simple given, and forever met with resistance. It was a collective social formation that was shot through and through with struggle and interdependence and that had built-in mechanisms for female agency. In terms of the question of continuity and break, the point is that resistance to polygamy was not simply or finally discovered at the end of the Qing. The polygamous regime was not a purely dark past that suddenly received light, nor was it suddenly and easily abandoned. Then I will address the *qing* aesthetic at the end of the Qing dynasty in terms of the formation of China the modern nation, especially in terms of the leveling effects shared by both the *qing* aesthetic and the ethos of modernity. Do the egalitarian ethic of the notion of *qing* and the image of the remarkable woman have any relevance in the formation of China as a nation among nations? Do the remarkable woman and her wanton counterparts have anything in common with the image of the modern woman? This will be followed by a reconsideration of Lacanian ideas discussed in the introduction, now using the evidence gathered thus far to make new and retrospective statements about late-Qing narrative as a historical and socially symbolic act. How does the notion of modes of enjoyment facilitate the understanding of the polygynous fantasy, the *qing* aesthetic, and the portrayal of historical destiny in late-Qing China? How do the concepts of the master, the university, the hysteric, and the analyst describe paradigmatic change at this time? Finally, I will end with some observations about the afterlife of polygyny and the *qing* aesthetic following the end of the Qing, finishing with the question, how are current and emergent sexualities still inscribed or forced into older sexual formations?

Polygyny and Women Writers

Since I have mainly discussed works written by men, we are left wondering what women writers have to say about the same topics men address, and also whether women even address those topics. Women writers of the Ming and Qing provide considerable evidence about resistance to male gender bias in general and also vast amounts of fantasy material in which women speak and act as if under no compulsion to remain hidden in the inner chambers or to act as if they must always yield to men. They also confirm the existence of something like the passive polygyny that male authors idealize and force us again to realize that polygyny, like footbinding, is more than a one-sided affair of a monolithically male fantasy. *Tanci* rhyme-narratives by women offer especially revealing glimpses of polygamy as something the woman wishes she could escape or actually does escape, but also as something in which she takes active part as if she can do so with little or no compromise to her integrity and talent. The following summary combines what I have learned from male-authored sources with what other scholars have noted in their references to polygamy in female-authored *tanci*.[3]

One of the most common features of *tanci* is the presence of cross-dressing heroines who leave the home and accomplish heroic tasks in politics and war. A split between cross-dressers who never return to female dress and those who not only do so but also marry as co-wives occurs in a handful of cases. The women who join polygamous marriages in general resemble the women in male-authored texts who put the virtue and excellence of the household above the pettiness of jealousy and scheming rivalry. One of the most famous *tanci* heroines is Meng Lijun of *Bonds of Karmic Reincarnation* (*Zaisheng yuan,* ca. 1770), who, when forced to leave her family before marriage, disguises herself as a man and decides never to dress as a woman again, even when her parents plead with her. The female author Chen Duansheng (1751?–1796?) left the story unfinished at this critical point, but in 1821 the female poet Liang Desheng (1771–1847) supplied an ending in which Meng Lijun resumes female attire and returns to the man she was originally meant to marry, who by then has two concubines, one of whom, to her resentment, is the daughter of their archenemy. But it turns out that there is a reason for the presence of the daughter of the archenemy. She is the reincarnation of a jealous concubine in an earlier *tanci* (*Yuchuan yuan*) and is punished for her jealousy by being reincarnated in *Zaisheng yuan.* Another female author, Hou Zhi (1764–1829), who disliked Meng Lijun's cross-dressing excesses, further polished *Zaisheng yuan* by removing the jealousy and insecurity of the daughter of the archenemy. The same split between cross-dressers occurs in Qiu Xinru's (1805?–1873?) *tanci,* in which the one who returns to female dress becomes the manager of a well-run polygamous household in which she tolerates no jealousy (Jiang Dehua's *Bi sheng hua,* first published in 1857), and in Sun Deying's (after 1841–?) *tanci,* in which one cross-dresser never wears women's clothes again and—like the author herself—vows never to marry, while the other two cross-dressers marry the same man, one becoming one of three concubines, the other the main wife and capable manager of the household (*Jin yu yuan,* 1860s).[4]

One of the chief characteristics of the *tanci* and women's writing in general, it is important to remember, is the pride in being a woman—thus, for example, the female author's extravagant portrayal of heroic women. If in Hou Zhi's and Qiu Xinru's eyes Meng Lijun was too extravagant, it was because she verged on what male and even female authors would call the shrew. When Hou Zhi created a daughter for Meng Lijun in her 1821 *tanci,* she came up with Feilong (Flying Dragon in *Zaizao tian*), whose outrageous behavior reads like the negative extreme of her mother's excesses. Modeling herself after the Tang empress Wu Zetian, Feilong reduces her husband the emperor to a puppet and supplants all other women until finally put in her place by her maternal aunt and mother-in-law, the empress dowager and exemplar of female moral authority. Although women writers also use shrews and other misbehaving women to voice resentment against male gender bias, their central model of womanhood nevertheless embodies the same voice of female moral authority as Feilong's dowager mother-in-law.[5] Hence the good woman, even if she is a member of a polygamous marriage, rises above jealousy and scheming rivalry, which are the traits of the female versions of the wastrel man, that is, shrews and wanton women. Hou Zhi's vision of social order is like that of other male and female writers of the last century of the Qing, for whom social morals and political harmony override the petty concerns of wastrels, shrews, and wanton women.

Passive Polygamy and a Concubine Author

Passive polygamy is a fantasy that I have reconstructed based on its recurrence in Qing texts by men. What about passive polygamy from the perspective of female agency, by which I mean the literary exercise of agency by female authors and both fictional and real historical situations in which women arrange or at least substantially contribute to the taking of concubines. The central question is, under the conditions of polygamy as a social given, what in passive polygamy is a matter of joint agency, or the partial yielding of male agency to women, or even of the primacy of the woman's role in the form of the dominant main wife? The *tanci* already provides examples of the strength of women in polygyny and the corresponding weakness or secondariness of men. Although the *tanci* is a case of fictional fantasy, its correlation with male-authored texts affirms the existence of a kind of accord between the sexes whereby everyone joins on a grander level, as it were, to enforce both domestic and civilizational harmony. The critical difference between male- and female-authored texts is that the *tanci* lacks the male fantasy's focus on the sexual availability of women and the women's eager support of his polygynous ambition.

For an example of mutual accord in the case of a nonfictional female member of a polygamous family, let us consider the concubine and poet Shen Cai, born in 1732. Famous concubine poets in Ming and Qing history include women who had been courtesans and as such had been trained to entertain literati clients. Such women succeeded in escaping the brothel, marrying into a literati family, and even continuing their artistic or poetic activities. Shen Cai differed in that she was never a courtesan but became a concubine at age twelve to a scholar and bibliophile named Lu Xuan, whose main wife, Peng Zhenyin, was a poet and who took on the role of maternal mentor to the girl. As soon as Shen entered the home, the wife became her teacher, and they had a close relationship. The occasion of Shen Cai's first intercourse with Lu Xuan in 1766 at age fifteen was marked by a ritual exchange between main wife and concubine, who recorded the occasion in a respectful address to the main wife.[6]

Evidence from male- and female-authored fiction would compel us to read the ritual exchange between main wife and concubine as a case of replacing jealousy and mistrust by what I have called female arrangement and cooperation. A form of mutual acknowledgment occurred between main wife, husband, and concubine when they knew that the time had come for Shen Cai to "pin up her hair," thus their three-way cooperation. Female arrangement took the form of the alliance the women cultivated between themselves and sanctified in this instance through an exchange of literary gifts. They thus avoided the potential of jealousy and rivalry on the women's part and callous favoritism on the man's. As a kind of two-wife polygyny, the triangular relationship took the form of a sublimated incest, in which husband and wife adopted a daughter who later served as secondary wife. As Grace Fong writes, Shen Cai treated Peng Zhenyin "more like a teacher and mother than a competitor for her husband's affection," even though Shen Cai's poetry included pieces about a night spent with Lu Xuan and sensuous poems about herself.[7] Shen Cai's harmonious membership in the polygamous family recalls the passive polygyny seen in male-authored fiction, in which the gentleman forgoes taking a concubine regardless of whether his wife might like her and the wife oversees and bonds with someone she knows will be a sexual partner to her husband. The situation receives a kind of public blessing in the form of Shen Cai's literary production and publication, which besides gaining appreciative readers also verifies in the observers' minds both the harmony of the polygynous family and the talent and worthiness of the nevertheless subordinate partner. Many copies of Shen's work circulated, and seven poems were included in a major anthology of women's poetry. Her writing is full of the minutiae of daily life in the "side room" (ceshi), the term for the concubine's, not main wife's, chamber. Absent are the tears, melancholy, and anxiety of waiting in isolation that are common to boudoir poetry. Instead, she turned her environment into an "energized, productive space," as Fong puts it, in which she avidly pursued her own interests.[8]

Another example of a wife's managing role in polygamy is that of Wang Duanshu (1621– before 1685), a professional female writer and anthologist, who used her own money to help purchase a concubine, Chen Yuan, for her husband, Ding Shengzhao (1621–ca. 1700), later adopting the couple's daughter as her own. She was the dominant figure in that she earned the most and was the most learned, as her husband acknowledged. The main wife's arrangement of polygyny in this case was a practical matter in that Wang Duanshu (author of a major anthology of women's poetry) desired more time on her own for her work but, we imagine, did not wish to flout the sexual and romantic interests of her husband and wanted to exert some control over his choice of concubine.[9] A third case is Shen Fu's wife Yun in Six Records of a Floating Life (Fusheng liuji), who requested that her husband take as concubine a young prostitute she herself loved. Although purporting to be pure autobiography, Fusheng liuji probably portrays parts of the relationship as Shen Fu nostalgically wishes it had been, thus staging passive polygyny from the perspective of the man creating his own self-image. In desiring a concubine for her husband, Yun was reportedly reacting to a friend of Shen Fu's who was proud of his new concubine, whom Yun thought lacked charm, thus Yun's "obsession" (chixin), in Shen's words, with finding a better concubine for her and her husband.[10] The effort failed, to Yun's great chagrin. Their attempt to recruit a concubine contrasts starkly with Shen Fu's father's attempt to find one without telling Shen Fu's mother. Because Yun helped in this attempt, misunderstandings developed between her and the mother-in-law. For this and other reasons, the young couple suffered ostracism from the family, after which Yun never recovered and finally died (a friend later presented Shen Fu with a concubine).

For Shen Fu and Yun, adopting a concubine was an open affair involving no deceit. It was a matter not of producing a son, since they already had one, but supposedly of Yun's securing herself a female companion to join her and her husband in their companionate marriage. Shen Fu fulfills the definition of the blank and unlustful polygynist in that he is a polygynist because he can be and is expected to be so, even by his wife, but he does not initiate finding a concubine. His behavior in a Cantonese brothel on a trip away from home confirms the picture of him as a gentle philanderer. While a friend of his goes from one prostitute to another, sometimes taking two in one night, Shen Fu stays with only one, choosing her because she looks like his wife and later being moved when he learns that she deeply lamented his departure.

In the above examples female agency takes the form of the woman's active contribution and even initiation. There is an accord between husband and main wife. The examples recall the cases of two-wife polygyny that I examined a few chapters ago where the limitation to two women was especially important. As was suggested, two-wife polygyny—whether involving two women of the same status or a main wife and a concubine—acted as a kind of relay between the polygynous hierarchy of multiple wives (three or more) and *qing* egalitarianism, as if to locate a compromise between multiple wives and just one. For the man to deserve polygyny, he must in general be unlustful or even asexual. For the woman to be willing to join such a marriage, she must play a managerial role. Stopping at two is as if to mark the limit of temperance or the limit up to which the participants can still adhere relatively well to the spirit of the *qing* aesthetic. Adhering "relatively well" means being fair to two women who marry the same humble man. Meanwhile, the pressure of equivalence exerts a tempering effect on the centrality of the man, who as a member of a triad, as I have said, is more like one of three rather than one over many.

China the Nation and the *Qing* Aesthetic at the End of the Imperial Era

How and why polygamy ended inevitably poses the question, was change in this regard defined as paradigmatic only if there was influence because of Western intrusion? The loudest and easiest answer is yes, but in fact a critique of polygamy already existed before the time of intrusion. A novel like *Shanghai Dust* proves the natural link between the modern notion of equality, on the one hand, and the long-existing link between the theme of the remarkable woman and the egalitarianism of the *qing* aesthetic, on the other. What had also already long been around included stories of cross-dressing women and gender fluidity, stories in which the male consort of the remarkable woman experienced the life-shattering effect of their love, and stories in which there was an implied message that "we are all women." The authors of such fantasies include Cao Xueqin, Wei Xiuren, Chen Sen, and Zou Tao. As a writer living in a period of unprecedented cultural dislocation, Wei Xiuren turned the shattering effect of love between two people into a de facto form of sublime monogamy. He inherited the radical *qing* aesthetic of the late Ming and used it to elevate the love of the loyalist couple. After the loyalists Wei and Liu die, other loyalist couples conquer the Taiping enemy, thereby diverging from fictional endings common elsewhere in which the reestablishment of social harmony is one and the same with the reaffirmation of polygamous harmony.

Let us at this point note the link between the *qing* aesthetic of radical subjectivity, with its ethics of egalitarianism, and the formation of China as a new modern nation in line with the sentence from *The Stone of Goddess Nüwa,* "If women change, so will the whole nation." At first glance the link appears improbable in that, by the end of the Qing, the formation of China the modern nation had little use for the feminine aspects of the *qing* aesthetic. If anything, the spirit of turning China into a strong nation had more to draw from Qing fiction's valiant and martial heroes and heroines than from the characters in Pu Songling's stories, *Dream of the Red Chamber,* and nineteenth-century works like *Precious Mirror of Boy Actresses, Traces of the Flowery Moon,* Wang Tao's imitations of Pu Songling's stories, and *Shanghai Dust.*[11] In the eyes of the proponents of strong national character, the latter group of works illustrated refuge from rather than adjustment to the advent of overwhelming change. For this reason, by the end of the Qing, the *qing* aesthetic was thrown together with the traditional regimes of polygyny and patronage of prostitutes, all of which were to be abandoned in light of the encounter with the European intrusion and the advent of modernity.

Yet *qing* and the remarkable woman, whether chaste or wanton, are still relevant to the dynamics of China and modern nation-forming, especially if we consider the leveling effects inherent in the notions of both *qing* universality and modern nationhood in one of its most fundamental senses, namely, the merging of a particular culture like China into the global, universal assemblage of other nations and cultures.[12] Let us consider, for example, the phenomenon in the mid- to late-nineteenth century of the gradual sense of the loss of Chinese civilizational centrality. This began around the Opium War of 1839–1842 with the perception of a categorically different kind of enemy in the form of the British and other

Western powers.[13] Later we see things like the Chinese government's reaction to discrimination against Chinese immigrants in the United States and elsewhere, which led to an increasing recognition from the 1860s to the 1890s of the legal and political status of the Chinese subject in an international setting. There was also the reaction to the rapid Westernization of Japan, which at first appeared in Chinese eyes to be a case of abandonment of "the universal order known as Civilization," but eventually led to the recognition of the inevitability of that trend.[14] By the end of the Qing we then witness the self-conscious framing of China as a modern nation among nations and the general notion both of China's place in Asia and "China in the world," that is, no longer China as the center of the world.[15] The fundamental implication of China in the world was the advent of a universal global subject that as such, in the core abstract sense, was shorn of all cultural particulars. To be shorn of cultural particulars gets at the notion I am driving at about the link between *qing* universality and modernity. Wang Tao evoked a similar image when he extended the meaning of the Chinese *dao* to the level of a neutral universal and claimed that the Chinese *dao* was everyone's *dao*, with no exclusive claim to a particular chosen people. Such a leveling effect demonstrates, in Terry Cochran's words, that the "ethos of modernity was born of a clash with the other."[16] Such a clash shatters the enclosure of the traditional cultural sphere. There is no alternative but the breaching of that wall of enclosure, with the result that all subjects are suddenly and permanently transported out of the time and space of their particular cultural past.

In spite of the difference in tenor between the "ethos of modernity" and the aesthetics of *qing*, the two notions nevertheless share a similar sense of the individual subject's radical dislocation. The displacement of the polygynist male in literature from the late Ming to the late Qing likewise involves the master figure in a "clash with the other." The remarkable woman plays a central role in this displacement by serving as the figural representative of both spatial and temporal transition. She is able to do so because of the universalizing and egalitarian features already present in the *qing* aesthetic and its motif of the male consort of the remarkable woman. Hence the instinctive link between the *qing* aesthetic and the newly introduced ideas of sexual egalitarianism in *Shanghai Dust* or the overlap between the old theme of female heroism in times of male decline and the female revolutionaries in *The Stone of Goddess Nüwa*. The link is likewise present in the form of the vilified Shanghai prostitute, who is an alternate version of the late-Qing female revolutionary. The self-certain master philanderer understands women, who he believes recognize in him the rare instance among men of the truly deserving polygamist. He registers the women's line of sight infallibly. The Shanghai prostitute, however, reads the man infallibly. As a new remarkable woman, she enforces a new concept of equality that, although condemned in literature about patrons and prostitutes, stipulates that she marries a man only under the condition that she stay in the Shanghai concessions; she will never return with the man to the home of his wife and mother, to whom she would have to kowtow; and she can leave the man if she wants, even absconding with his money and valuables.[17]

What, however, happened to the sexual agency of the wanton woman in the transition to modern nationhood? More generally, what happened to the agency of sexual pleasure? The answer in brief is that the polygynist-philanderer did not easily surrender his sexual primacy; and the prostitute-concubine did not pass her sexual incorrigibility to the modern woman. Gao Xianglan of *Tracks of the Snowgoose,* Fu Caiyun of *Flower in a Sea of Karma,* and Lin Daiyu or Sai Jinhua of *Nine-times Cuckold* are roughly the same incorrigibly free and self-indulgent woman portrayed in these and other novels, city guidebooks, pictorials, and journalistic accounts.[18] As girls and women of "good families" (*liangjia funü*) appeared on the streets alongside them in the early 1900s, the good women suffered from the slippage that occurred between them and the wanton prostitute. The good woman, as noted, struggled to free herself from the perception that the woman who appeared in public was by definition loose. The new egalitarian woman had in general to rise above the sexual, therefore, where sexual was still defined according to the roles of the polygynist-philanderer and the prostitute-concubine. The trajectory of the new woman pointed to female separatism, that is, exclusion of sexual relationships with men. Hence the anarchist assassin in *Heroines of Eastern Europe (Dong'ou nühaojie),* the woman who murders her husband in *Flower in a Woman's Prison (Nüyu hua),* and the inhabitants of a brothel in *The Stone of Goddess Nüwa* that turns out to be a scientific utopia ruled by women who vilify sex and relations with men.[19]

Why can't we add one more radical to this group, the prostitute-concubine who cuckolds the patron-husband? If she was not considered a radical like the others, it is because of her pollution by what was still considered the base sexuality of the prostitute-concubine. When Jin Wenqing catches Fu Caiyun committing adultery, she replies that she is a concubine, not a main wife, and that because she is a plaything, she follows no rules. "This is the way I am, and I can't be changed" (*benxing nan yi*).[20] Given the supreme value placed upon female chastity in the Qing dynasty and after, this is an extremely outrageous statement. Given the context of Shanghai and the new possibilities it offers women like Fu Caiyun, her ability to say such things could potentially be read as a sign of a radically new kind of female subjectivity. Nevertheless, the words "this is the way I am" never become what a woman like her is honored for. The new man's equal is the superior woman who compels the man to forget about polygyny and patronizing prostitutes. *Nine-times Cuckold* denigrates such an egalitarianism by simply not mentioning it. The only type of egalitarianism that occurs in *Nine-times Cuckold* takes minor form in the secret love affair between the prostitute and the actor, that is, a man of the prostitute's same social level who pays her nothing and whom she loves more than her elite paying patrons. In the discourse of polygyny, monogamy and egalitarianism amount to no more than the relationship between the base male actor and the base prostitute. By the same logic, a man who is monogamous is such because he is a fool who lacks the aptitude for philandering. Egalitarianism is thus the unsatisfactory compromise between the sophisticate's self-confidence and the fool's melancholy and resentment.

Fantasy and the Battle of Modes of Enjoyment

This book has been a study of narrative as historical and socially symbolic act, mainly focusing on fictional but also some biographical sources. The terms and tools of psychoanalytic theory discussed in the introduction have been lurking under the surface and need to be openly engaged once again both to prove their relevance and to provide an alternate type of clarity to what has been said so far. The courtesan's or boy actress's depression because of their entrapment in the brothel or opera troupe, for example, recalls the position of the Lacanian hysteric. Hong Shanqing, the brothel facilitator, speaks in the discourse of the analyst. Zhang Qiugu's brothel mastery, especially as embodied in his knowing eye, is a case of the master's denial of the fundamental state of split subjectivity. The mental turn that occurs in the brothel patron when he decides upon a certain prostitute has to do with the university discourse, the producers of which emulate the example of the man with the most women, carry out his laws, and build their reputations among each other by means of the particular choices of woman they make. All these instances of subjective discourse presume a special understanding of the function of fantasy in framing and supplying consistency to narrative reality. Fantasy in this particular sense has to be understood as a general word standing for all narratives, from myth to dream and including fiction as well as history. It is a question of the fundamental organizing function of fantasy and its framing and construction of desire, which *Traces of the Flowery Moon* and *Shanghai Dust* particularly exemplified in their crystallizations of one cultural order against another and *Tale of Filial Heroes* showed in its portrayal of modes of enjoyment, as in Deng Jiugong's disgust with boy actresses.

The notion of modes of enjoyment is key in illustrating fantasy's organizing function. To recapitulate the definition given above, modes of enjoyment have to do with a character's or a group's preferences and habits of sexual and marital custom, eating and hygiene, also including music, clothing, and other areas of art, pleasure, and physical well-being. The word "enjoyment" in this special sense needs to be understood to include more than pleasure, but also other modes of sensation such as sorrow and loss, and courage and dedication, even if painful. The *ernü* kind of *qing*, the utter abstinence from opium smoking among the star characters of *Tale of Filial Heroes*, and opera about military heroes are all examples of modes of enjoyment organized by the fantasy narrative of not only the novel but also the ideological discourse it represents. Opera about military heroes opposes opera about sentimental beauties and scholars, where the former is loved by those who embody the energy that will maintain China in its supposedly original wholesomeness and the latter is loved by decadent and depraved people who represent China in a state of decay. Nevertheless, *Precious Mirror of Boy Actresses* and *Traces of the Flowery Moon*, as opposed as they are to *Tale of Filial Heroes* in terms of the interpretation of *qing*, resemble *Tale of Filial Heroes* in their portrayal of heroes who never smoke opium. In the late Qing, abstinence from opium was in general the sign of an ideological fantasy of a purified China, opposed both to the foreigners who imposed opium upon China from the outside and to the Chinese who smoked it and ruined the empire from within. Though neither *Tale of Filial Heroes* nor *Precious Mirror of Boy Actresses* self-consciously engages the historical realities of the opium trade and China's interactions with Europe, opium in itself carries the weight of that historical meaning. *Traces of the Flowery Moon* engages those realities explicitly. Opium as a pregnant signifier in this period, plus juxtaposition with *Traces of the Flowery Moon*, thus allows us to say that the mere portrayal in *Precious Mirror of Boy Actresses* of the contrast between the vulgar, rapacious, and opium-smoking Xi Shiyi, on the one hand, and the chaste, opium-abstaining heroes of sublime love, on the other, in itself enunciates the same highly charged moral position of *Traces of the Flowery Moon* and the later *Shanghai Dust*. *Tale of Filial Heroes* takes an equally charged moral stance, but in the mode of the remarkable warrior woman who does not even smoke tobacco, much less opium, and who saves the world by restoring it to proper Confucian values.[21]

Qing plays a role similar to opium. As a mode of enjoyment, *qing* in these novels is a signifier of Chinese civilizational purity. In their various declensions of the *qing* aesthetic, the sublime lover of the boy actress, the polygynous man and his final courtesan lover, and the passive polygynist and his protective co-wives all take the same side in the battle taking place throughout nineteenth-century literature between China as a civilizational center and the invading forces of the West. Although only *Traces of the Flowery Moon, Later Tales of Liaozhai,* and *Shanghai Dust* actually describe this battle, the others participate in the same structure of the fantasy of the polygynist-philanderer and his female counterparts who stand for the essence of Chinese cultural character. Wang Tao's portrayals of the philanderer's inalienable pursuit of pleasure among Chinese courtesans, not Japanese or Swiss, aligns his characters with the heroic lovers of *Traces of the Flowery Moon* in their battle against the Taipings and their monstrous states of sexual being. A central motif in such battles, regardless of cultural setting or historical era, is the theft of pleasure. The vile enemy steals too much pleasure and even replaces our mode of enjoyment with theirs. The opium smoker is again an example. He or she exemplifies obscene enjoyment, replacing even sex with the ecstasy of the opium high. They enjoy themselves more than pleasure should properly be enjoyed, and thereby take more than their allotment. As I have shown elsewhere, opium the cultural signifier always carried within it the notion that it was from the "West" (as in the widely used terms for opium, "Western smoke," *yangyan,* and "Western medicine," *yangyao,* even though most opium in the late Qing was grown in China).[22] As such, it could never be accepted or normalized in the symbolic universe of late-Qing China and was always an inherent sign of degrading and obscene desire. *Qing* lovers never smoked opium, or, if they did, as in *Seductive Dreams,* they represented eroded forms of love destined for dire and inglorious endings.

Qing plays a central role in the battles of modes of enjoyment because of its sense of radical subjectivity. The prostitute and boy actress who hate the role they are forced to play exemplify the Lacanian discourse of the hysteric, that is, the subject who occupies a fundamentally impossible social position. Their core question is, "Why am I what you are saying I am?"[23] Qinyan, the most famous boy actress, hates being a *dan* and hates the men he attracts, hence his sublime state of depression and illness, which his true lover Mei Ziyu shares as they suffer together in a world in which they lead a fractured existence. It is not far from the hysteria of their roles to that of Wei Chizhu and Liu Qiuhen in *Traces of the Flowery Moon,* Wang Tao's patrons and courtesans in *Later Tales of Liaozhai,* or Gu Lansheng and Han Qiuhe in *Shanghai Dust.* The feminine subjectivity of these men and women is not just part of a sublime love affair; it is also part of a larger fantasy of China as a social and cultural whole in a state of fundamental social and political crisis.

The deradicalized forms of *qing* in *Tale of Filial Heroes* and *Nine-times Cuckold* recall the function of Lacan's master discourse, which represses the inherent state of split subjectivity, the hysteric's in particular. The Master is comfortable in his enforcement of social law and, like Zhang Qiugu in *Nine-times Cuckold,* possesses a knowing eye, which is the most telling feature of the master figure. The Lacanian notion of gaze best describes the function of the knowing eye. Gaze refers to the fact that people never look at me from where I expect them to.[24] No one is seen in the way she wants to be seen. The important distinction here is between the *look* and the *gaze,* where the gaze comes from the perspective of what is looked at, which never coincides with the subject's look. The split between the look of the eye (the subject's) and the gaze (the object's, that is, other people's) is the visual form of the split of split subjectivity. The knowing eye looks at an object but disrecognizes how that object is looking back at him. The three women who swear sisterhood in *Flowers of Shanghai* enact the gaze when they comment on the horrible appearance of the half-open eyes of the napping Grand Master of Love, Qi Yunsou, and how he can never know what is truly in their hearts. The look back is particularly missing in the novels portraying the most brazen and knavish polygynist-philanderers, *Revisiting the Silken Chambers, Courtesan Chambers,* and *Nine-times Cuckold.* Thus, in *Courtesan Chambers* we see one of the most farcical examples of the absence of the gaze in nineteenth-century fiction when Jin Yixiang's disembodied soul looks at his own corpse as his wives weep over him. It is a case of the knowing eye that sees himself without others returning his look, as if he sees all, but they see nothing.

Flowers of Shanghai stands out among all the novels I have examined because of the way in which it crystallizes the moment of historical transition in which one master begins to pass away as another inevitably arrives. The in-between moment, as Lacan says, exposes the arbitrariness of all masters, the past one especially, and hence this novel's stark difference from others about patrons and prostitutes in Shanghai, especially *Nine-times Cuckold.* The gaze is omnipresent in *Flowers of Shanghai,* especially in the form of the brothel facilitator, Hong Shanqing. This is not to say that he qualifies as a kind of psychoanalyst, an anachronistic notion, not to mention that Hong Shanqing himself is also caught up in the discourse of the master and is never purely in the position of the analyst. Nevertheless, as the facilitator of brothel affairs, he and his prostitute-mistress repeatedly examine the love fantasy of the others surrounding them, doing so in a way that exposes it as something artificial and contingent. They expose people to their entrapment in the fantasy, which amounts to exposing them to the fantasy/contagion of the world of Shanghai. Although he serves the supposed master philanderers frequenting the brothels, he never emulates them or strives to be one like them, but instead stands for a new type of man who adapts to the new world of Shanghai without missing the old China or resenting what Zhang Qiugu calls the "incorrigibly wanton" prostitute.

After the Verge of Modernity

The final question of this book is, what form will sexuality take after the late Qing in terms of sexual agency and pleasure? This can be addressed on two levels, one that of the future of the *qing* aesthetic after the end of the Qing, the other that of the residual and shadowy effects of polygamous sexuality.

Versions of the *qing* aesthetic continued in the sentimental Mandarin Duck and Butterfly fiction that followed the Qing. One of the most famous examples is *Jade Pear Spirit (Yuli Hun),* the novel inspired by *Traces of the Flowery Moon.* As Rey Chow puts it, love in this and other Butterfly fiction is no longer a "cherished state of being." Instead, it is a sign of disaster that must be hidden completely from sight—hence the lovers in *Jade Pear Spirit* never even hold hands. May Fourth intellectuals condemned this fiction, seeing the authors as anachronistic in their placement of the impossibility of love within the framework of the Confucian virtue that their stories elevate.[25] In Butterfly fiction, the radical nature of sublime passion gets subsumed under the backward-looking vision of Confucian chastity. Or, instead of backward looking, we should say frozen, as the lovers in their arrested state display their inability to enter the modern era. The excess of the feminine that is prized by the *qing* aesthetic goes against the flow of the new modern subject advocated by late-Qing ideologues, and thus the necessary death of that aesthetic.

But there is another way of looking at their affair in that the *qing* lovers were in fact uncomfortable both before and after modernity. The same dubious relation between *qing* in its most radical forms and the centrist force of Confucian values continued in the love stories of Butterfly fiction, where modernity takes the place of Confucian values. In other words, modernity shares the same hegemonic effect as patriarchal Confucianism with respect to the intricately intimate world of the *qing* aesthetic. So, for example, if the lovers in *Jade Pear Spirit* and other early-Republican sentimental fiction can only enjoy sad and unfulfilled love, this is not simply a case of anachronistic sexual repression. Instead, as I have said, the lovers in their arrested state display their inability to enter the modern era, but that inability represents heroic defiance and refusal. In their arrested state, deliberately refusing to consummate, they signal their refusal to choose between village and metropolis, or Chinese *qing* and foreign love. They are like loyalist lovers who reject the forced choice, even if to many they seemed impossibly maudlin. Their nostalgia and excess of emotion—for which May Fourth intellectuals rejected them—concealed a radical effect recalling that of the late-Ming notion of *qing*.

As for the after effects of polygamous sexuality, in recent work Ding Naifei considers the positionalities of the polygynist-philanderer and the main wife, concubine, and prostitute in vestigial and recombinant forms in contemporary Taiwan. She refers to the Taipei prostitutes who took to the streets in 1997 to protest the city's proposal to revoke their licenses, while feminists in Taiwan at the time opposed licensed prostitution.[26] In her critique of the feminist position, Ding writes of the "affective power of a hierarchic principle that although no longer at work as dominant ideology nonetheless functions in the manner of a shadow force." In other words, even if no longer dominant, the sexual regime of the polygynist-philanderer still exerts a shadowy force on the logic of banning prostitution. The baseness of the wanton woman, which is a fundamental feature of the regime that scripts the roles of main wife versus concubine and prostitute, still functions in the contemporary Taiwanese feminist who calls for the suppression of prostitution. The contemporary intellectual-professional feminist makes "universalist liberatory claims" for the bondmaid-concubine and the prostitute, and thereby assumes the unself-critical stance of the traditional "good woman" (*liangjia funü*), meanwhile denying rights of protection and livelihood to the concubine and the prostitute. In short, the modern feminist uncritically occupies the position of the good woman/main wife. Ding's points can be clarified by furthering the question asked above about the possible parallels between the Shanghai prostitute and the female separatists of the early 1900s: In the terms of the wanton woman of Ming and Qing fiction, how is "a sexually opportunist and incidentally murderously vengeful succubus of the concubine-bondmaid denomination [like Pan Jinlian in *Jin Ping Mei*] to become 'useful' for present day feminists in Taiwan?" In other words, can the sex worker who demonstrates on the streets for her rights in 1990s Taipei also be "recognized as 'feminist?'"[27]

My final point is a hypothesis about the future of a polygynous discourse like that found in late-Qing novels. In what forms will the insistence on the primacy of polygynous pleasure persist after the end of the Qing? This question applies not only to men who carry on with various echoes of so-called past behavior but also to women who continue as their "base" polygamous counterparts as well as women who in their antipolygamy still follow the mode of the chaste "good woman." Let us speculate about how chastity continued to be a dominant virtue after the fall of the Qing by going back to a common lament of late-Qing- and Republican-period intellectuals, the backwardness of the Chinese national character. In literary and nonliterary contexts alike, the Chinese man and woman were generalized as slavish, selfish, ignorant, and utterly lacking in self-consciousness. They had no sense of individualism and moral autonomy, the basic elements for forming a new and democratic nation.[28] To forge a modern sense of Chinese national identity, the major mottoes became the healthy reproduction of the race and the strengthening of the population.[29] Modern morality would liberate people from feudal practices and mentalities like footbinding and polygamy, while medicine and the science of hygiene would liberate the people from poor health and disease. In all this, the question of sexual pleasure was in general marginalized, especially, as Rey Chow emphasizes, that of the woman.[30] The erotic tradition known until then was dismissed, along with the polygamist and brothel patron on the one hand and the concubine and prostitute on the other. My point is that the cost of dismissing the polygamist-philanderer and his female counterparts was never adequately paid. They were condemned too easily and unquestioningly. A step was skipped in the transition to a new paradigm of citizenship in terms of unanswered questions: What was salvageable and what was resistant to change in the traditions of polygamy, the patronage of prostitution, and their definitions of sexual pleasure? How was one to separate the question of the sexual pleasure of women from its identification with wanton baseness or from its centuries-long portrayal in the art of the bedchamber? The problematic nature of sexual pleasure had to do with the profound influence of polygamy upon sexuality in general, making the same theorem apply in late-Qing China that applied before: namely, the equation of the transcendence of polygamous sexuality and the transcendence of sexual pleasure.

In regard to the residual forms of concubinage and primary wifehood in Taiwan, Ding writes, "Sexuality, that is, all non-reproductive pleasurable sexuality, seems an all-male domain that is either bad polygamous consumption (preying upon the weak and innocent), or good procreative sex in marriage."[31] She points, in other words, to a troublesome dichotomy that still persists between the stigmatized zone of polygynous sexuality and the exalted zone of heterosexual marriage, with little room left for other sexualities to emerge—hence the fact that gays and lesbians accompanied prostitutes on the streets of Taipei in 1997, all demonstrating against the banning of licensed prostitution. Taiwan may differ from mainland China, Hong Kong, Singapore, and concentrated Chinese communities elsewhere, but consideration of these other areas must still keep in mind the continually productive forces of polygyny and prostitution as residually dominant regimes. The new and the old "jostle and struggle in and between different space-times,"[32] surprising us with remnants, renewals, and recombinations of what we may have thought was abandoned long ago. Just as polygamy and the patronage of courtesans were about to be abandoned as relics of the past, in other words, they had already begun to exert shadowy and residual effects on sexuality afterwards.

Notes

Introduction. The Male Consort of the Remarkable Woman

1. Modified versions of the first three sections of this chapter, plus a digest of parts of chapters 2, 5, and 9, appeared in "The Concept of Chinese Polygamy," in Olga Lomova, ed., *Paths to Modernity* (Prague: Karolinum Press, 2008), pp. 127–147.

2. On the image of the peaceful addict, see Keith McMahon, *The Fall of the God of Money: Opium Smoking in Nineteenth-century China* (Lanham, Md.: Rowman and Littlefield, 2002), especially chapter 5; and McMahon, "Opium Smoking and Modern Subjectivity," *Postcolonial Studies* 8.2 (2005): 165–180. On the bound-footed woman as an icon of purity, see Dorothy Ko, *Cinderella's Sisters: A Revisionist History of Footbinding* (Berkeley: University of California Press, 2005), p. 34.

3. The Chinese sources I use also refer to it as *qiqie chengqun* (droves of wives and concubines) or *yiqi shuqie* (one wife and several concubines), for example. The term *fengliu caizi* also exists, which resembles philanderer or libertine, but too narrowly connotes a man who is "dashing and talented."

4. See Matthew Sommer, "Making Sex Work: Polyandry as Survival Strategy in Qing Dynasty China," in Bryna Goodman and Wendy Larson, eds., *Gender in Motion: Divisions of Labor and Cultural Change in Late Imperial and Modern China* (Lanham, Md.: Rowman and Littlefield, 2005), pp. 29–54; see pp. 31–33. The practice stretched from Taiwan to Gansu, and it often involved actual written contracts.

5. See Peter Bretschneider, *Polygyny: A Cross-Cultural Study* (Stockholm: Almqvist and Wiksell, 1995), who refers to a large number of studies, among which I have found the following also useful: Thomas Hakansson, "Family Structure, Bridewealth, and Environment in Eastern Africa: A Comparative Study of House-Property Systems," *Ethnology* 28.2 (1989): 117–134; and Douglas R. White, "Rethinking Polygyny: Co-wives, Codes, and Cultural Systems," *Current Anthropology* 29.4 (1988): 529–558. I also consulted Joseph Chamie, "Polygyny and Arabs," *Populations Studies* 40.1 (Mar. 1986): 55–66, which notes that polygyny "decreases with higher educational attainment of husbands" (p. 62).

6. In the first type, bridewealth is also a prominent factor. Women are valued for their labor and hence the exchange based on a bridewealth payment. This type

of polygyny occurs mainly in sub-Saharan Africa. White calls it "wealth-increasing polygyny," but others scholars disagree with this term, saying that it is better thought of as an inexpensive form of polygyny (White, "Rethinking Polygyny").

7. In real life, many polygynous men were not necessarily elite. Artisans and small-scale storeowners, as well as rich peasant farmers, could be polygynists. On polygyny and concubinage in China, see Maria Jaschok, *Concubines and Bond-servants: A Social History* (London: Zed Books, 1988); and Rubie S. Watson and Patricia Buckley Ebrey, eds., *Marriage and Inequality in Chinese Society* (Berkeley: University of California Press, 1991), especially Watson's chapter, "Wives, Concubines, and Maids: Servitude and Kinship in the Hong Kong Region, 1900–1940," pp. 231–255. Also see Keith McMahon, *Misers, Shrews, and Polygamists: Sexuality and Male-Female Relations in Eighteenth-century Chinese Fiction* (Durham, N.C.: Duke University Press, 1995); and Ding Naifei, *Obscene Things: Sexual Politics in Jin Ping Mei* (Durham, N.C.: Duke University Press, 2002).

8. See Chen Yiyuan's study, *Yuan Ming zhongpian chuanqi xiaoshuo yanjiu* (Hong Kong: Xuefeng wenhua shiye gongsi, 1997), especially concerning Ming novellas like *Zhong qing liji, Huashen sanmiao zhuan, Xun fang yaji, Wu jin yu zhuan,* and especially *Tianyuan qiyu* and *Li Sheng liuyi tianyuan.* It is out of works like these that grew the polygynist fantasies of vernacular fiction such as *Xinghua tian, Taohua ying,* and *Nao hua cong,* to name a few. The progress of the man's encounters with a series of women was called *yanyu* or *yanyou,* "encounters with beauties" or "tour of beauties."

9. The discussion of Lacanian psychoanalysis and the late Qing appeared in expanded form, using some of the same language, in McMahon, trans., Li Yuzhen, ed., "Cong Lagangde xingbie chayi lilun kan wanQing Zhongguo" [Lacan's Theory of Sexual Difference in Late Imperial China], *Tsinghua Journal of Chinese Literature* 1 (Sept. 2007): 294–313.

10. Joan Copjec, *Read My Desire: Lacan against the Historicists* (Cambridge, Mass.: MIT Press, 1995), p. 204.

11. For a good summary of these ideas, see Mark Bracher, "On the Psychological and Social Functions of Language: Lacan's Theory of the Four Discourses," in Bracher et al., eds., *Lacanian Theory of Discourse, Subject, Structure, and Society* (New York: New York University Press, 1994), pp. 107–128, especially p. 113.

12. Quoted from Slavoj Žižek, *The Metastases of Enjoyment: On Women and Causality* (London: Verso, 2005), p. 127.

13. From Slavoj Žižek, *Tarrying with the Negative: Kant, Hegel, and the Critique of Ideology* (Durham, N.C.: Duke University Press, 1993), p. 2.

14. The notion of crowd comes from Žižek, "Four Discourses, Four Subjects," in Žižek, ed., *Cogito and the Unconscious* (Durham, N.C.: Duke University Press, 1998), pp. 74–113.

15. See Bracher, "On the Psychological and Social Functions of Language," pp. 121–122.

16. On the uses and advantages of Lacan's four discourses, see ibid., pp. 126–128. In

Lacanian terms, the hysteric is the ultimate model of subjectivity. This gets back to the idea of split subject: no one escapes the condition of being split. The master is oblivious to this fact but is nevertheless just as split as anyone else. If anyone, the hystericized subject is the most aware that the emperor wears no clothes, that is, that the master is equally split. Still, the hysteric is not necessarily able to act on that awareness, but remains subject to the discourse of the master.

17. Lacan, trans. Alan Sheridan, *Écrits: A Selection* (New York: W. W. Norton, 1977), p. 514.

18. See Lacan's *Encore* (Paris: Editions du Seuil, 1975), pp. 73–75; Bruce Fink's translation, *On Feminine Sexuality: The Limits of Love and Knowledge* (New York: Norton and Company, 1998), pp. 78–81; and the excellent account in Copjec, *Read My Desire,* chap. 8, especially p. 214.

19. The best exposition of these ideas is in Ding, *Obscene Things.*

20. This is but one way to look at bound feet. See McMahon review of Dorothy Ko, *Cinderella's Sisters: A Revisionist History of Footbinding, Nan Nü: Men, Women and Gender in Early and Imperial China* 9.2 (2007): 395–400.

Chapter 1. Sublime Passion and the Remarkable Woman

1. The best recent treatment of the idealization of the woman is Li Wai-yee's *Enchantment and Disenchantment: Love and Illusion in Chinese Literature* (Princeton, N.J.: Princeton University Press, 1993), chapter 1. Other discussions include Kang-i Sun Chang, *The Late-Ming Poet Ch'en Tzu-lung: Crises of Love and Loyalism* (New Haven, Conn.: Yale University Press, 1991), pp. 9–18; Maram Epstein, "Reflections of Desire: The Poetics of Gender in *Dream of the Red Chamber,*" *Nan Nü: Men, Women, and Gender in China* 1.1 (1999): 64–106, and *Competing Discourses: Orthodoxy, Authenticity, and Engendered Meanings in Late Imperial Chinese Fiction* (Cambridge, Mass.: Harvard University Press, 2001); Martin Huang, "Sentiments of Desire: Thoughts on the Cult of Qing in Ming-Qing Literature," *Chinese Literature: Essays, Articles, and Reviews* 20 (1998): 153–184; and Dorothy Ko, *Teachers of the Inner Chamber* (Stanford, Calif.: Stanford University Press, 1994), in which Ko writes that *qing* can be referred to as a "gender equalizer," but with important qualifications (pp. 111–112), and notes the subtle differences between male and female perspectives on *qing* (p. 78). For a broad discussion including earliest definitions (also found in Huang, "Sentiments"), see Anthony Yu, *Rereading the Stone: Desire and the Making of Fiction in* Dream of the Red Chamber (Princeton, N.J.: Princeton University Press, 1997), pp. 56–66.

2. Li Wai-yee observes that the late Ming was "the age that discovered radical subjectivity" (*Enchantment and Disenchantment,* pp. 45–46).

3. As noted by Martin Huang, the reverence toward chaste women was extreme in the Ming; women were regarded as "*natural* exemplars of . . . loyalty and chastity" (original emphasis). See Huang, *Negotiating Masculinities in Late Imperial China* (Honolulu: University of Hawai'i Press, 2006), pp. 6, 72.

4. To "ride" women is the term *yu* from the classic art of the bedchamber.

5. In her discussion of the cult of *qing*, Maram Epstein refers to the "power of *qing* to feminize" and the "ideological appropriation of the feminine" as a counter hegemonic movement. See *Competing Discourses*, pp. 88–92.

6. See Feng Menglong, *Qingshi leilue* (Changsha: Yuelu shushe, 1984), preface, pp. 1–2, p. 324 (the end of *juan* 11), and p. 652 (the end of *juan* 19).

7. See Ding's *Obscene Things*, pp. 138 and 184. Pan Jinlian engages in the art of abjection (p. 218), using the "art of maneuvering" (*quanshu*), which "is no mere resistance of power, but an active using of it in the contrary, or reverse, direction. It is a sending it back along the same connecting line whence it came, except in such a way as to make the receiving point accept it *as if it were its own*" (original emphasis, p. 175).

8. It is "as if sexual desire were a 'femininity' within, a tendency toward dissolution and death" (ibid., p. 221).

9. See articles in the 1992 special issue of *Late Imperial China* (13.1); Dorothy Ko, *Teachers of the Inner Chambers;* and articles in Ellen Widmer and Kang-I Sun Chang, ed., *Writing Women in Late Imperial China* (Stanford, Calif.: Stanford University Press, 1997), among many other works on the topic of women writers, artists, and educators.

10. Poetry is one of the best places to find these voices. See, for example, the *ci*-lyrics written in the heroic or *haofang* style of the *Manjianghong* mode. Usually considered appropriate for heroic masculine expression, the mode is a favorite of women voicing strong feelings of loyalism, ambition, frustration, and rage. See Li Xiaorong, "Engendering Heroism: Ming-Qing Women's Song Lyrics to the Tune Man Jiang Hong," *Nan Nü: Men, Women, and Gender in China* 7.1 (2005): 1–39, especially pp. 29–30 and 32. On Shen Shanbao, see Grace Fong, "Writing Self and Writing Lives: Shen Shanbao's (1808–1862) Gendered Auto/biographical Practices," *Nan Nü: Men, Women, and Gender in China* 2.2 (2000): 259–303; see p. 267. Shen also turned poetry writing into a means to earn a living, herself conscious of numerous other non-courtesan women who did so in the centuries since the Ming, though a woman like her always had to be careful to distinguish herself from appearing like a courtesan (ibid., pp. 268, 278).

11. One of them uses the word "steal" (*tou*), as in to steal time. See Hu Siaochen, *Cainü cheye weimian* (Taibei: Maitian renwen, 2003), pp. 117, 192, referring to Qiu Xinru, author of *Bi sheng hua*. Most of my evidence of dating is based on Hu's great work. Also useful were Bao Zhenpei's *Qingdai nüzuojia tanci xiaoshuo lungao* (Tianjin: Tianjin shehui kexueyuan chubanshe, 2001) and Ellen Widmer's *The Beauty and the Book: Women and Fiction in Nineteenth-century China* (Cambridge, Mass.: Harvard University Press, 2006).

12. The section on *Liaozhai zhiyi* appeared in earlier form with slightly different contents in a book chapter, "The Remarkable Woman in Pu Songling's *Liaozhai zhiyi*," in Paolo Santangelo (with Donatella Guida), ed., *Love, Hatred, and Other Passions: Questions and Themes on Emotions in Chinese Civilization* (Leiden: Brill,

2006), pp. 212–228. A modified version was translated by Xu Huilin and edited by Li Yuzhen for publication as "Qinüzide nanban yu nüxing qizhide bentilun" [The Male Consort of the Remarkable Woman and the Ontology of the Feminine], in *Tsinghua Journal of Chinese Literature* 1 (Sept. 2007): 315–326.

13. See Kang-i Sun Chang, *The Late-Ming Poet Ch'en Tzu-lung*; Li Wai-yee, "The Late Ming Courtesan: Invention of a Cultural Ideal," in Widmer and Chang, eds., *Writing Women in Late Imperial China*, pp. 46–73; and especially idem, "Heroic Transformations: Women and National Trauma in Early Qing Literature," *Harvard Journal of Asiatic Studies* 59.2 (1999): 363–443.

14. Writers anyway did not need the direct experience of the 1640s in order to bear witness to the impact of those times, as can be seen in Pu's contemporaries such as the dramatists Hong Sheng (?–1704) and Kong Shangren (1648–?).

15. Also Gong Dingzi and Gu Mei, Mao Xiang and Dong Bai, or Hou Fangyu and Li Xiangjun.

16. For Wu's poems about Bian Sai, see "On Listening to the Daoist Nun Bian Yujing Play the Zither" of 1651, in Wu Weiye, *Meicun jiacangji*, Sibu congkan jibu (1680–1683) (Shanghai: Shangwu yinshuguan, 1922), *juan* 3.4a–4b; and "In the Brocade Woods, Passing the Tomb of the Daoist Yujing," *Meicun jiacangji, juan* 10.2b–3b. See also Kang-i Sun Chang, "The Idea of the Mask in Wu Wei-yeh (1609–1671)," *Harvard Journal of Asiatic Studies* 48.2 (1988): 289–320; and Li Wai-yee, "Heroic Transformations," on Wu's poetry about his relationship with Bian Sai. For "Praising the Buddha," see *Meicun jiacangji, juan* 3.9b–10a. For more on Chen Yuanyuan, including other renditions and expansions upon her affair with Wu Sangui, see Li Wai-yee, "The Late Ming Courtesan," pp. 67–69. For excellent annotation on "Praising the Buddha," see Qian Zhonglian, *Mengtiao'an zhuanzhu erzhong* (Beijing: Zhongguo shehuikexue chubanshe, 1984), pp. 123–144; and Qian Zhonglian and Qian Xuezeng, *Qingshi sanbaishou* (Changsha: Yuelu shushe, 1994), pp. 33–43.

17. On the after effects see, for example, the story "Gui ku" (Weeping Ghosts; 76–77), which recalls the Xie Qian revolt of 1646–1647, or "Yegou" (Wild Dogs; 70–71) and "Gongsun jiuniang" (Ninth Maiden Gongsun, 477–483), which recall the Yu Qi rebellion and its bloody suppression in 1661–1662. See Lu Dahuang, *Pu Songling nianpu* (Jinan: Qilu shushe, 1980), pp. 6, 13. Page numbers here and hereafter refer to Pu Songling, ed. Zhang Youhe, *Liaozhai zhiyi* (Shanghai: Shanghai guji chubanshe, 1978, originally 1962).

18. As Li Wai-yee shows, the woman's liminality can be taken back to the Han in the figure of the "ambivalent divine woman" of the Han *fu*, who is "defined by her liminal state" (*Enchantment*, p. 29).

19. This story reenacts the motif of a woman revenging her father's murder, as seen for example in the Tang tale "Xie Xiao'e zhuan" by Li Gongzuo. An excellent study of the female knight-errant that has inspired my thinking about this and other stories is Roland Altenburger's "The Sword or the Needle: The Female Knight-Errant (*Xia*) in Traditional Chinese Fiction" (Habilitationsschrift, University of Zu-

rich, 2000; on this story see pp. 159–166). A similar story is Pu Songling's "Shang Sanguan" (373–375), in which a woman murders the man who killed her father and then hangs herself when the mission is done.

20. See "Dongsheng" (133–136) and Rania Huntington's discussion, "Foxes and Sex in Late Imperial Chinese Narrative," *Nan Nü: Men, Women, and Gender in China* 2.1 (2000): 82 and 89–90.

21. Other examples include "Gejin" (1436–1444), in which the woman denies that she is an immortal and insists that all she wants is secrecy, but the man's suspicions cause her finally to disappear. In "Jiaping gongzi" (1588–1591), the woman persuades the man to accept that she is a ghost, but later leaves him when she notices his writing full of miswritten characters.

22. In "Xihu zhu" (646–655) a young man releases a wounded alligator that he later learns is a princess of Lake Dongting, whom he then eventually joins in her immortal realm of water-world beauties. Other cases of the man eventually joining the woman are in "Zhuqing," "Xiangyu," and "Zhu Suiliang."

23. In several stories she bears a child that she gives to the earthly wife to raise, as in "Hua Guzi," "Zhuqing," and "Fang Wenshu."

24. See also "Qiaoniang," in which the young man is "like a eunuch" (256) but still has a "tiny tip" (259) which suffices for growth to normal size when an older woman gives him a special pill, and "Hehua sanniangzi" (Lotus Lady the Third; 682–686), in which a goddess changes into stone whenever the man is brazen with her. When he learns to restrain himself, they become intimate, and she bears him a son; but she finally disappears, leaving him her name, which, if he calls it out, causes her smiling image to appear to him, though she will not speak.

25. In "Yunluo gongzhu" (Princess Yunluo), the woman gives him a choice between playing chess or having sex, on the condition that having sex means living a shorter life; he chooses sex. In "Shi Qingxu" the hero is granted ownership of a precious rock, but he must surrender three years of his life.

26. The most encyclopedic study of the shrew can be found in Yenna Wu, *The Chinese Virago: A Literary Theme* (Cambridge, Mass.: Harvard University Press, 1995). See also McMahon, *Misers*, which treats the shrew and jealousy mainly in the context of Qing vernacular fiction about polygamy.

27. For Wang Dao's story, see Lü Zhan'en's annotation (733). See also Richard Mather, *A New Account of Tales of the World* (Minneapolis: University of Minnesota Press, 1976), pp. 430–431; and Liu Yiqing, *Shishuo xinyu jiaojian* (Beijing: Zhonghua shuju 1984), p. 444. Dan Minglun's commentary appeared in 1842, while Feng Zhenluan's, written in 1818, was not published until 1891 (*Liaozhai zhiyi*, pp. 1723–1724).

28. From "Jiangcheng" (858), in which the fault lies with what the man did to her in a previous incarnation. In "Ma Jiefu" the man says it is his wife's beauty that keeps him attached to her in spite of her abuse of both him and his father.

29. See "Qiaoniang," "Xing Ziyi," and "Xiaoxie," at the end of which the Historian of the Strange says, "Only the man who is not always lusting after women will meet with such fortune" (779).

30. E.g., "Chen Yunqi" and "Xiangyu."
31. See "Lianxiang," "Qiaoniang," "Chen Yunqi," and "Jisheng." On alliances, see McMahon, *Misers*, pp. 121, 208–211; on favoritism, pp. 49, 136, 211.
32. Li Wai-yee writes, "The negation of carnal desire is thus taken to be the best metaphor for obsessive attachment" or *chi*. See *Enchantment*, p. 92, citing Feng Menglong.
33. Zeitlin, *Historian of the Strange: Pu Songling and the Chinese Classical Tale* (Stanford, Calif.: Stanford University Press, 1993).
34. This comment is found in the Qingke ting edition, but not the hand-copied Zhuxue zhai edition, so may or may not be Pu Songling's, but is apt nevertheless.

Chapter 2. *Qing* Can Be with One and Only One

1. See Susan Mann, *Precious Records: Women in China's Long Eighteenth Century* (Stanford, Calif.: Stanford University Press, 1997), p. 20. The period "reaches its zenith during the decades after the 1720's and begins a downward turn sometime in the mid 1770's, declining rapidly after the 1790's, when White Lotus and Miao rebellions began to undermine the power of the central government."
2. Shang Wei, *Rulin waishi and Cultural Transformation in Late Imperial China* (Cambridge, Mass.: Harvard University Press, 2003), p. 147.
3. See Mann, *Precious Records*, p. 12. Mann cites the shortage of women as a prominent factor in the eighteenth-century "marriage crunch." Sommer refers to the same phenomenon as the "skewed sex ratio" ("Making Sex Work," p. 32).
4. The edition used is *Honglou meng* (Beijing: Renmin wenxue chubanshe, 1982); the in-text references cite chapter and page (e.g., 3.16) or refer to the entire chapter (e.g., 3). This translation is Li Wai-yee's in *Enchantment*, p. 164. Although Cao Xueqin may not have written these prefatory words, the theme of female superiority is consistent with the rest of the novel and many other writings of the period.
5. See Zhu Yixuan, *Honglou meng ziliao huibian* (Nanjing: Nankai daxue chubanshe, 1985), p. 427, the Gengchen edition dating from 1760. On this theme, Shu Wu provides a complete list of their quarrels in *Shuo meng lu* (Shanghai: Guji chubanshe, 1982), pp. 128–131, writing that for them, "love is all about quarreling."
6. As translated by Hawkes, *The Story of the Stone* (Harmondsworth: Penguin Books, 1977), vol. 2, p. 134. Li Wai-yee refers to the "impossibility of articulation in the world of *ch'ing*" (*Enchantment*, p. 185). Other cases include when the imperial concubine sends gifts to the Jia family children, Baochai receives more than Daiyu, but Baoyu is helpless to repair the imbalance. Even though he swears to Daiyu that she is the only one for him, she will not believe it (28). When several of the cousins submit poems for judgment, everyone ranks Daiyu's first. But Li Wan, the judge, immediately declares that Baochai's is better and rejects Baoyu's request to reconsider (37).
7. Hawkes, *Story of the Stone*, vol. 2, p. 142, with slight modifications.
8. See Maram Epstein's excellent discussion of the "dissolution of ritual identities" in *Competing Discourses*, pp. 163–173 and 90–91.

9. Even though the title gives the sense of words offered as humble but worthy advice, the additional sense of exposure in the word *pu*, plus the novel's general celebration of its superhero, lead me to choose "radiant words" as the best translation of *puyan*.

10. I follow the work of Giovanni Vitiello and Martin Huang on this convergence. See Vitiello, "Exemplary Sodomites: Chivalry and Love in Late Ming Culture," *Nan Nü: Men, Women, and Gender in China* 2.2 (2000): 207–257; and Huang, "From Caizi to Yingxiong: Imagining Masculinities in Two Qing Novels, *Yesou puyan* and *Sanfen meng quan zhuan*," *Chinese Literature: Essays, Articles, and Reviews* 25 (2003): 61–100. Huang lists earlier and later novels that perform the same convergence, e.g., *Huatu yuan, Tiehua xianshi, Jinshi yuan, Xue Yue Mei quanzhuan,* and *Lingnan yishi* ("From Caizi to Yingxiong," pp. 67–68 and 73). The convergence of these scenarios does not always result in the desentimentalization of *qing*, but my focus is on the cases that do. See also Maram Epstein's discussion of the "masculinization" of the scholar-beauty genre, in *Competing Discourses,* pp. 229–238.

11. Martin Huang puts it aptly: *Radiant Words* "is a curious product of audacious self-celebration carefully framed in the straitjacket of the rigid orthodoxy of Cheng-Zhu neo-Confucianism" (*Literati and Self-re/presentation: Autobiographical Sensibility in the Eighteenth-century Chinese Novel* [Stanford, Calif.: Stanford University Press, 1955], p. 141).

12. The main points of comparison between Wen and Wang include Wen's emphasis upon being a sage over passing the exams, his ability to convert others to his brand of Confucianism, the episodes in which he fakes his death by drowning in order to avoid the murderous plot of his eunuch enemy, and finally his participation in the suppression of rebellions, bandits, and aborigines. The time frame of the novel precedes that of Wang Yangming's active life by a few decades, perhaps to avoid too obvious an overlap. See Huang, *Literati,* pp. 131–133; and Wang Qiongling, *Qingdai sida caixue xiaoshuo* (Taipei: Taiwan Shangwu yinshuguan, 1997), pp. 133–135, for examples. The words "de facto ruler" come from Huang, who also points to the intermarriage between Suchen's offspring and the royal family, in *Literati,* p. 116.

13. See the 1881 Piling huizhen lou edition, Beijing University Library, 6.11ab; and McMahon, *Misers,* p. 157.

14. Numerous passages depict his tremendous strength, but his overall aura is that of a refined man of *wen*. The references to his yang strength can be seen in 7, 67, 95, 96, and 98, and include descriptions of the potency of his urine and semen (see 20, 67, 68, and 70).

15. Shang Wei, *Rulin waishi and Cultural Transformation,* p. 230.

16. See Mann, *Precious Records,* pp. 219, 22. As Mann observes, the method of selection in Wanyan Yun Zhu's anthology *Correct Beginnings: Women's Poetry of Our August Dynasty* "denies and erases the destructive possibilities so clear in *Red Chamber*'s indulgent and ineffectual maternal figures" (*Precious Records,* p. 102).

17. The following section on sequels appeared in longer form in the chapter "Eliminating Traumatic Antinomies: Sequels to *Honglou meng*," in Martin Huang, ed., *Snakes' Legs: Sequels, Continuations, Rewritings, and Chinese Fiction* (Honolulu: University of Hawai'i Press, 2004), pp. 98–115. I benefited from personal communication with Ellen Widmer, from her "*Honglou meng* Sequels and Their Female Readers in Nineteenth-Century China," in Martin Huang, *Snakes' Legs,* pp. 116–142, and from her *Beauty and the Book,* especially part 2. See note 21 below for a list of sequels with dates and with titles translated. Since this section deals with a large group of overlapping works known to few readers, I will refer to them by their Chinese titles, translating the titles into English only in the first mention in parentheses.

18. Only one of these sequels, the only one known to be by a woman, concludes on something less than a positive note. At the end of *Honglou meng ying* (*In the Shadow of the Dream of the Red Chamber*), Baoyu looks up at Baochai, Daiyu, and two other women talking and laughing by a balcony railing, ignoring Baoyu, who sadly discovers that there is no stairway leading up to them.

19. If women wrote narratives, they usually wrote *tanci.* See Ellen Widmer about the meaningfulness of *Honglou meng* to female readers and the hypothesis that *Honglou meng* may have brought women closer to being able to write in the narrative form of the vernacular novel: Widmer, "Ming Loyalism and the Woman's Voice in Fiction after *Honglou meng,*" in Widmer and Chang, eds., *Writing Women in Late Imperial China,* and *Beauty and the Book.* Gu Chun (style name Taiqing, 1799–1877) was a Manchu and a well-known writer of *ci* lyrics. She was married as concubine, niece of the main wife, to a great-grandson of the Qianlong emperor, Yihui (1799–1838). When the main wife died, Gu Taiqing became in effect the main wife for the last nine years of her husband's life. See Zhao Botao, "*Honglou meng* de zuojia ji qita," *Honglou meng xuekan* 4.1 (1989): 243–251. She belonged to a poetry society with other female poets, including Shen Shanbao, who wrote the 1861 preface to Gu's novel.

20. *Xu Honglou meng xinbian,* the exception, instead concentrates on Baoyu's exam success and career.

21. The list of sequels is as follows (see bibliography at the end of this book for contemporary publishing data): *Hou Honglou meng* (*The Later Dream of the Red Chamber*), by Xiaoyaozi; *Xu Honglou meng* (*Sequel to Dream of the Red Chamber*), written sometime between 1797 and 1798, published 1799, by Qin Zichen; *Qilou chongmeng* (*Revisiting the Silken Chambers*), completed no earlier than 1797, published in 1805, by Wang Lanzhi of Hangzhou (*jinshi* of 1780); *Honglou fumeng* (*Return to Dream of the Red Chamber*), preface 1799, by Chen Shaohai; *Xu Honglou meng xinbian* (*New Sequel to Dream of the Red Chamber*), preface 1805, by Haipu zhuren; *Bu Honglou meng* (*Patching the Dream of the Red Chamber*), preface 1814, published 1820, and *Zengbu Honglou meng* (*The Sequel to Patching the Dream of the Red Chamber*), preface 1820, published 1824, both by Langhuan shanqiao; *Honglou yuanmeng* (*The Resolution of the Dream of the Red Chamber*), published

1814, by Mengmeng xiansheng; *Honglou meng bu* (*Dream of the Red Chamber Revisited*), published 1819, by Guichuzi; *Honglou huanmeng* (*The Illusion of the Dream of the Red Chamber*), published 1843, by Huayue chiren; *Honglou meng ying* (*In the Shadow of Dream of the Red Chamber*), preface 1861, published 1877, by Gu Taiqing (1799–1876); and *Xu Honglou meng gao* (*Draft Sequel to Dream of the Red Chamber*), unfinished, by Zhang Yaosun, born 1807.

22. The most complete surveys of *Honglou meng* sequels are Zhao Jianzhong's *Honglou meng xushu yanjiu* (Tianjin: Tianjin guji chubanshe, 1997) and Lin Yixuan's *Wu cai ke bu tian: Honglou meng xushu yanjiu* (Taibei: Wenjin chubanshe, 1999). Other sequels may have existed which do not survive, including one possibly by a woman (see Zhao Jianzhong, *Honglou meng xushu yanjiu,* pp. 31–36). For general bibliography, surveys, synopses, and other information, see Sun Kaidi, *Zhongguo tongsu xiaoshuo shumu* (Beijing: Renmin wenxue chubanshe, 1982), pp. 138–141; Yisu *Honglou meng shulu* (Shanghai: Shanghai guji chubanshe, 1981), pp. 86–131; Feng Qiyong et al., eds., *Honglou meng da cidian* (Beijing: Wenhua yishu, 1990); Ouyang Jian et al., eds., *Zhongguo tongsu xiaoshuo zongmu tiyao* (Beijing: Zhongguo wenlian chubanshe, 1990); Liu Shide et al., *Zhongguo gudai xiaoshuo baike quanshu* (Beijing: Zhongguo dabaike quanshu, 1993); and the scholarly notes to the Beijing University Press editions. Other studies include Chen Angni, "You *Honglou meng* ji qi xushu tantao Jia Baoyu zhi juese bianqian," *Guowen tiandi* 9.7 (1993): 33–44; Huang Jinzhu, "*Honglou meng* de jindai xushu," *Taibei Shiyuan xuebao* 9 (1996): 171–196; Li Zhongchang, *Gudai xiaoshuo xushu manhua* (Shenyang: Liaoning jiaoyu chubanshe, 1993); and Zhao Jianzhong, "*Honglou meng* xushu de yuanliu shanbian ji qi yanjiu," *Honglou meng xuekan* 4 (1992): 301–335. Widmer provides a concise summary of the sequence of sequels in *Beauty and the Book,* pp. 220–225.

23. In *Honglou huanmeng* Daiyu tells him that he must no longer "yearn for the company of actors" (4.53). In *Honglou meng bu* he burns his racy books; and "his temperament completely changes from what it was in the old days" (7.78).

24. Respectively, see *Honglou fumeng* and *Honglou yuanmeng;* for hours of leisure, see *Xu Honglou meng xinbian, Bu Honglou meng, Zengbu Honglou meng,* and *Honglou meng ying;* for philanthropy, see *Honglou meng bu;* for study for exams, see *Xu Honglou meng xinbian* and *Xu Honglou meng gao,* in the latter of which Baochai and Daiyu are more learned than Baoyu. The erotic sequels also include a number of these nonromantic pursuits. *Honglou huanmeng* has Baoyu and Daiyu engage in philanthropy, while *Qilou chongmeng* has women engaging in battle.

25. He is compassionate with all women, moreover, including old ones and ugly ones (13.139). Chapter 13 contains the first major explication of his nature, including the fact that the women "forget that he is a man" (13.139–140). See Lin Yixuan, *Wu cai ke bu tian,* pp. 63–64, for a fuller discussion of his relations with his wives.

26. First published in 1799, *Qilou chongmeng* also has an 1805 edition that refers to the two prior sequels, *Hou Honglou meng* and *Xu Honglou meng.* Yisu mentions a nineteenth-century commentator who believed that the author wrote the book

as a roman à clef targeting an enemy of his embodied in Xiaoyu—in other words, that the lewdness of the book was by way of insulting his enemy (*Honglou meng shulu*, p. 99). Whether the hypothesis is true or not, the same or a similar man appears elsewhere, as we will see in *Courtesan Chambers* and *Nine-times Cuckold*, and thus confirms him as a type, a late-Qing version of the master polygamist and master of the brothel.

27. As in *Hou Honglou meng, Xu Honglou meng, Qilou chongmeng, Honglou yuan-meng, Honglou meng bu, Honglou huanmeng,* and *Xu Honglou meng gao,* in which she returns to life either as herself or in reincarnated form. *Honglou fumeng* alone favors Baochai over Daiyu, drastically reducing Daiyu's role in her reincarnation. In three sequels, although favored over Baochai, Daiyu never returns to life at all (*Bu Honglou meng, Zengbu Honglou meng,* and *Honglou meng ying*). In *Bu Hong-lou meng,* Baoyu and Daiyu meet as immortals but instead of being passionately in love have now reached what is termed an ultimate stage of "bland" love (*dan,* 30.276–277). Ellen Widmer emphasizes the presence of capable female manage-ment in almost all of the sequels (*Beauty and the Book,* p. 220).

28. See also *Honglou meng bu,* in which she no longer suffers from insomnia or con-stant worries (4.39); *Honglou meng bu,* in which she arranges for Baoyu to take four maids as concubines; and *Xu Honglou meng,* in which she joins Baochai to discuss methods of keeping their husband in check by arranging the living quar-ters of the concubines so that none will be able to monopolize him (22).

29. When Xiren later asks him who is better in bed, Baochai or Daiyu, he replies that Baochai is better because she is more voluptuous ("carved out of lamb's fat"). Then he says that Daiyu is nevertheless better because when they make love, "it is marvelous beyond words" (5.58).

30. Other such examples can be found in 9.57, 27.174–175, 38.247–248, 39.257, 41.266, 45.291 and 296. *Honglou huanmeng* also features an instance in which Baoyu helps a young woman having her first menstruation (16.244).

31. Early reactions to *Qilou chongmeng* are summed up by Baochai, who at the end of *Bu Honglou meng* (ca. 1814) describes the author of *Qilou chongmeng* as "a deranged maniac who has lost all sense of humanity" (48.430).

32. After Baochai tells Daiyu how much she loves her now, Daiyu responds, "I love you as much as he does" (5.55). After she bears twins, Daiyu tells Baoyu why she figures she did so, recalling to him a night of pleasure in which they made love twice. The first time she climaxed first: "I felt your surging warm essence shoot into me, and then we fell into a deep sleep"; they later "had orgasm at the same time" (22.328). On another occasion they whisper to each other about the plea-sures of the night before (7.96). By chapter 12, the three of them routinely sleep together. Once Baochai sucks on Daiyu's breasts (19.279). For intimacy between Daiyu and Qingwen, as Baochai looks on, see 16.237–238 and 23.343; they are said to be "just like female lovers," making reference to Li Yu's play *Lianxiang ban* (*The Fragrant Companion*), in which a man's two wives are lovers.

33. On this point, see McMahon, *Misers,* pp. 190–191.

34. On childbirth, see especially *Honglou meng ying,* 4 and 9; *Honglou huanmeng,* 22; and *Qilou chongmeng,* 3 (and 6 for a scene of women nursing).

35. In previous work I argued that two-wife polygamy marked the limit between two types of beauty-scholar romances, the chaste and the erotic, of which works with explicit erotic detail tend to be about men with more than two wives or sexual partners. I also argued that two-wife polygamy marked the limit of maintaining the scenario of gender fluidity (see *Misers,* pp. 113–122). The current discussion adds to the earlier one by placing two-wife polygamy in the larger framework of passive polygamy, a term I introduce in this book.

36. A man could have two wives in the special case in which he carried on the family line of a deceased brother, for example. In *Haishanghua liezhuan,* Shi Tianran tricks Zhao Erbao into thinking that he will marry her as wife, not concubine, based on this logic. The man's marriage to two wives has both legendary and real basis in the situation in which the man marries two sisters, the most famous mythical example being Emperor Shun's marriage to the two daughters of Emperor Yao.

37. See Baoyu, 1.22; Liu Xianglian, 5.66; and Qiongyu, 9.122. In an analogous situation, Qiongyu is first in the *jinshi* exams, while Baoyu is second, but the emperor decides to make an exception and allow both to have the status of *zhuangyuan* (7.99).

38. In "Xiaoxie" (772–779), the widowed young man likes courtesans but will never sleep with them. He remains chaste with two women who seek refuge with him (772), as does a poor and upright scholar in "Xing Ziyi" (1141–1144). Both are cases of *yeben,* "seeking refuge at night," in which a woman flees an undesirable situation, such as an abusive madam, if she is a prostitute, or an abusive husband or main wife, if a concubine.

39. In recent years, some scholars have floated the idea that Pu Songling himself had two wives. Based on evidence in Pu's piece "Inscription for the Portrait of Chen Shuqing," Tian Zechang tries to prove that Chen Shuqing was Pu's second wife whom he met during the chaos of the suppression of the Yu Qi rebellion (1661–1662). See Tian, "Pu Songling he Chen Shuqing," *Pu Songling yanjiu jikan* 1 (1980): 264–280. Because Pu's parents did not approve of the relationship, Pu and Chen lived separately but kept in secret contact, then managed to live together and have children when Pu lived in Jiangsu Province working as secretary for a friend in 1670–1671. Chen died in Jiangsu, and thus the writing of this piece in memory of her. Wang Zhizhong refutes Tian's evidence, also citing others on both sides of the issue (the topics argued include whether or not Pu's wife was "shrewish"); see Wang, *Pu Songling lunji* (Beijing: Wenhua yishu chubanshe, 1990), pp. 52–75, p. 75, n. 10.

40. See "Feng Sanniang" (610–617). Although the immortal disappears in the end, until then the plot resembles other stories in which the man actually marries the two women.

41. "Chen Yunqi" (1496) is about the Daoist nuns; "Xiangyu" (1548–1555), about the

flower spirits. In this case, the man has a mortal wife, whom he eventually leaves to join the two spirits, the three of whom finally die.

42. Even the larger polygamies of Qing vernacular fiction reflect some form of pressure to fairness. The man makes sure to have no favorites and shares his nights equally with each wife. Each woman embodies a particular quality or skill that provides her with an unassailable position within the grand marriage (e.g., *Yesou puyan* and *Lin Lan Xiang*; see McMahon, *Misers*, pp. 137, 155). No woman can feel that she is useless or expendable unless she herself actively takes on the role of being expendable, as in "Shaonü" or "Da'nan," in which self-sacrificing concubines accept the abuse of the shrew and thereby finally gain her respect.

Chapter 3. The Otherworldliness of the Courtesan

1. See McMahon, *The Fall of the God of Money*, and "Opium Smoking and Modern Subjectivity."

2. Between 1784 and 1841 male authors wrote a series of courtesan accounts in which, as Susan Mann writes, "The most prized courtesans were especially admired for guarding their solitude, for the continual retreat from 'city dust,' for their refusal to open their doors to any man." See *Precious Records*, pp. 130–131.

3. Troubadour poetry flourished from circa 1100 to circa 1300 in the language of Occitania stretching from northwest Italy to southwestern France and consisting of a repertoire of about twenty-five hundred songs. My source for this comparison is the medievalist Sarah Kay, who evaluates Jacques Lacan's and Slavoj Žižek's reference to this motif in her book *Žižek: A Critical Introduction* (London: Polity, 2003). The words "too far away from me" are "trop mes lunhada," from Bernart Marti's "Na Dezirada" (My Desired Lady), cited in Sarah Kay, "Desire and Subjectivity," in Simon Gaunt and Sarah Kay, eds., *The Troubadours: An Introduction* (Cambridge, Mass.: Cambridge University Press, 1999), pp. 212–227 (quoted phrase p. 218). See also Sarah Kay, *Subjectivity in Troubadour Poetry* (Cambridge, Mass.: Cambridge University Press, 1990), pp. 85–111.

4. See Mann, *Precious Records*, p. 125.

5. From the ninth essay of a set written in 1815 and 1816, "Yi bing zhi ji zhuyi," in Sun Qinshan, ed., *Gong Zizhen shi wen xuan* (Beijing: Renmin wenxue chubanshe, 1993), pp. 303–309. For the biography of Gong Zizhen I have consulted Arthur W. Hummel, *Eminent Chinese of the Ch'ing Period* (Washington, D.C.: U.S. Government Printing Office, 1943), pp. 431–434; Shirleen Wong, *Kung Tzu-chen* (Boston: Twayne Publications, 1975); and Wu Changshou's *Dingan xiansheng nianpu*, in Zhu Jieqin, ed., *Gong Dingan yanjiu* (Hong Kong: Chongwen shudian, 1971), pp. 201–255. My thanks to Kang-i Sun Chang, who in 2002 shared a paper she wrote on Gong Zizhen's love poetry, "The Problematic Self-Commentary: Gong Zizhen and His Love Poetry," which provided an excellent summary and discussion of these poems.

6. On the literary inquisition, see his 1825 poem "Yong shi," in Sun Qinshan, *Gong*

Zizhen shi wen xuan, pp. 91–93. For the rest, see poems 24, 123, 125, 294 in the collection *Jihai zashi,* in Wan Zunyi, ed., *Gong Zizhen Jihai zashi zhu* (Beijing: Zhonghua shuju, 1978). Henceforth I will refer to the poem number using this edition unless otherwise noted.

7. On the Platonic affair, see Wang Zhenyuan's discussion in his *Jianqi xiaoxin: xi shuo Gong Zizhen shi* (Beijing: Zhonghua shuju, 1990), pp. 55–58. On the poems about his grief, see poems 182–197 in *Jihai zashi* and Wang Zhenyuan, *Jianqi xiaoxin,* pp. 59–63, referring to thirteen years earlier, which would be the same 1826 of the reference to the Platonic affair. Wang Wenru suggests that Gong is referring to a maternal cousin (cited in Wan Zunyi, *Gong Zizhen Jihai zashi zhu,* p. 268). See Wang Zhenyuan, *Jianqi xiaoxin,* pp. 79–82, and Wong, *Kung Tzu-chen,* pp. 34–36, for summaries of the extensive discussions about Gong's supposed affair with Gu Taiqing.

8. See also poem 253, in which he writes that she is not one to affect frail charm or sickliness to win him over.

9. See poem 262, in which Gong declares in the first line that he has a wife and in the next line that has a "fairly" literate concubine.

10. He writes of doing the same on another occasion, which according to Wan Zunyi refers to his affair with a courtesan in Yangzhou (poems 241–243); see *Gong Zizhen Jihai zashi zhu,* pp. 331–333.

11. On his return to Yuanpu, see his note to poem 278, in which he says that he will no longer write about her. On the sketchy evidence, see Sun Qinshan, *Gong Zizhen shi wen xuan,* p. 251; and Wan Zunyi, *Gong Zizhen Jihai zashi zhu,* pp. 358–359, referring to a note later appended to poem 276. A note on a piece of calligraphy from 1840 also says, "With A Xiao of Suzhou in attendance." These two records supply the only evidence that he might have continued with her.

12. This summary is based on Benjamin Elman, *Classicism, Politics, and Kinship: The Ch'ang-chou School of New Text Confucianism in Late Imperial China* (Berkeley: University of California Press, 1990). Besides Duan Yucai, for example, in 1819 he studied the Gongyang commentary under Liu Fenglu, who also taught Wei Yuan, a peer of Gong's and a major statesman in the mid-nineteenth-century period. Some say he left Beijing because of impending political danger. See Qian Mu, *Zhongguo jin sanbai nian xueshu shi* (Taipei: Shangwu yinshu guan, 1976, originally 1937), p. 552. See Wong, *Kung Tzu-chen,* pp. 35–36, for a summary of speculation on why he left Beijing.

13. For the motif of the scatterer of flowers, see Wang Zhenyuan's discussion in *Jianqi xiaoxin,* pp. 40–44 and 68–69, and poem 97 in *Jihai zashi.*

14. On his gambling, see poem 267, in which he writes of a "jade woman," that is, Lingxiao, encouraging him to stop; and Wang Zhenyuan, *Jianqi xiaoxin,* pp. 75–78.

15. See Zeng Pu's 1907 *Flowers in a Sea of Sin (Niehai hua;* Taibei: Sanmin shuju, 1998), chapters 2–3.

16. The best study of this novel is Patrick Hanan's "*Fengyue Meng* and the Courtesan

Novel," *Harvard Journal of Asiatic Studies* 58.2 (1998): 345–372. Hanan's forthcoming translation of the novel is with Columbia University Press. On the role of opium in the novel, see McMahon, *The Fall of the God of Money,* pp. 144, 151, 162–165.

17. See Hanshang Mengren, *Fengyue meng* (Beijing: Beijing daxue chubanshe, 1990), 5.30, where several characters, for example, refer to earlier days recorded in the famous *Yangzhou huafang lu* of the late-Qianlong era. See Antonia Finnane, who cites sources from 1817 through 1844 which record a decline since 1795, in *Speaking of Yangzhou: A Chinese City, 1550–1850* (Cambridge, Mass.: Harvard University Press, 2004), p. 298. She also notes Gong Zizhen's comments in his 1839 visit, however, when he found Yangzhou still a pleasant place in spite of the negative reports he had heard.

18. Only two earlier novels have come to my attention that figure opium prominently: *Sanfen meng quanzhuan* (earliest extant edition 1835) and *Yaguan lou* (circa 1821), which also takes place in Yangzhou. On the former, see Martin Huang, "From Caizi to Yingxiong," pp. 79–80, 87–88, 92, n. 47. A glancing mention of opium can be found in Shen Fu's *Fusheng liuji* during his trip to Canton in 1792–1794; for other mentions beginning in the seventeenth century, see McMahon, *The Fall of the God of Money,* chapter 2. Gong Zizhen and numerous other poets only begin writing of it in the 1830s (*Jihai zashi,* poems 85–86).

19. The woman who commits suicide is what is called a *fenzhang huoji,* that is, a prostitute who leases herself to the brothel, in contrast to the *kunzhang huoji* in the next piece of news, that is, one who has been kidnapped and forced to enter the brothel (2.12). Her father practices what is known in Yangzhou of the time as "putting out the hawk" (*fang ying,* 2.12).

20. This section is an abbreviated and modified version of "Sublime Love and the Ethics of Equality in a Homoerotic Novel of the Nineteenth Century: *Precious Mirror of Boy Actresses,*" *Nan Nü: Men, Women, and Gender in Early and Imperial China* 4.1 (2002): 70–109. Many thanks to *Nan Nü*'s editors and outside readers, to Giovanni Vitiello and Andrea Goldman for helpful comments on early versions of this chapter, and to them and Sophia Volpp for supplying me with copies of their work on topics closely related to this chapter. The edition I use is Chen Sen, *Pinhua baojian* (Taibei: Guiguan tushu gufen youxian gongsi, 1986). "Boy actress" comes from the English translation of the 1925 French novel *Pei Yu Boy Actress,* by George Soulié de Morant, originally *Bijou-de-Ceinture,* trans. Gerald Fabian and Guy Wernham (San Francisco: First Alamo Square Press, 1991). Chen Sen reportedly wrote the novel during the ten years between 1837 and 1848, but may have started it earlier. For other discussions of the novel, see Lu Xun, *A Brief History of Chinese Fiction* (Beijing: Foreign Languages Press, 1976), pp. 319–322; and Zhao Jingshen, *Zhongguo xiaoshuo congkao* (Jinan: Qilu shushe, 1980), pp. 454–463. More recent references include Lei Yong, "Xiaxie xiaoshuo de yanbian ji qi chuangzuo xintai," *Zhongguo gudai jindai wenxue yanjiu* 2 (1997): 131–136; and Wu Cuncun, "Qingdai shiren xiayou xutong fengqi xulue," *Zhongguo wenhua* 15, 16

(1997): 231–241, and *Ming Qing shehui xing'ai fengqi* (Beijing: Renmin wenxue chubanshe, 2000). Recent studies in English include David Wang, *Fin-de-siècle Splendor: Repressed Modernities of Late Qing Fiction, 1849–1911* (Stanford, Calif.: Stanford University Press, 1997), pp. 61–71; Chloe Starr, "Shifting Boundaries: Gender in *Pinhua baojian*," *Nan Nü: Men, Women, and Gender in Early and Imperial China* 1.2 (1999): 268–302; and Martin Huang, *Negotiating Masculinities*, pp. 139–146.

21. For sources on the theatrical world, see Wu Cuncun, *Ming Qing shehui xing'ai fengqi*, chap. 14; Colin Mackerras, *The Chinese Theatre in Modern Times: From 1840 to the Present Day* (London: Thames and Hudson, 1975), *Chinese Theater: From Its Origins to the Present Day* (Honolulu: University of Hawai'i Press, 1983), and *Chinese Drama: A Historical Survey* (Beijing: New World Press, 1990); and Andrea Goldman, "Opera in the City: Theatrical Performance and Urbanite Aesthetics in Beijing 1770–1900" (Ph.D. diss., University of California, Berkeley). See also the compilation of materials on opera and actors by Zhang Cixi, *Qingdai yandu liyuan shiliao* (Beijing: Zhongguo xiju chubanshe, 1991). Colin Mackerras says that the high period of the role of the *dan* was between 1790 and the 1830s, after which the emphasis shifted from boy actors toward an interest in more mature male roles (*Chinese Drama*, p. 67). But the south, especially Jiangsu and Anhui, continuously supplied *dan* to Beijing until the Taiping Rebellion in the 1850s and 1860s interrupted that connection (Wu, *Ming Qing shehui xing'ai fengqi*, pp. 182–183).

22. Male same-sex love was held in high regard by prominent literati in the Ming and Qing. On this point, see Wu Cuncun, *Ming Qing shehui xing'ai fengqi*, pp. 155–178; Vitiello, "Exemplary Sodomites," pp. 253–254, and "The Fantastic Journey of an Ugly Boy: Homosexuality and Salvation in Late Ming Pornography," *positions* 4.2 (1996): 291–320, p. 300, where he notes the "salvational" nature of this sort of high passion. See also Sophie Volpp, "The Male Queen: Boy Actors and Literati Libertines" (Ph.D. diss., Harvard University, 1995); Michael Szonyi, "The Cult of Hu Tianbo and the Eighteenth-century Discourse of Homosexuality," *Late Imperial China* 19.1 (1998): 1–25; and Vitiello, "The Forgotten Tears of the Lord of Longyang: Late Ming Stories of Male Prostitution and Connoisseurship," in Peter Englefriet and Jan de Meyer, eds., *Linked Faiths: Essays on Chinese Religions and Traditional Culture in Honour of Kristofer Schipper* (Leiden: Brill, 2000), pp. 227–247.

23. In general, the equality I refer to existed only in the imagination of the novel. In real life, status inequality was the rule. But the context for the possibility of something like the egalitarianism I am discussing did exist at the time of the creation of *Precious Mirror*. Andrea Goldman's study of *zidi shu* (scion's tales) in nineteenth-century Beijing supplies evidence regarding a stronger sense of "peer identity between performers/writers and audiences" than for opera. As she shows, even a "grizzled" male opium addict could play either a man or a woman in erotic encounters, performance being more important than appearance. See

Goldman, "The Nun Who Wouldn't Be: Representations of Female Desire in Two Performance Genres of *Si Fan*," *Late Imperial China* 22.1 (2001): 71–138, especially pp. 114, 117–119. In real life, leaving the profession (also called *gai ye*) was common enough for actors, especially when they matured, but becoming a literatus like his patron was unlikely. Before the Yongzheng emperor's abolition of the laws differentiating the status categories of *jian* (base person) and *liang* (good commoner), it was illegal to change "professions," although people managed to do so anyway. By the time of *Precious Mirror,* changing professions was mainly a monetary matter. For more detail on the laws of status, see Matthew Sommer, *Sex, Law, and Society in Late Imperial China* (Stanford, Calif.: Stanford University Press, 2000). Goldman discusses the practice of buying boys out, but mentions that sometimes the actor became no more than a page boy; see her "Opera in the City," p. 103.

24. Hence the fact that the refined characters are chaste but not above making suggestive remarks about the penis (7.86), boy lovers (*longyang,* 7.94), or anal sex (12.150). Even women use racy language (11.141–142). As Gregory Pflugfelder says of male love in Edo Japan, sexual intercourse was "not even a sine qua non element of the *wakashū-nenja* relationship;" see *Cartographies of Desire: Male-Male Sexuality in Japanese Discourse, 1600–1950* (Berkeley: University of California Press, 1999), p. 43.

25. Xu Ziyun "hasn't the slightest deviant thought" when with his favorite *dan,* Baozhu (5.58). When Tian Chunhang spends the night with Su Huifang, Chunhuang suppresses "deviant urges" (*xienian,* 14.171).

26. He comes from Hainan Island in Guangdong and travels to Beijing to purchase an official title (3.36, 39–40). Since his father is a "merchant in foreign goods" (*yangshang*), Xi Shiyi has the connections to deal in "foreign goods" (*yanghuo*), the sale of which earns him a great profit (18.231). He makes this profit, moreover, from a "foreign ship" (*yangchuan*) that docks in nearby Tianjin, one of five treaty ports by the time the novel was published (27.327). On opium in *Precious Mirror,* see McMahon, *The Fall of the God of Money,* pp. 151–152, 153–154, 160–162, 165–167.

27. For censored portions of the Guiguan and other editions, I have consulted the edition in traditional binding, Gest Library, Princeton University (n.d.).

28. The practice of stuffing orifices can also be found in Ida Pruitt's *Daughter of Han: The Autobiography of a Chinese Working Woman* (Stanford, Calif.: Stanford University Press, 1967), where Ning Lao T'ai-t'ai tells of a wanton woman who was punished by having her vagina stuffed with hot peppers.

29. For other uses of the word *hun* in this sense, see *Flowers of Shanghai,* where a prostitute and her client "fool and tussle for a bit" (*guihun yizhen*), in Han Bangqing, *Haishanghua liezhuan* (Changsha: Hainan chubanshe, 1997), 6.43. In *Dream of the Red Chamber,* Baoyu says he once "fooled around" (*hunle*) with You Erjie and You Sanjie for a month, which does not necessarily mean he had sex with them, perhaps only that they flirted or fondled (66.944).

30. The word *baorong* is also used with this sense (53.672). A person like Hua Guang-

su has no capacity to *titie* (33.403), the best illustration of which is his intolerance of Qinyan's constant moodiness.

31. Also, when Ziyu and Qinyan first meet, Ziyu confuses the positions of host and guest (10.129). When Tian Chunhang first meets the *dan* Su Huifang, Su's carriage splashes mud on Tian, whose anger melts into adulation when he sees how beautiful Su is (12.153). When Tian the scholar becomes destitute, Su the indentured opera player comes to his rescue. A famous affair between an early-Qing literatus and an actor is an earlier example of the same effect, about which Volpp writes of the affectation of "ignorance of the gulf in social status." See Volpp, "The Male Queen," pp. 118, 128. For "romantic egalitarianism" in the context of male same-sex love in Edo Japan, see Pflugfelder, *Cartographies of Desire*, pp. 37–38, 82; and on "egalitarian mutuality" in *Precious Mirror*, see Starr, "Shifting Boundaries," p. 284.

32. See Xu in chapter 12 and Hua in chapter 41. Two of these occasions take up nearly entire chapters (11 and 57; see also 6, 41, and 52).

33. See Anthony Yu's discussion of Baochai in this regard: *Rereading the Stone*, pp. 186–188, 246. Starr notes the idealization of masculine intelligence in women like Qionghua ("Shifting Boundaries," pp. 298, 299). Aware of Ziyu's relationship with Qinyan, Qionghua sees through Ziyu's prevarication about the affair, but never displays jealousy or anger.

34. David Wang states that the novel "gravitate[s] toward a conservative discourse in which sexuality is safely compartmentalized" (*Fin-de-siècle Splendor*, p. 56). He also sees a "usurp[ation of] feminine discourse for men's use" and states that the novel's "happy ending underlies nothing more than a male-centered fantasy" (*Fin-de-siècle Splendor*, pp. 66–71). My point is that, as severe as the compartmentalization indeed is, the young scholar's chastity and the *dan*'s virginity can be seen as signs not of conservative repression but of radical liberation. Similarly, Chloe Starr notes the troublesome ambiguity of the ending in which the young men marry women who look like their male lovers ("Shifting Boundaries," pp. 224, 298). I would say that if we focus only on the marginalization of women and femininity in general, we risk attaching too much significance to the superficiality of the attributes adopted by boy actresses in their female impersonations and thereby fail to understand the radically ontological aspects of *qing* femininity that I have stressed throughout this book.

Chapter 4. The Love Story and Civilizational Crisis

1. It was only after 1860 that a substantial number of writers, statesmen, and members of the gentry stated that China was faced with unprecedented change. See Yen P'ing Hao, "Changing Chinese Views of Western Relations, 1840–95," in John K. Fairbank and Kwang-ching Liu, eds., *The Cambridge History of China*, vol. 11, part 2 (Cambridge, Mass.: Cambridge University Press, 1989), pp. 142–201, especially p. 156.

2. The edition I use is Wei Xiuren, *Huayue hen* (Fuzhou: Fujian renmin chuban-

she, 1981). The in-text references cite chapter and page (e.g., 29.256) or refer to the entire chapter (e.g., 29). According to some scholars, Wei Xiuren, style name Zi'an, wrote chapters 2 to 44 by 1858, when his preface was written, and finished the remaining chapters in 1864, after the Taipings had been defeated (see Du Weimo's essay in the 1981 edition). Other scholars slightly disagree, but in general believe the last chapters were finished later than the first forty or so. The earliest printed edition bears the date 1888 and contains upper-margin and chapter-final commentaries. See Rong Zhaozu, "*Huayue hen* de zuozhe Wei Xiuren zhuan," in Wang Junnian, ed., *Zhongguo jindai wenxue lunwenji, 1919–1949, xiaoshuo juan* (Beijing: Zhongguo shehui kexue chubanshe, 1988), pp. 194–206, especially pp. 199–201. The original edition contains a brief biography of a courtesan named Liu Xufeng of Taiyuan, whose life leading to her residence in a brothel corresponds to Liu Qiuhen's in the novel. Wei Zi'an (named Buke in the biography) fell in love with her but could not afford to redeem her, lamented the loss, and thus wrote the novel, which also primarily takes place in Taiyuan.

3. On the passages copied, see Chi Chongqi, "Shi lun *Huayue hen* dui *Pinhua baojian* de mofang he chaoxi," *Henan shifan xuebao (shehui kexueban)* 4 (1997): 53–131.

4. The novel especially inspired *Shanghai Dust* (chaps. 16, 49) and *Jade Pear Spirit* (*Yuli hun*). For the latter, see C. T. Hsia, "Hsu Chen-ya's *Yu-li hun*: An Essay in Literary History and Criticism," *Renditions* 17 and 18 (1982): 199–240. A number of prominent literary figures of Republican times recorded their appreciation of the novel, including Cai Yuanpei, Zhang Chunfan, Zheng Yimei (listing *Traces of the Flowery Moon, Dream of the Red Chamber*, and *Romance of the Three Kingdoms* as his three favorite novels), Xu Zhenya, and Zhang Henshui. See Yuan Jin, "Fuchen zai shehui lishi dachaozhong—lun *Huayue hen* de yingxiang," *Shehui kexue* 4 (2005): 112–118.

5. See 31.273; Yuan Jin, "Fuchen"; and David Wang, *Fin-de-siècle Splendor*, p. 73.

6. Both C. T. Hsia and David Wang discuss this point in terms of the influence of *Traces of the Flowery Moon* on *Jade Pear Spirit*. See Hsia, "Hsu Chen-ya's *Yu-li hun*," p. 224; and Wang, *Fin-de-siècle Splendor*, pp. 73–81, especially p. 75.

7. See David Wang, *Fin-de-siècle Splendor*, pp. 75–81.

8. See ibid., p. 358, n. 45; Liu Oubo, "*Huayue hen* zuozhe zhi sixiang," in Wang Junnian, *Zhongguo jindai wenxue lunwenji*, pp. 182–193; and Rong Zhaozu, "*Huayue hen*," ibid., pp. 194–206. The ending was early on criticized for its excess of fantasy, although Liu Oubo defended it in "*Huayue hen* zuozhe zhi sixiang."

9. Li Wai-yee uses a wide range of sources from poetry (e.g., Qian Qianyi, Liu Rushi, and Wu Weiye) and drama (Kong Shangren's "Peach Blossom Fan") to confirm the relation between the romantic-erotic attachment and loyalism in the late Ming. See Li, "The Late Ming Courtesan," and "Heroic Transformations," especially pp. 403, 414–415. The author of Wei Xiuren's epitaph, Xie Zhangting, wrote that Wei took his frustrations with the times and "entrusted them to a love story" (cited in Rong Zhaozu, "*Huayue hen*," p. 200).

10. A friend of Chizhu attempts to redeem Qiuhen on behalf of Chizhu, but Qiuhen's madam drives too hard a bargain. This is followed by the incident in which

the villainous Goutou ("Dog Head," who later joins the Taipings) tries to rape Qiuhen.

11. In a sentiment frequently evoked in women's poetry, Qiuhen reflects that after Chizhu dies his fame will endure in his writings, but as for a woman like her, "there will not even be a trace of her left" (9.65). In the event called "Ranking of Flowers," in which men rank the beauty and talent of ten Taiyuan prostitutes, Liu Qiuhen comes last while the sexy opium-addict Bitao comes first. Liu sneers at the process, saying, "To begin with we are men's playthings. If he loves us, then he sits us on his knee; if he tires of us he tosses us into the abyss" (6.37).

12. See 20.162 and 28.245–256; on the adumbrative description of sex as a sign of the high erotic, see McMahon, *Misers,* pp. 45–46, 138–139, 244–246, and passim.

13. Chizhu writes a memorial to the emperor that includes a condemnation of the opium evil (46.383). See also 20.165, on *afurong,* one of the numerous names for opium, and 31.270–371.

14. Chen Yinke, *Chen Yinke xiansheng wenshi lunji* (Hong Kong: Wenwen chubanshe, 1973), pp. 335–336, written after Wang's suicide.

15. See 40.343 and the commentary at 33.291.

16. On the *tanci* in this regard, see Hu Siaochen, *Cainü cheye weimian,* p. 278.

17. The edition I use is Wang Bin, Chen Fu, Guo Yinghai, and Li Siying, eds., *Hou liaozhai zhiyi quanyi xiangzhu* (Harbin: Heilongjiang chubanshe, 1988). The original title is *Songyin manlu,* which was first published serially in *Shenbao* between 1884 and 1887 and finally as a complete volume in 1893, after which other editions appeared using the title *Hou liaozhai zhiyi.* Wang wrote other stories, but I concentrate on the ones in this anthology. In-text references are to page number.

18. These words are from the story "Xiangu" (Fairy Gorge, 414). In general he avoids describing the sexual aspects of love affairs except in a very few cases such as "A Lian and A Ai" (568) where he writes of courtesans known for their skills in *neimei,* that is, giving sexual pleasure (see also "Yelai xiang").

19. On his relationship with foreigners, see Catherine Yeh, "The Life-style of Four Wenren in Late Qing Shanghai," *Harvard Journal of Asiatic Studies* 57.2 (1997): 419–470, especially 430–431; and Patrick Hanan, "The Bible as Chinese Literature: Medhurst, Wang Tao, and the Delegates' Version," *Harvard Journal of Asiatic Studies* 63.1 (2003): 197–239, especially 222–231. On his Christianity, see Paul Cohen, *Between Tradition and Modernity: Wang T'ao and Reform in Late Ch'ing China* (Cambridge, Mass.: Harvard University Press, 1974), pp. 82–83; and Hanan, "The Bible as Chinese Literature," p. 227.

20. See Yeh, "Life-style," pp. 432–433. Almost a third of his fiction is about courtesans. I have also consulted Xin Ping, *Wang Tao pingzhuan* (Shanghai: Huadong shifan daxue chubanshe, 1990); Zhang Hailin, *Wang Tao pingzhuan* (Nanjing: Nanjing daxue chubanshe, 1993); and Christian Henriot, *Belles de Shanghai: Prostitution et sexualité en Chine aux XIXe–XXe siècles* (Paris: CNRS editions, 1997).

21. See Cohen, *Between Tradition and Modernity,* pp. 32–56.

22. John Fryer, for example, asked him in 1886 to be the curator of the Shanghai Polytechnic Institute and Reading Room, which was designed to provide students

with reading materials in science and technology, and which pointedly excluded both Confucian and missionary learning. See Cohen, *Between Tradition and Modernity,* p. 182; and Xin Ping, *Wang Tao pingzhuan,* pp. 207–228.

23. He makes the same point about the development of communication between all parts of the world, with no place left untouched, in his essay "On the *Dao,*" from the 1883 collection *Taoyuan wenlu waibian* (Shenyang: Liaoning renmin chubanshe, 1994), p. 5.

24. See "Xiaoyun yishi," "He Huixian," or "Hu Qionghua."

25. See Roland Altenburger's fine discussion in "The Sword or the Needle," pp. 44–68.

26. See respectively "Hua Xi nüshi," "Sanshi liu yuanyang puxia," "Dongbu chuling," "Ershi si hua shi shang."

27. See his essay, "Ji busidieni jiao" (On Positivism) in *Taoyuan wenlu waibian,* pp. 236–238; and Cohen, *Between Tradition and Modernity,* pp. 138–139. In the essay "On the *Dao,*" he writes, "The *dao* of the world is one and the same everywhere. How could there be more than one!? . . . There is no *dao* beyond the human, nor is there any human beyond the *dao.*" He adds that Confucianism is not the only *dao* and that "there is a *dao* beyond Confucianism" (*Taoyuan wenlu waibian,* p. 3).

Chapter 5. Passive Polygyny in Two Kinds of Man-child

1. The edition I use is Yu Da, *Qinglou meng* (Beijing: Beijing daxue chubanshe, 1990). Citations are to chapter and page or to chapter.

2. Zou Tao appears in the novel under the name of Zou Bailin, the hero Jin Yixiang's soul mate in the brothels. Zou Tao, who wrote that Yu Da was "the supreme soul mate of my life," is the main source of our meager knowledge about Yu Da, such as the fact that in his later years he was too poor to sustain himself in the city and moved with his elderly mother and sisters to the countryside, where he rented or perhaps owned land to live on. In 1883 and 1884 Zou received two letters from Yu lamenting his lot in life and his inability to make ends meet, 1884 being the year Yu died. Zou reports in his commentary that Yu Da was originally a man of practical political ambition whose "submersion in *qing*" (*lei yu qing*) was a result of frustration with current affairs and corrupt leadership, as Yu himself asserts. The above information on Yu Da can be found in Lin Wei, *Qingdai xiaoshuo lungao* (Beijing: Beijing guangbo xueyuan chubanshe, 2000), pp. 151–157.

3. At the beginning of the dream, the hero and his best friend Zou Bailin pay their respects to the goddess Lin Daiyu, Bailin meaning "worshipper of Lin [Daiyu]."

4. In Chinese numerology, nine denotes the peak of yang power, thus for the grand gathering of thirty-six women to occur in the twenty-ninth chapter is hardly an accident, especially since the novel has the same number of chapters as hexagrams in the *Book of Changes.* Six is the prime yin number, which figures in the thirty-third chapter (two threes add up to six), in which Yixiang dies. See Maram Epstein on numerological patterns in Chinese fiction (*Competing Discourses,* pp. 57–59).

5. The novel appeared in 1878 but was begun as early as 1851. See *Ernü yingxiong zhuan* (Jinan: Qilu shushe, 1989), with commentary by Dong Xun. For a review of

the last one hundred years of scholarship on the novel, see Chang Xueying, "Ershi shiji *Ernü yingxiong zhuan* yanjiu huigu," *Neimenggu shida xuebao (zhexue shehui kexue ban)* 30.6 (Dec. 2001): 3–6. See also Lin Wei's overview of Wen Kang in her article "*Ernü yingxiong zhuan* zuozhe Wen Kang jiashi, shengping ji zhushu kaolue," reprinted in her *Qingdai xiaoshuo lungao,* pp. 1–22.

6. Hu Siaochen's article on the novel has inspired my discussion, especially her observations on the role of women in practical affairs in spite of the nominal authority of Confucian patriarchy. Besides the most prominent of such women, He Yufeng, Hu Siaochen also notes relatively minor characters like the old aunt (*jiu taitai*), who plays a similar role in relation to the elder and younger men of the household. See "Pinfan riyong yu daotong lunli—lun *Ernü yingxiong zhuan,*" in Wang Ayling, ed., *Ming Qing wenxue yu sixiangzhong zhi zhuti yishi yu shehui, wenxue pian* (Taipei: Institute of Chinese Literature and Philosophy, 2004), pp. 589–638.

7. Nüwa is referred to along with Sakyamuni as one of the two exemplars of the combination of "boyish- and girlishness" (that is, the *ernü* kind of *qing*) and "heroism" (*yingxiong*, prologue chapter, pp. 5–6).

8. Three points sum up the novel's self-stated reasons for its superiority to *Dream of the Red Chamber:* the women are free of the poison of jealousy, father and son commune in joyful discussions of classical learning, and the maids do not connive for secret liaisons with their young masters. On Wen Kang's critique of *Dream of the Red Chamber,* see Epstein, *Competing Discourses,* pp. 293–296. On the idea of the purity of the first humans on earth, see Hu Siaochen's discussion in "Pinfan riyong yu daotong lunli."

9. The split between the didactic statement and the subject who enunciates the contents of the statement is of course a reference to Jacques Lacan's method of locating the message of the unconscious in the split between the subject of enunciation, that is the subject who speaks, and the subject of the enunciated, that is, the contents of what is spoken, as mentioned in the introduction. See Lacan, *Écrits: A Selection,* pp. 269–270. This split is similar to that of the separate planes of male and female existence that I have just referred to.

10. That is, *zhongyuan wanli wu shengqi, xiagu gangchang sheng nü'er.*

11. Another expression is *yidongle xingqing,* meaning to suffer a "shift" or "mutation" of one's original good nature (30.660).

12. David Wang discusses the novel and briefly refers to the modern attacks upon it in *Fin-de-siècle Splendor,* p. 159. See also Maram Epstein, who refers to Lu Xun's and Hu Shi's dismissal of the novel's inconsistency and its affirmation of Confucian values (*Competing Discourses,* p. 278).

13. A common scene is one in which An Xuehai breaks into pedantic lecture, quoting the classics, while others listen half-laughing, even making fun of him (e.g., 33.757–759).

14. Using the word *ai* recalls Daiyu in one of the sequels to *Dream of the Red Chamber, Honglou huanmeng,* when she says that she loves (*ai*) Baochai as much as Baoyu loves her (5.55).

15. The Jade Emperor hears a man talking about enjoying "the company of my gorgeous wife and beautiful concubines, and playing with our sons and daughters from morning to night" (24.497). The Jade Emperor doubts such a life can be had, but when the man insists it can, the emperor asks where to go because he would like to enjoy it himself. Elsewhere, when An Ji refers to harmony between husband and co-wives as "life's greatest pleasure" (*rensheng diyi leye*, 30.659), his wives take him to task for treating them like a man would treat courtesans.

16. His story is in chapter 15. See Maram Epstein's excellent summary of his character (*Competing Discourses*, pp. 291–292).

17. Wang points out the great continuity between the filial swordswoman like Thirteenth Sister and her modernized form in the revolutionary heroine. The motif of the righteous martial hero combines with the motif of the remarkable woman to produce heroines who, minus traditional Confucian attributes, will bring about China's transformation into a modern nation. See Wang, *Fin-de-siècle Splendor*, pp. 156–174.

18. The term for buckteeth is *banlabaoya*, literally "half" buckteeth; hunchbacked is *gongzhe jian'er* and later *gongjian suobei*.

19. A parallel example lies in the novel's reference to the imperial examination halls' lack of toilet facilities. Scholars should be like soldiers and endure deprivation in order to prove their mettle. Unread women cannot possibly understand this, as An Xuehai says to his unread wife, who feels that she is sensibly bewildered by the lack of toilets (35.809–810).

20. Thanks to Ding Naifei for the idea of correction from within (personal communication, October 24, 2005).

21. For fascinating and extensive details about Manchu customs and characteristics, see Hu Siaochen's article cited above, "Pinfan riyong yu daotong lunli," and the works of the following scholars: Ding Yizhuang, *Manzude funü shenghuo yu hunyin zhidu yanjiu* (Beijing: Beijing daxue chubanshe, 1999); Li Ting, "Lun *Ernü yingxiong zhuan* zhong de manzu nüxingguan," *Manzu yanjiu* 2 (2003): 72–78; and Lin Wei, "*Ernü yingxiong zhuan* zuozhe Wen Kang jiashi, shengping ji zhushu kaolue," in *Qingdai xiaoshuo lungao*, pp. 1–22.

22. See chapter 9 herein and the case, for example, of *Yu lian huan*, in which there are three polygynous marriages, one with two wives and a concubine, and two with two wives.

Chapter 6. Fleecing the Customer in Shanghai Brothels of the 1890s

1. The edition I use is Han Bangqing, *Haishanghua liezhuan* (Changsha: Hainan chubanshe, 1997), with an interlinear translation of Shanghai dialect into Mandarin. I have used the Wu dialect dictionary compiled by Wu Liansheng et al., eds., *Wu fangyan cidian* (Beijing: Hanyu da cidian chubanshe, 1995), but in my romanization have used Mandarin pinyin because of my lack of competence in the Wu sound system. I have also consulted the translation into Mandarin by Zhang Ailing (Eileen Chang), *Haishanghua kai, Haishanghua luo* (Taibei: Huang-

guan, 1997), which abridges the original into sixty chapters; and her translation into English, revised and edited by Eva Hung, *Singsong Girls of Shanghai* (New York: Columbia University Press, 2005). This chapter appeared in earlier form as "Fleecing the Male Customer in Shanghai Brothels of the 1890s," *Late Imperial China* 23.2 (2002): 1–32.

2. My understanding of this milieu has benefited from two major studies of prostitution in Shanghai in the nineteenth and twentieth centuries: Gail Hershatter's *Dangerous Pleasures: Prostitution and Modernity in Twentieth-Century Shanghai* (Berkeley: University of California Press, 1997); and Christian Henriot's *Belles de Shanghai*. Also helpful were Chen Bohai, Yuan Jin, et al., *Shanghai jindai wenxue shi* (Shanghai: Shanghai renmin chubanshe, 1993); Catherine Yeh, "Reinventing Ritual: Late Qing Handbooks for Proper Customer Behavior in Shanghai Courtesan Houses," *Late Imperial China* 19.2 (1998): 1–63, "Life-style," "Cong shijiu shiji Shanghai ditu kan dui chengshi weilai dingyi de zhengduozhan," *Zhongguo xueshu* 1.3 (2000): 88–121, and her key recent work, *Shanghai Love: Courtesans, Intellectuals, and Entertainment Culture, 1850–1910* (Seattle: University of Washington Press, 2006); Paola Zamperini, "But I Never Learned to Waltz: The Real and Imagined Education of a Courtesan in the Late Qing," *Nan Nü: Men, Women, and Gender in China* 1.1 (1999): 107–144, and "Lost Bodies: Images and Representations of Prostitution in Late Qing Fiction" (Ph.D. diss., University of California, Berkeley, 1999). See also David Wang, *Fin-de-siècle Splendor,* pp. 89–90, 99.

3. This fact is notable because of the relative novelty of the literary magazine, many more of which would soon come into existence. The novel was published in book form in 1894. For details on the connection between changes in narrative style and serialization (which had already begun in *Shenbao* in 1872 and 1873) and the professionalization of writers, see Chen Bohai, Yuan Jin, et al., *Shanghai jindai wenxue shi,* pp. 235, 238–239, 241; and David Wang, *Fin-de-siècle Splendor,* pp. 89 and 360, n. 80.

4. Preceding Han are figures like Wang Tao, Qian Zheng, and Cai Erkang. Han himself was a *xiucai* who failed the provincial exams and served in the low echelons of the bureaucracy before settling in Shanghai. According to Liu Bannong and Hu Shi, Han reportedly spent his inherited wealth in the brothels of Shanghai (Liu Bannong, "Du *Haishanghua liezhuan*," in Han Bangqing, *Haishanghua liezhuan,* p. 28; and Hu Shi, "Hu Shi xu," in Han Bangqing, *Haishanghua liezhuan,* pp. 1–18). As Catherine Yeh notes, the novelist Zeng Pu was an addict who, according to Bao Tianxiao, wrote *Niehai hua* in the midst of his habit. See Yeh, "Life-style," p. 455.

5. Yuan Jin considers it the best novel of the *jindai* period (Chen Bohai, Yuan Jin, et al., *Shanghai jindai wenxue shi,* p. 236).

6. Around the early 1860s, the main locale of the business of prostitution began moving from the walled Chinese city of Shanghai to the foreign concessions, one of the main reasons being the instability caused by the Taiping Rebellion. As Yeh notes, courtesans gained a new sense of power in the foreign concessions, to the displea-

sure of officials in the Chinese city. In 1870, a circuit intendant tried to order the closure of all brothels there, where he had no real jurisdiction (Yeh, "Reinventing Ritual," pp. 2–3, 6–7; and Henriot, *Belles de Shanghai*, p. 315). In the 1880s, officials again tried to control the freedom of movement among prostitutes, issuing orders (likewise ineffective) that no women be employed in teahouses (Henriot, *Belles de Shanghai*, p. 316).

7. The words about the village are by Hong Shanqing to the naïf Zhao Puzhai (12.101–102, 13.105). Passages about feelings include "The closer you are to your mistress, the less long-lasting your affair will be," and "The closer you are, the more trouble you get yourself into," both said about the couple Tao Yufu and Lin Shufang (7.58; 42.354).

8. As Yeh notes in reference to Shanghai city guidebooks, "The *changsan* were not shy about the professional aspect of their life, referring to their entertaining clients as 'doing business,' *zuo shengyi.*" ("Reinventing Ritual," p. 29).

9. Henriot writes that women did not remain as prostitutes for very many years *(Belles de Shanghai,* pp. 152, 257–258). Women who could free themselves independently were rare, age and ill-health being the main reasons for their high rates of replacement (p. 38).

10. In focusing on Hong Shanqing in this way, I disagree with Eileen Chang's view of him as a lesser character with an opportunistic merchant's mentality (see Zhang, *Haishanghua luo,* p. 710). She instead sees Hua Tiemei as a possible self-representation of the author (pp. 719–721). Hong Shanqing is indeed opportunistic in that he profits—sometimes quite blithely—from the transactions between customers and prostitutes. But my point is not to insist on precise and consistent correspondence between author and Hong Shanqing, or on a necessarily flattering self-image, since even Hua is described by his mistress as neurotically indecisive (see her comments in chapter 52). Hong and Hua are in fact similar in that neither pretends to be a master philanderer; and both are more prone to see brothel transactions from the woman's perspective than from the man's, though like the prostitute both mainly serve the interests of the men with money and power.

11. According to the author's "Postscript" (pp. 555–556), however, Wu later marries someone else. Zhang Ailing speculates that Ge dies, after which Wu keeps the child to raise with a husband she marries uxorilocally, which in Zhang's sense tends to mean a husband in poor circumstances who marries a woman on her conditions. See Zhang, *Zhang Ailing wencui* (Beijing: Wenhua yishu chubanshe, 2003), p. 406.

12. Zhang Ailing speculates that the suicide potion is fake, probably based on the fact that actual prostitutes did such things. Zhu still drinks the counterpoison that the others bring to her, which makes her vomit. See Zhang's endnote in *Haishanghua luo,* p. 694.

13. The original story is by Li Gongzuo (ca. late eighth–early ninth centuries); see "The Governor of Nanke" (Nanke taishou zhuan), in Li Fang, *Taiping guangji* (Beijing: Zhonghua shuju, 1986), pp. 3910–3915.

Chapter 7. Cultural Destiny and Polygynous Love
in Zou Tao's *Shanghai Dust*

1. This chapter is a modified version of a journal article, "Cultural Destiny and Polygynous Love in Zou Tao's *Shanghai Dust*," *Chinese Literature: Essays, Articles, and Reviews* 27 (2005): 117–135. The edition I use is Zou Tao, *Haishang chentian ying* (Nanchang: Baihuazhou wenyi chubanshe, 1993). Zou Tao was a well-known reformist thinker who wrote on the customs and political principles of foreign nations in *Wanguo jinzheng kao* (Modern Governments Abroad), *Wanguo fengsu kaolue* (Customs of the World's Nations), and *Diqiu fangyu kaolue* (World Geography). In his later years he taught at a Catholic girls' school in Shanghai. The earliest known edition dates from 1904, but Wang Tao's 1896 preface indicates that the book existed in manuscript form at that time already.

2. Su Yunlan is the name of the courtesan Zou Tao supposedly failed to marry; she wrote a critique of his novel, which Zou Tao appends at the beginning. Wang Tao's preface details her life. Numerous features of the brothel recall earlier Ming and Qing scenarios in which men and women drop the formalities of hierarchical appellations. They socialize, write poetry, and conduct their love affairs there, though some of the women never have sex with their patrons. One of them knows martial arts, as she demonstrates when she subdues an unruly customer (24). The women tolerate no insults from men (32). A new element is the brothel's protection by Shanghai's foreign laws, which are "precise and objective" (*shi shi qiu shi*, 22.357–358).

3. The Boxers had been active since the early 1800s, but they became especially antiforeign in the 1890s. They are still called *yihe quan* here, not *yihe tuan*, the name they received in 1899, when members of the imperial government began to enlist them in antiforeign activities.

4. In one case it is a matter of implying to her mother that she would rather have married Han instead of the wastrel (11.154–155); in another case, she implies that she would willingly have become his concubine (31.509); and, finally, in speaking to Han she almost utters the words, "'if we were husband and. . . ,' but then she cut herself off" (49.851).

5. See "Maiyoulang duzhan huakui," in Feng Menglong, ed. Li Tien-yi, *Xingshi hengyan* (Taibei: Shijie shuju, 1959), story 3.35a.

6. See Yu Dafu quoted in Yang Yi, *Zhongguo xiandai xiaoshuo shi* (Beijing: Renmin chubanshe, 1986), p. 557, using the word *rouma*.

Chapter 8. The Polygynous Politics of the Modern Chinese Man
in *Nine-times Cuckold*

1. Prominent critics dismissed *Nine-times Cuckold* as a mere guidebook for rakish brothel patrons, but it remained popular from its first appearance up to at least the 1920s. Zhang Chunfan serialized it in newspapers from 1906 to 1910. He was by

then already writing short stories for newspapers and was also an educational and provincial-level official in both the late-Qing and early-Republican governments. The edition used is *Jiuwei gui* (Nanchang: Baihua wenyi chubanshe, 1993).

2. Thus the examples of women such as Kang Aide (1873–1931), Lü Bicheng (1883–1943), and Zhang Zhujun (1871–?). On Kang and Zhang, see Hu Ying, *Tales of Translation: Composing the New Woman in China, 1899–1918* (Stanford, Calif.: Stanford University Press, 2000); on Lü Bicheng, see Grace Fong, "Alternative Modernities, or a Classical Woman of Modern China: The Challenging Trajectory of Lü Bicheng's (1883–1943) Life and Song Lyrics," *Nan Nü: Men, Women, and Gender in China* 6.1 (2004): 12–59. On the legal deconstruction of polygamy in the early-Republican period, see Lisa Tran, "Concubines under Modern Chinese Law" (Ph.D. diss., University of California, Los Angeles, 2005).

3. See the special theme issue of *Nan Nü: Men, Women, and Gender in China* 6.1 (2004), with articles by Grace Fong, "Alternative Modernities"; Qian Nanxiu, "'Borrowing Foreign Mirrors and Candles to Illuminate Chinese Civilization': Xue Shaohui's Moral Vision in the *Biographies of Foreign Women*," pp. 60–101; Joan Judge, "Blended Wish Images: Chinese and Western Exemplary Women at the Turn of the Twentieth Century," pp. 102–135; and Ellen Widmer, "Inflecting Gender: Zhan Kai/Siqi Zhai's 'New Novels' and Courtesan Sketches," pp. 136–168.

4. Modern feminism first gathered momentum in the mid-1890s and found a regular voice in journals beginning around 1902. See, for example, Liang Qichao's biographies of Madame Roland (1902) and Kang Aide (1897) as discussed in Hu Ying's *Tales of Translation*, pp. 3, 123–126, and pp. 172–179; on the new man, see pp. 150–151. On anarcho-feminism in this period, see Peter Zarrow, "He Zhen and Anarcho-Feminism in China," *Journal of Asian Studies* 47.4 (1988): 796–813.

5. See Zhang Jingyuan, *Psychoanalysis in China: Literary Transformations 1919–1949* (Ithaca, N.Y.: Cornell University Press, 1992), pp. 37–38. The term *xinlixue* "did not enter Chinese usage until shortly before 1900." The first translated book on psychology was in 1889, using the term *xinlingxue*. The Guangxu emperor included psychology among the courses to be taught in schools of higher education.

6. In *Nine-times Cuckold*, see 23.172–173; and in Li Boyuan's *Tracks of the Snowgoose*, see *Li Boyuan quanji* (Nanjing: Jiangsu guji chubanshe, 1997), vol. 3, 16.92, referring to a prostitute's *waijiao shouduan*.

7. Zeng Pu's (1872–1935) *Flower in a Sea of Karma* was likewise popular, selling tens of thousands of copies in the several years after 1905 and continuing in popularity for the next several decades. Jin Tianhe (1873–1947) was the author of the first six chapters, but Zeng took over the novel after Jin abandoned it.

8. These are the words used in his seduction of the prostitute Lin Daiyu, after they watch the opera performance of the seduction scene of Pan Jinlian and Ximen Qing.

9. Another example of language switching can be found in the passage in which Chen Wenxian is angry at Zhang Qiugu, who—proving his sensitivity and savoir

faire—then turns from masculine Mandarin to feminine Suzhou dialect and softens her by simply telling her, "Don't get mad now" (34.257). In another scene, when a prostitute asks him where he is going, he responds in Suzhou dialect that he is going to "do" her and another woman at the same time (against the prostitute's usual insistence that the patron patronize one woman at a time, 44.320).

10. See Lu Xun, "Shanghai wenyi zhi yibie," in *Erxin ji* (Shanghai: Hezhong shudian, 1932), pp. 124, 126; and Hu Shi's preface in Han Bangqing, *Haishanghua liezhuan,* p. 17. David Wang translates Lu Xun's words as "talented young man plus rascal" (*Fin-de-siècle Splendor,* p. 88).

11. To someone who challenges him, he insists that he is above the actor who becomes the prostitute's secret lover without spending any money on her, even taking money from her (31.231). Zhang Qiugu maintains the bearing of a patron who actually spends money, miserliness being one of the traits he most detests. "Canon of whoring" occurs in the title to chapter 31 (31.229).

12. David Wang refers to *Nine-times Cuckold* as not a "sequel" to *Flower in a Sea of Karma,* but nevertheless as consciously taking up where the earlier novel left off (*Fin-de-siècle Splendor,* pp. 109–110).

13. Which forms the title of another well-known novel of the time, the 1898 *Haishang mingji sida jingang qishu* (*The Four Courtesan Door-gods of Shanghai*).

14. The term, which describes Lin Daiyu in the scene just referred to, was in use from the late Qing through the first several decades of the Republic. For a definition with illustration, see Wang Zhongxian, *Shanghai suyu tushuo* (Shanghai: Shanghai shudian, 1999, original edition 1935), pp. 139–141.

15. The original formula is *yi yi dai lao.* See the brilliant French translation and commentary by Francois Kircher (pseudonym of Francois Wildt), *Les trente-six stratagèmes: traité secret de stratégie chinoise* (Paris: Editions du Rocher, 2001), pp. 50–53, which has "Attendre tranquillement un ennemi qui s'épuise" (to wait quietly as the enemy exhausts himself; p. 50).

16. See Lu Xun, "Shanghai wenyi zhi yibie," p. 126.

17. That is, *xiaoqi, dong shou dong jiao,* and *yiwei waichan* (9.70).

18. The unmarried Zhao Erbao was a *renjiaren* (*nin'ga'nin*) in *Flowers of Shanghai* before becoming a full-fledged prostitute. In her case, she was lured by a man who took advantage of her gullibility.

19. On the point that Zeng Pu is less radical than the original author of *Flower in a Sea of Karma,* see Ouyang Jian's discussion of the novel in *WanQing xiaoshuo shi* (Hangzhou: Zhejiang guji chubanshe, 1997), pp. 187–224.

Conclusion. The Postpolygnous Future

1. *Nüwa shi,* by Haitian duxiaozi, can be found with other novels in Lingnan yuyi nüshi et al., *Dongou nühaojie etc.* (Nanchang: Baihuazhou wenyi chubanshe, 1991); for this quote, see p. 441.

2. On the evolution of the actor-patron relationship during the Republican period,

see Kang Wenqing, *Obsession: Male Same-Sex Relations in China, 1900–1950* (Hong Kong: Hong Kong University Press, 2009).

3. Both Hu Siaochen and Bao Zhenpei discuss women and polygamy specifically: in Hu, *Cainü cheye weimian;* in Bao, *Qingdai nüzuojia tanci xiaoshuo lungao,* which contains three subsections on polygamy and concubinage (pp. 123–126).

4. On Sun Deying, see Hu Siaochen, *Cainü cheye weimian,* pp. 181, 207–210. Once her mother died, Sun disavowed marriage and from 1863 to 1868 devoted herself to writing *Jin yu yuan,* never leaving the inner chambers during that time. In *Liu-hua meng* (1841), the heroine refuses to return to female dress until the emperor orders her to join a polygynous household. She still involves herself in political affairs until she fulfills her ambitions and in Pu Songling–style becomes an immortal. *Mengying yuan*'s (1843) author profoundly regrets being a woman. Ten of her twelve heroines never marry; all of them and the two who do marry die before the end. *Zixu ji*'s (1883) cross-dressing heroine commits suicide rather than go back to being a woman.

5. Hu Siaochen discusses shrews in female-authored texts in a 2005 conference paper, "Xiong jiu, fengdian yu dushen—lun Qingdai nüxing tanci xiaoshuozhong de jiduan nüxing renwu."

6. My information on Shen Cai relies on Grace Fong's scholarship in *Herself an Author: Gender, Agency, and Writing in Late Imperial China* (Honolulu: University of Hawai'i Press, 2008), pp. 69–83. As Fong translates, Shen Cai wrote that it was in 1766 "when I first had my hair pinned up and paid my respects to Madam. Madam gave me this calligraphy as a token of her friendship in return" (p. 76). There is also the suggestion that Shen Cai's younger sister became a concubine in the household (p. 70). The sisters came from a good family that suffered decline; as Fong reports, it is impossible to tell from the records if either had children.

7. Ibid., pp. 78–83.

8. See ibid., pp. 81–82.

9. As Dorothy Ko writes, when Wang discovered husband and concubine becoming too intimate, she wrote a poem expressing her displeasure. My information on Wang comes from Ko, *Teachers of the Inner Chamber,* pp. 129–136. Yet another case is that of the poet Qu Bingyun, who frequently discussed and exchanged poetry with her husband, who had a concubine. Although Qu did not introduce or choose the concubine, she maintained steady contact with the young woman, especially through poetry, giving her the courtesy name Lianqing, a homonym for "loving you." The two were constant companions, thus demonstrating the situation of rising above jealousy in which the main wife takes the lower-class, less-well-educated concubine under her wing. My information on Qu Bingyun comes from Liuxi Meng, *Poetry as Power: Yuan Mei's Female Disciple Qu Bingyun (1767–1810)* (Lanham, Md.: Lexington Books, 2007).

10. See Shen Fu, *Fusheng liuji* (Beijing: Renmin wenxue chubanshe, 1980), p. 14; and Shen Fu, trans. Leonard Pratt and Chiang Su-hui, *Six Records of a Floating Life* (Harmondsworth: Penguin Books, 1983), p. 48, which uses the word "obsession."

11. The novels of valiant heroes and heroines include *An Old Man's Radiant Words* and the late-Qing novels about martial heroes such as *Tale of Filial Heroes, Routing the Brigands* (*Dangkou zhi*), and *Judge Bao and His Valiant Lieutenants* (*Sanxia wuyi*). Numerous late-Qing figures (e.g., Zhang Taiyan, Huang Zunxian, and Liang Qichao) promoted the ideal of the valiant hero prominent in such works.

12. The ideas in this paragraph were combined with a brief digest of the rest of this book as a book chapter, "Love Martyrs and Love Cheaters at the End of the Chinese Empire," in Doris Croissant, Catherine Vance Yeh, and Joshua S. Mostow, eds., *Performing "Nation": Gender Politics in Literature, Theater, and the Visual Arts of China and Japan, 1880–1940* (Leiden and Boston: Brill, 2008), pp. 135–142.

13. This perception was accompanied by the sense among many Chinese intellectuals of the senescence and corruption of the Manchu empire. As cited in Guo Yanli, *Zhongguo jindai wenxue fazhanshi* (Jinan: Shandong jiaoyu chubanshe, 1990), volume 1, see, for example, the poetry of Wei Yuan (1794–1856), p. 125; Zhang Weiping (1780–1859), p. 161; and references to Lu Song (1791–1860), pp. 214–216; Lu Yitong (1804–1863), p. 218; and Bei Qingqiao (1810–1863), pp. 225–227 (e.g., satirical poems about the ridiculous tactics of the Qing military against the British).

14. On the legal and political status of the Chinese subject in an international setting, see Rebecca Karl, *Staging the World: Chinese Nationalism at the Turn of the Twentieth Century* (Durham, N.C.: Duke University Press, 2002), pp. 54–55. The quote is from D. R Howland's *Borders of Chinese Civilization: Geography and History at Empire's End* (Durham, N.C.: Duke University Press, 1996), p. 2.

15. See Karl, *Staging the World,* regarding the idea that "China became thinkable as specifically national at the same time as, and only when, China became consciously worldly," that is, at the end of the nineteenth century. Such a framing also has to do with the "incipient understanding of how imperialism worked to ideologically create its object"; see pp. 13 and 151–152.

16. See Cochran, *Twilight of the Literary: Figures of Thought in the Age of Print* (Cambridge, Mass.: Harvard University Press, 2001), p. 135. These points derive from Cochran's discussion of Kant and his "world idea as the conceptual framework of modernity." Cochran refers to Kant's creation of "the modern science of man as an autonomous agent . . . derived from the idea of an *abstract human without local limitations*" (pp. 169, 20; emphasis mine).

17. These stipulations can be found in numerous novels besides *Flowers of Shanghai,* including the 1899 *Tracks of the Snowgoose,* the 1908 *Nine-tailed Fox* (*Jiuwei hu*), and Sun Jiazhen's 1903 *Shanghai Splendor* (*Haishang fanhua meng*). For the second and third stipulations, see *Haishang fanhua meng* (Changchun: Shidai wenyi chubanshe, 1993), I.28.326 and II.21.597, referring to the two parts in this edition as I and II, followed by chapter and page number. "Equality," called *pingdeng,* appears in this novel in a reference to the use of status appellations between the prostitute and the man's family, including his main wife (II.14.510). *Shanghai Splendor,* to be

sure, ultimately emulates the truly *qing*-inspired couple who leave the cold world of Shanghai and return to Suzhou, where the man's wife awaits him patiently with their newborn child, while the prostitute agrees to kowtow as concubine to the wife (II.22).

18. Such portrayals continued for several decades, as shown in studies by Ellen Laing, "Women in 'Shanghai *manhua*' (Shanghai sketches)" and Barbara Mittler, "The New Woman: Dreams, Nightmares (and Realities) in Women's Magazines from the Republican Period," from a 2004 conference at Heidelberg University, "New Gender Constructs in Literature, the Visual and the Performing Arts of Modern China and Japan."

19. *Nüyu hua,* however, eventually abandons the activist heroine and opts (though not entirely) for female characters who marry and engage in conventional careers. See Widmer, *Beauty and the Book,* pp. 264–265. The point about slippage comes from Joan Judge, "The Culturally Contested Student Body: *Nü Xuesheng* at the Turn of the Twentieth Century," in Croissant, Yeh, and Mostow, *Performing "Nation,"* pp. 105–132.

20. See *Niehai hua,* 21.245. She also says, "You haven't got what it takes to make me stay by you for good!"

21. For further elaboration about who smokes and who does not, and of the significance of opium versus tobacco, see McMahon, *The Fall of the God of Money,* pp. 155–162.

22. See ibid., p. 20; and for a discussion of opium and sex, pp. 114, 129–132, 162–169.

23. See Žižek's summation of Lacan's meaning in Lacan's seminar on ethics and psychoanalysis in Žižek, *Tarrying with the Negative,* p. 254, n. 39.

24. That is, "You never look at me from the place from which I see you," in Lacan, trans. Alan Sheridan, *The Four Fundamental Concepts of Psychoanalysis* (New York: W. W. Norton, 1981), p. 103. These ideas are based on the assumption that there is no transcendental position of neutrality. The gaze, in other words, stands for the absence of the transcendental perspective. See Joan Copjec, *Imagine There's No Woman: Ethics and Sublimation* (Cambridge, Mass.: MIT Press, 2002), pp. 210–212; and Dylan Evans, *An Introductory Dictionary of Lacanian Psychoanalysis* (London: Routledge, 1996), p. 72.

25. Rey Chow, *Women and Chinese Modernity: The Politics of Reading between West and East* (Minneapolis: University of Minnesota Press, 1991), pp. 54–55, and her wording for this point in terms of the "split between upholding Confucian virtue and dramatizing that which undermines those virtues." Chow's point is that the act of punishing the self by disallowing romantic fulfillment is the effect of historic trauma (something also seen in *Traces of the Flowery Moon* and *Shanghai Dust*). Chow also notes the idea of woman "as the locus of social change" (p. 39). "Because women are the fundamental support of familial social structure, the epochal changes that historians document are most readily perceived through the changing status of Chinese women" (p. 53). She sees "women's lives as the place

where the most intense ideological issues can be dramatized" (p. 104) and notes that the woman problem is the kind of issue that "culture either dismisses point-blank or subsumes under the largest and most irresponsible terms" (p. 119).

26. See "Feminist Knots: Sex and Domestic Work in the Shadow of the Bondmaid-concubine," *Inter-Asia Cultural Studies* 3.3 (2002): 449–467, which discusses the question that arose when Taipei prostitutes protested: could they be considered feminists and radicals, or were they examples of false consciousness and mere remnants of a former base existence that had not evolved properly? Could "sex work and sexual service . . . be validated as a 'right'"? (p. 452). On the further relevance of late-imperial sexual formations in contemporary Taiwan, see also Zhang Jiarong, "Guoqu guoqu yizhi lai: 80 niandai nüxing xiaoshuode qingfu shuxie" (M.A. thesis, National Tsinghua University, 2006).

27. See "Feminist Knots," pp. 460, 450–451, 455.

28. See Lydia Liu's *Translingual Practice: Literature, National Culture, and Translated Modernity—China, 1900-1937* (Stanford, Calif.: Stanford University Press, 1995), which examines the debates on individualism and humanism in early-twentieth-century China. She sums up the traits as follows, paraphrasing Sun Yat-sen: "servile, ignorant, self-centered, and lacking in the ideal of freedom" (pp. 48–49). Liu discusses the development of a new stylistics in fiction which focused on a character as an individual in possession of psychological and moral truth, and not a mere element in a kinship hierarchy (p. 94).

29. Frank Dikötter discusses the role of science in his *Sex, Culture and Modernity in China* (Honolulu: University of Hawai'i Press, 1995), pp. 7, 17, 110. In the new science of the healthy citizen, women were to become healthy mothers (pp. 17–18), while the new habits of hygiene still maintained the dangerous qualities of female sexuality (p. 61). The division was still made between the man with his brainy capacities and public role and the woman and the function of her womb and her sequestration from the public world (p. 29). Sex was transformed into a "medical category denoting degeneracy, disease and contamination" (p. 122). As for European knowledge, in general it was "selectively appropriated," especially in terms of the distinction between procreative and nonprocreative sex, including homosexuality and heterosexuality (p. 139). The individual's right to pleasure was bracketed as a European notion.

30. *Women and Chinese Modernity*, p. 149.

31. See "Concubinage and New Feminist Imaginaries," p. 19 (talk presented at the Sixth International Super-Slim Conference on Politics of Gender/Sexuality, National Central University, November 27, 2004). Many thanks to Ding Naifei for supplying me with this manuscript.

32. See "Feminist Knots," pp. 450–451.

Character Glossary

"A Bao" 阿寶
"A Lian A Ai" 阿憐阿愛
"A Xian" 阿纖
afurong 阿芙蓉
ai 愛
"Ainu" 愛奴
an buwang wei 安不忘危
An Ji 安驥
An Xuehai 安學海
Ba Yingguan 巴英官
ba Yixiang kanle yi kan 把悒香看了一看
"Bai Qiulian" 白秋練
Bailin 拜林
bajie 巴結
banlabaoya 半拉包牙
Bao Tianxiao 包天笑
Baochai 寶釵
baorong 包容
Baozhu 寶珠
bashi 把勢
Bei Qingqiao 貝青喬
benshi 本事
benxing nan yi 本性難移
Bi sheng hua 筆生花
bi yeyou 避冶遊
Bian Sai 卞塞
bianfa ziqiang 變法自強
bifa 筆法
biji 筆記
Bitao 碧桃
Bu Honglou meng 補紅樓夢
Buke 逋客
bumie 不滅
bushi yuanjia buju tou 不是冤家不聚頭
buzhi wei ren 不知為人
Cai Erkang 蔡爾康
cainü 才女
caizi jia liumang 才子加流氓
Cao Xueqin 曹雪芹
ceshi 側室
"Chang E" 嫦娥
changsan 長三
Chen Duansheng 陳端生
Chen Sen 陳森
Chen Shaohai 陳少海
Chen Shiwen 陳詩雯
Chen Wenxian 陳文仙
Chen Xiaoyun 陳小雲
Chen Yinke 陳寅恪
Chen Yuan 陳元
Chen Yuanyuan 陳圓圓
"Chen Yunqi" 陳雲棲
Chen Zilong 陳子龍
Cheng-Zhu 程朱
chi 痴
chixin 痴心
chou 愁
chu jia 出家
chu ju 出局
chushi 處士

Cui Hu　崔護
daidaide kanzhe　呆呆的看着
daixiang　呆想
Daiyu　黛玉
dajia bangzhe ban shi　大家幫著辦事
dan　淡
dan　旦
Dan Minglun　但明倫
"Da'nan"　大男
dandang　旦黨
dang　蕩
Dangkou zhi　蕩寇志
daren　大人
dazhangfu　大丈夫
Deng Jiugong　鄧九公
Ding Shengzhao　丁聖肇
dingqing shi　定情詩
Diqiu fangyu kaolue　地球方域考略
Dong Bai　董白
Dong E　董鄂
dong shou dong jiao　動手動腳
Dong Xun　董恂
"Dongbu chuling"　東部雛伶
Dong'ou nühaojie　東歐女豪傑
"Dongsheng"　董生
"Dongying cainü"　東瀛才女
Du Caiqiu　杜采秋
Du Liniang　杜麗娘
Du Qinyan　杜琴言
Duan Yucai　段玉裁
Duo Guniang　多姑娘
duoqing　多情
Ernü yingxiong zhuan　兒女英雄傳
"Ershi si hua shi shang"　二十四花史上
Fang Bosun　方伯蓀
"Fang Wenshu"　房文淑
fang ying　放鷹
fangdang guanle　放蕩慣了
fanhua　繁華
fei　肥
fei　妃
Feilong　飛龍
Feng Menglong　馮夢龍

"Feng Peibo"　馮佩伯
"Feng Sanniang"　封三娘
Feng Zhenluan　馮鎮巒
Feng Zipei　馮子佩
fengcheng　奉承
Fenglin　鳳林
fengliu caizi　風流才子
Fengliu guangda jiaozhu　風流廣大
　教主
fengqing　風情
Fengyue meng　風月夢
fenle niwo de en'ai　分了你我的恩愛
fenzhang huoji　分賬伙計
Fu Caiyun　傅彩雲
Fusheng liuji　浮生六記
gai hang　改行
gai jia　改嫁
gai ye　改業
Gao Xianglan　高湘蘭
Ge Zhongying　葛仲英
"Gejin"　葛巾
geming　革命
Gong Cheng　龔橙
Gong Dingzi　龔鼎孳
Gong Zizhen　龔自珍
gongjia　功架
gongjian suobei　拱肩縮背
"Gongsun jiuniang"　公孫九娘
gongzhanli　攻戰力
gongzhe jian'er　拱着肩兒
Goutou　狗頭
Gu Chun (Taiqing)　顧春 (太清)
Gu Lansheng　顧蘭生
Gu Mei　顧媚
Gu Taiqing　顧太清
guan　管
guanren zui fanjide shi shuo ta chi cu
　倌人最犯忌的是說他吃醋
"Gui ku"　鬼哭
Gui Peishan　歸佩珊
Guichuzi　歸鋤子
guihun yizhen　鬼混一陣
guixiu　閨秀

guojia   國家
guomin sixiang   國民思想
"Haidi qijing"   海底奇境
Haipu zhuren   海圃主人
Haishang chentian ying   海上塵天影
Haishang fanhua meng   海上繁華夢
Haishang mingji sida jingang qishu   海
　上名妓四大金剛奇書
Haishanghua kai   海上花開
Haishanghua liezhuan   海上花列傳
Haishanghua luo   海上花落
Haitian duxiaozi   海天獨嘯子
Haitian hongxue ji   海天鴻雪記
"Haiwai zhuangyou"   海外壯游
Han Bangqing   韓邦慶
Han Hesheng   韓荷生
Han Qiuhe   韓秋鶴
Hanshang Mengren   邗上蒙人
hao   好
hao yin   好淫
haofang   豪放
haoxiang yige shenti meiyou fangchu
　yiban   好像一個身體沒有放處一
　般
"He Huixian"   何惠仙
He Xinyin   何心隱
He Yufeng   何玉鳳
"Hehua sanniangzi"   荷花三娘子
hong   哄
Hong Liangji   洪亮吉
Hong Shanqing   洪善卿
Hong Sheng   洪昇
Honglou fumeng   紅樓復夢
Honglou huanmeng   紅樓幻夢
Honglou meng   紅樓夢
Honglou meng bu   紅樓夢補
Honglou meng sanjia pingben   紅樓夢
　三家評本
Honglou meng ying   紅樓夢影
Honglou yuanmeng   紅樓圓夢
hou   后
Hou Fangyu   侯方域
Hou Honglou meng   後紅樓夢

Hou Liaozhai zhiyi   後聊齋誌異
Hou Zhi   侯芝
houtian de xin   後天的心
"Hu Qionghua"   胡瓊華
Hu Shih   胡適
Hua Guangsu   華光宿
"Hua Guzi"   花姑子
Hua Teimei   華鐵眉
"Hua Xi nüshi"   花蹊女史
Huang Cuifeng   黃翠鳳
Huang Yuanjie   黃媛介
Huang Zunxian   黃尊憲
huangjin   黃巾
Huashen sanmiao zhuan   花身三妙傳
Huatu yuan   畫圖緣
Huayue chiren   花月痴人
Huayue hen   花月痕
hui yi   會意
"Humeng"   狐夢
hunao   胡鬧
hunle   混了
huyu   浴浴
"Ji busidieni jiao"   紀卜斯迭尼教
Jia Baoyu   賈寶玉
Jia Lian   賈璉
Jia Ming   賈銘
Jia She   賈赦
Jia Zheng   賈政
jian   賤
jian bian   剪邊
Jiang Dehua   姜德華
Jiang Youchun   蔣又春
Jiangbei   江北
"Jiangcheng"   江城
"Jiaping gongzi"   嘉平公子
jiaren caizi xiaoshuo   佳人才子小說
jieguo   結果
jieti   戒體
Jihai zashi   己亥雜詩
Jin Cuiwu   金翠梧
Jin Hanliang   金漢良
Jin Ping Mei   金瓶梅
Jin Tianhe   金天翮

Jin Wenqing 金雯青
Jin Yixiang 金悒香
Jin yu yuan 金魚緣
Jin Yun Qiao zhuan 金雲翹傳
jing 敬
jinri de guanchang 今日的官場
Jinshi yuan 金石緣
"Jinü" 績女
"Jisheng" 寄生
jiu taitai 舅太太
Jiuwei gui 九尾龜
Jiuwei hu 九尾狐
ju nei 懼內
jucu 侷促
jue wu yanhua sutai 絕無煙花俗態
jue wu yishide chusheng 絕無意識的畜生
Kang Aide 康愛德
Kang Jisheng 康己生
kangkai huisa tantu 慷慨揮洒談吐
kao nanren yizhang paizi 靠男人一張牌子
Keqing 可卿
Kong Shangren 孔尚任
kunzhang huoji 捆賬伙計
Langhuan shanqiao 鄉嬛山樵
"Le Zhong" 樂仲
"Le Zhongshan" 樂仲贍
lei yu qing 累於情
Li Boyuan 李伯元
Li Gongzuo 李公佐
Li Ping'er 李平兒
Li sheng liuyi tianyuan 李生六一天緣
"Li Siniang" 李四娘
Li Wan 李紈
Li Xiangjun 李香君
Li Yu 李漁
Li Zhi 李贄
"Liancheng" 連城
liang 良
Liang Desheng 梁德繩
Liang Qichao 梁啟超
liangzhi 良知
Lianqing 蓮卿
"Lianxiang" 蓮香
Lianxiang ban 憐香伴
Liaozhai zhiyi 聊齋誌異
Lin Daiyu 林黛玉
Lin Lan Xiang 林蘭香
Lin Shufang 林淑芳
Lingnan yishi 嶺南逸史
Lingxiao 靈簫
Liu Mengmei 柳夢梅
Liu Qiuhen 柳秋痕
Liu Rushi 柳如是
Liu Xufeng 劉栩鳳
Liuhua meng 榴花夢
longluo 籠絡
longyang 龍陽
Lü Bicheng 呂碧城
Lu Shu 陸書
Lu Song 陸嵩
Lu Sulan 錄素蘭
"Lü Wubing" 呂無病
Lu Xiangshan 陸象山
Lu Xuan 陸烜
Lu Xun 魯迅
Lu Yitong 魯一同
Lü Zhan'en 呂湛恩
Luo Zifu 羅子富
luopo caizi 落魄才子
"Ma Jiefu" 馬介甫
mai zai Shanghaile 賣在上海了
"Maiyoulang duzhan huakui" 賣油郎獨占花魁
Manjianghong 滿江紅
Mao Xiang 冒襄
Mei Ziyu 梅子玉
meiren duoluo, mingshi kanke 美人墮落,名士坎坷
Meng Lijun 孟麗君
Mengmeng xiansheng 夢夢先生
Mengying yuan 夢影緣
menmen 悶悶
miao miao miao 妙妙妙
milian 迷戀

mingdan　名旦

mingji　名妓

mingshi　名士

mu xuan shen jing　目眩神驚

Mudan ting　牡丹亭

Nanke jun　南柯郡

"Nanke taishou zhuan"　南柯太守傳

nannü bingzhong　男女並重

Nao hua cong　鬧花叢

neimei　內媚

Ni ke ai ta? . . . Wo ai ta　你可愛他？
　. . . 我愛他.

ni yu zhifen　溺於脂粉

niaonuo duozi　嫋娜多姿

"Nie Yinniang"　聶隱娘

Niehai hua　孽海花

Niu Aiqing　鈕愛卿

nuli xingzhi　奴隸性質

Nüwa shi　女媧石

nüxia　女俠

Nüyu hua　女獄花

pa po　怕婆

Pan Jinlian　潘金蓮

Pan Qiguan　潘其觀

Pei Rang　佩攘

Pei Xing　裴鉶

Peng Zhenyin　彭貞隱

piaojie zhinan　嫖界指南

piaojing　嫖經

pin xizi　姘戲子

pingdeng　平等

Pinhua baojian　品花寶鑑

Pu Songling　蒲松齡

qi　妻

Qi Yunsou　齊韻叟

Qian Qianyi　錢謙益

Qian Zheng　錢徵

Qian Zigang　錢子剛

qiao　敲

"Qiaoniang"　巧娘

qibing　奇兵

qichang baduan qiuqiu dandan de daile
　dao you taniangde yidaqun xiaodan

七長八短球球蛋蛋的帶了倒有他娘
的一大群小旦

qie　妾

Qiguan　琪官

Qilou chongmeng　綺樓重夢

Qin Keqing　秦可卿

Qin Zichen　秦子忱

qing　情

qingdai meiren　輕待美人

qingfu　輕浮

Qingjiang　清江

Qingke ting　青柯亭

Qinglou meng　青樓夢

Qingshi leilue　情史類略

Qingwen　晴雯

qinü　奇女

Qiongyu　瓊玉

qiqie chengqun　妻妾成群

qiqie fangwei zhi le yi lingluejinle　妻妾
　房帷之樂已領略盡了

qiqie zhidu　妻妾制度

Qiu Xinru　邱心如

Qu Bingyun　屈秉筠

quanshu　權術

rengjiu xiao er buyan　仍舊笑而不言

renjiaren　人家人

renmian taohua zhi hen　人面桃花之
　恨

renpin　人品

rensheng diyi leye　人生第一樂業

rensheng zhi zhili　人生之至理

rouma　肉麻

"Ruiyun"　瑞雲

Rulin waishi　儒林外史

Sai Jinhua　賽金花

saile tade kou'er　賽了他的口兒

Sanfen meng quanzhuan　三分夢全傳

sanren tongxin　三人同心

"Sanshi liu yuanyang puxia"　三十六鴛
　鴦譜下

Sanxia wuyi　三俠五義

se　色

"Shang Sanguan"　商三官

"Shaonü"　邵女
Shen Cai　沈彩
Shen Fu　沈復
Shen Shanbao　沈善寶
Shen Xiaohong　沈小紅
Shenbao　申報
shengyi bense　生意本色
shenpin　神品
"Shi Qingxu"　石清虛
shi shi qiu shi　實事求是
Shi Tianran　石天然
Shisan mei　十三妹
shuaishi　衰世
Shuanglin　雙林
"Shuchi"　書痴
shudaizi　書呆子
Shunhua　舜華
sihun yizhen　廝混一陣
siwen qiangdiao　斯文腔調
sixin aimu　私心愛慕
Songyin manlu　淞隱漫錄
Su Huifang　蘇惠芳
Su Shi　蘇軾
Su Yunlan　蘇韻蘭
Sun Deying　孫德英
Sun Jiazhen　孫家振
Suyu　素玉
Taichisheng　太痴生
Taizhou　泰州
tanci　彈詞
Tang Xianzu　湯顯祖
Tao Yufu　陶玉甫
Taohua ying　桃花影
taoren　討人
Taoyuan wenlu waibian　弢園文錄外編
Tian Chunhang　田春航
Tianxiang　天香
Tianyuan qiyu　天緣奇遇
Tianzhu jiao　天主教
tiao cao　跳槽
tiaodou　挑逗
Tiehua xianshi　鐵花仙史
titie　體貼

tongbao　同胞
tongjufa　同居法
tongxin　童心
tou　偷
Tu Mingzhu　屠明珠
waijiao shouduan　外交手段
Wang Boshen　王伯神
Wang Dao　王導
Wang Duanshu　王端淑
Wang Gen　王艮
"Wang Guian"　王桂菴
Wang Ji　王幾
Wang Lanzhi　王蘭沚
Wang Liansheng　王蓮生
Wang Tao　王韜
Wang Yangming　王陽明
Wanguo fengsu kaolue　萬國風俗考略
Wanguo jinzheng kao　萬國近政考
wanwu ru sanqian, yiqing wei xian-
　suo　萬物如散錢, 一情為線索
Wanyan Yun Zhu　完顏惲珠
Wei Chizhu　韋痴珠
Wei Xiaxian　衛霞仙
Wei Xiuren　魏秀仁
Wei Yuan　魏源
Wei Zi'an　魏子安
weiwei ruirui　葳葳蕤蕤
Wen Junyu　文君玉
Wen Kang　文康
Wen Suchen　文素臣
wenming　文明
wenrou　溫柔
wensheng　瘟生
wo bugai yuyan jianli　我不該語言尖
　利
wo yi bi lao　我逸彼勞
wo zhidaole　我知道了
woyi　倭夷
Wu Jianren　吳趼人
Wu jin yu zhuan　五金魚傳
Wu Sangui　吳三桂
Wu Weiye　吳偉業
Wu Wushan　吳吳山

Wu Xuexiang 吳雪香
Wu Zetian 吳則天
wu zhangfu qi 無丈夫氣
Wuke 五可
Xi Shiyi 系十一
Xia Jingqu 夏敬渠
xianggong 相公
"Xiangu" 仙谷
"Xiangyu" 香玉
"Xianren dao" 仙人島
xiantian benxing chizi zhi xin 先天本
　性赤子之心
"Xianü" 俠女
xiao er buyan 笑而不言
xiao hun 銷魂
"Xiaocui" 小翠
xiaodan 小旦
xiaoqi 小氣
"Xiaoxie" 小謝
Xiaoyaozi 逍遙子
Xiaoyu 小鈺
"Xiaoyun yishi" 小雲軼事
Xiashang 霞裳
Xie Qian 謝遷
"Xie Xiao'e zhuan" 謝小娥傳
Xie Zhangting 謝章鋌
xienian 邪念
xiguo funü 西國婦女
"Xihu zhu" 西湖主
Ximen Qing 西門慶
xindang 新黨
xinfa gezhijia 新法格致家
"Xing Ziyi" 邢子儀
Xinghua tian 杏花天
Xingshi hengyan 醒世恆言
Xingshi yinyuan zhuan 醒世姻緣傳
Xinlingxue 心靈學
xinlixue 心理學
xinwen 新聞
xinxu koufei 心許口非
Xiren 襲人
xiucai 秀才
Xu Honglou meng 續紅樓夢

Xu Honglou meng gao 續紅樓夢稿
Xu Honglou meng xinbian 續紅樓夢
　新編
"Xu Shuangfu" 徐雙芙
Xu Zhenya 徐枕亞
Xu Ziyun 徐子雲
Xue Pan 薛蟠
Xue Yue Mei quanzhuan 雪月梅全傳
Xun fang yaji 尋芳雅集
Yaguan lou 雅觀樓
"Yan Exian" 嚴蕚仙
Yan Huasheng 顏華生
Yang Shuangqiong 洋雙瓊
yangchuan 洋船
yanghuo 洋貨
yangshang 洋商
yangyan 洋煙
yangyao 洋藥
Yangzhou huafang lu 揚州畫舫錄
yanyou 艷遊
yanyu 艷遇
Yao Jichun 姚季蓴
yao'ni 幺二
yeben 夜奔
"Yecha guo" 夜叉國
"Yegou" 野狗
"Yelai xiang" 夜來香
Yesou puyan 野叟曝言
"Yi bing zhi ji zhuyi" 乙丙之際著議
yi jian ru gu 一見如故
yi lai shen shou, fan lai zhang kou 衣來
　伸手, 飯來張口
yi lao mai lao 倚老賣老
yi seshen shi ren 以色身示人
yi yi dai lao 以逸待勞
"Yici" 㜝詞
yidongle xingqing 移動了性情
yifu duoqi 一夫多妻
yihe quan 義和拳
yihe tuan 義和團
Yihui 奕繪
yinci 淫詞
yindang 淫蕩

yinfu　淫婦
Ying'er　鶯兒
yiqi shuqie　一妻數妾
yiqie dou yao gongping　一切都要公平
yituan siyu choumen qise　一團思慾愁
　　悶氣色
yiwei waichan　一味歪纏
"Yong shi"　咏史
You Erjie　尤二姐
You Sanjie　尤三姐
youtou huanao　油頭花腦
yu　欲
yu　御
Yu Da　俞達
Yu Dafu　郁達夫
Yu lian huan　玉連環
Yu Qi　于七
yu shao fu qingchi　余少負情痴
Yuan Hongdao　袁宏道
Yuan Mei　袁枚
Yuan You　袁猷
Yuan Zhongdao　袁中道
"Yuandao"　原道
Yuanpu　袁浦
Yuanyang　鴛鴦
Yuchuan yuan　玉釧緣
Yuesu　月素
yuli　餘瀝
Yuli hun　玉黎魂
Yuling shanguan　羽陵山館
Yun　蕓
"Yunluo gongzhu"　雲羅公主
Zaisheng yuan　再生緣
Zaizao tian　再造天
Zeng Pu　曾朴
Zengbu Honglou meng　增補紅樓夢
zhan　沾
Zhang Ailing　張愛玲
Zhang Chunfan　張春帆
Zhang Henshui　張恨水

Zhang Huizhen　張惠貞
Zhang Jinfeng　張金鳳
Zhang Qiugu　章秋谷
Zhang Taiyan　章太炎
Zhang Weiping　張維屏
Zhang Yaosun　張曜孫
Zhang Zhujun　張竹君
Zhang Zhupo　張竹坡
zhanzhi　粘滯
Zhao Erbao　趙二寶
Zhao Puzhai　趙樸齋
zheng qi　爭氣
Zheng Yimei　鄭逸梅
zhenghong　征鴻
zhengzhengde wangzhe　怔怔的望着
zhi yao meimei guoyidequ jiu shile　只
　　要妹妹過意得去就是了
zhiji　知己
zhishi　支使
zhong qing　種情
Zhong qing liji　鍾情麗集
zhongyuan wanli wu shengqi, xiagu
　　gangchang sheng nü'er　中原萬里無
　　生氣, 俠骨剛腸生女兒
Zhou Shuangyu　周雙玉
Zhou Shuangzhu　周雙珠
zhu　貯
Zhu Shuren　朱淑人
"Zhu Suiliang"　楮遂良
zhuangyuan　狀元
zhuguanle Shanghai　住慣了上海
"Zhuqing"　竹青
Zhuxue zhai　鑄雪齋
zidi shu　子弟書
zijiaren　自家人
Zijuan　紫鵑
Zixu ji　子虛記
Zou Tao　鄒弢
zuo shengyi　做生意

Bibliography

Altenburger, Roland. "The Sword or the Needle: The Female Knight-Errant (*Xia*) in Traditional Chinese Fiction." Habilitationsschrift, University of Zurich, 2000.

Bao Zhenpei. *Qingdai nüzuojia tanci xiaoshuo lungao*. Tianjin: Tianjin shehui kexueyuan chubanshe, 2001.

Bracher, Mark. "On the Psychological and Social Functions of Language: Lacan's Theory of the Four Discourses." In Mark Bracher et al., eds., *Lacanian Theory of Discourse: Subject, Structure, and Society*, pp. 107–128. New York: New York University Press, 1994.

Bretschneider, Peter. *Polygyny: A Cross-Cultural Study*. Stockholm: Almqvist and Wiksell, 1995.

Cao Xueqin. *Honglou meng*. Beijing: Renmin wenxue chubanshe, 1982.

———. *Honglou meng baishihui jiaoben*. Hong Kong: Zhonghua shuju, 1985.

———. *Honglou meng sanjia pingben*. Shanghai: Guji chubanshe, 1988.

Carlitz, Katharine. "Desire and Writing in the Late Ming Play *Parrot Island*." In Widmer and Chang, eds., *Writing Women in Late Imperial China*, pp. 101–130. Stanford, Calif.: Stanford University Press, 1997.

Chamie, Joseph. "Polygyny and Arabs." *Populations Studies* 40.1 (Mar. 1986): 55–66.

Chang, Chun-shu, and Shelley Hsueh-lun Chang. *Redefining History: Ghosts, Spirits, and Human Society in Pu Sung-ling's World, 1640–1715*. Ann Arbor: University of Michigan Press, 1998.

Chang, Kang-i Sun. "The Idea of the Mask in Wu Wei-yeh (1609–71)." *Harvard Journal of Asiatic Studies* 48.2 (1988): 289–320.

———. *The Late-Ming Poet Ch'en Tzu-lung: Crises of Love and Loyalism*. New Haven, Conn.: Yale University Press, 1991.

———. "Ming and Qing Anthologies of Women Poetry and Their Selection Strategies." In Ellen Widmer and Kang-i Sun Chang, eds., *Writing Women in Late Imperial China*, pp. 147–170. Stanford, Calif.: Stanford University Press, 1997.

Chang Xueying. "Ershi shiji *Ernü yingxiong zhuan* yanjiu huigu." *Neimenggu shida xuebao (zhexue shehui kexue ban)* 30.6 (Dec. 2001): 3–6.

Chen Angni. "You *Hou Honglou meng* ji qi xushu tantao Jia Baoyu zhi juese bianqian." *Guowen tiandi* 9.7 (1993): 33–44.

Chen Bohai, Yuan Jin, et al. *Shanghai jindai wenxue shi.* Shanghai: Shanghai renmin chubanshe, 1993.

Chen Sen. *Pinhua baojian.* Taibei: Guiguan tushu gufen youxian gongsi, 1986.

———. *Pinhua baojian.* Edition in Gest Library (n.d.), Princeton University.

Chen Shaohai. *Honglou fumeng.* Beijing: Beijing daxue chubanshe, 1988.

Chen Yinke. *Chen Yinke xiansheng wenshi lunji.* Hong Kong: Wenwen chubanshe, 1973.

Chen Yiyuan. *Yuan Ming zhongpian chuanqi xiaoshuo yanjiu.* Hong Kong: Xuefeng wenhua shiye gongsi, 1997.

Chi Chongqi. "Shi lun *Huayue hen* dui *Pinhua baojian* de mofang he chaoxi." *Henan shifan xuebao (shehui kexueban)* 4 (1997): 53–131.

Chow, Rey. *Women and Chinese Modernity: The Politics of Reading between West and East.* Minneapolis: University of Minnesota Press, 1991.

Cochran, Terry. *Twilight of the Literary: Figures of Thought in the Age of Print.* Cambridge, Mass.: Harvard University Press, 2001.

Cohen, Paul. *Between Tradition and Modernity: Wang T'ao and Reform in Late Ch'ing China.* Cambridge, Mass.: Harvard University Press, 1974.

Copjec, Joan. *Imagine There's No Woman: Ethics and Sublimation.* Cambridge, Mass.: MIT Press, 2002.

———. *Read My Desire: Lacan against the Historicists.* Cambridge, Mass.: MIT Press, 1995.

Dikötter, Frank. *Sex, Culture and Modernity in China.* Honolulu: University of Hawai'i Press, 1995.

Ding, Naifei. "Concubinage and New Feminist Imaginaries." Talk presented at the Sixth International Super-Slim Conference on Politics of Gender/Sexuality, at National Central University, November 27, 2004.

———. "Feminist Knots: Sex and Domestic Work in the Shadow of the Bondmaid-Concubine." *Inter-Asia Cultural Studies* 3.3 (2002): 449–467.

———. *Obscene Things: Sexual Politics in Jin Ping Mei.* Durham, N.C.: Duke University Press, 2002.

Ding Yizhuang. *Manzude funü shenghuo yu hunyin zhidu yanjiu.* Beijing: Beijing daxue chubanshe, 1999.

Dong Wencheng. "*Jin Yun Qiao zhuan* dui *Honglou meng* yishu chuangxin de duochong yingxiang." Two parts. *Honglou meng xuekan* 3 (1999): 178–195; 4 (1999): 247–272.

Edwards, Louise. "Representations of Women and Social Power in Eighteenth-Century China: The Case of Wang Xifeng." *Late Imperial China* 14.1 (1993): 34–59.

———. "Women in *Honglou meng:* Prescriptions of Purity in the Femininity of Qing Dynasty China." *Modern China* 16.4 (1990): 407–429.

Elman, Benjamin. *Classicism, Politics, and Kinship: The Ch'ang-chou School of New Text Confucianism in Late Imperial China.* Berkeley: University of California Press, 1990.

Epstein, Maram. *Competing Discourses: Orthodoxy, Authenticity, and Engendered Meanings in Late Imperial Chinese Fiction.* Cambridge, Mass.: Harvard University Press, 2001.

——. "Reflections of Desire: The Poetics of Gender in *Dream of the Red Chamber*." *Nan Nü: Men, Women, and Gender in China* 1.1 (1999): 64–106.

Evans, Dylan. *An Introductory Dictionary of Lacanian Psychoanalysis*. London: Routledge, 1996.

Feng Menglong. *Qingshi leilue*. Changsha: Yuelu shushe, 1984.

——. Li Tien-yi, ed. *Xingshi hengyan*. Taibei: Shijie shuju, 1959.

Feng Qiyong et al., eds. *Honglou meng da cidian*. Beijing: Wenhua yishu, 1990.

Finnane, Antonia. *Speaking of Yangzhou: A Chinese City, 1550–1850*. Cambridge, Mass.: Harvard University Press, 2004.

Fong, Grace. "Alternative Modernities, or a Classical Woman of Modern China: The Challenging Trajectory of Lü Bicheng's (1883–1943) Life and Song Lyrics." *Nan Nü: Men, Women, and Gender in China* 6.1 (2004): 12–59.

——. *Herself an Author: Gender, Agency, and Writing in Late Imperial China*. Honolulu: University of Hawai'i Press, 2008.

——. "Writing from a Side Room of Her Own: The Literary Vocation of Concubines in Ming-Qing China." *Hsiang Lectures on Chinese Poetry*, vol. 1, pp. 41–63. Montreal: Centre for East Asian Research, McGill University, 2001.

——. "Writing Self and Writing Lives: Shen Shanbao's (1808–1862) Gendered Auto/biographical Practices." *Nan Nü: Men, Women, and Gender in China* 2.2 (2000): 259–303.

Francis, Sing-chen Lydia. "Body and Identity in *Liaozhai zhiyi*." *Nan Nü: Men, Women, and Gender in China* 4.2 (2002): 206–231.

Goldman, Andrea Sue. "The Nun Who Wouldn't Be: Representations of Female Desire in Two Performance Genres of *Si Fan*.'" *Late Imperial China* 22.1 (2001): 71–138.

——. "Opera in the City: Theatrical Performance and Urbanite Aesthetics in Beijing 1770–1900." Ph.D. dissertation, University of California, Berkeley, 2005.

Gong Zizhen. Wan Zunyi, ed. *Gong Zizhen Jihai zashi zhu*. Beijing: Zhonghua shuju, 1978.

Gu Bingquan. *Shanghai yangchang zhuzhici*. Shanghai: Shanghai guji chubanshe, 1996.

Gu Meigao. *Liaozhai zhiyi yu Pu Songling*. Tianjin: Tianjin guji chubanshe, 1988.

Gu Taiqing. *Honglou meng ying*. Beijing: Beijing daxue chubanshe, 1988.

Guichuzi. *Honglou meng bu*. Beijing: Beijing daxue chubanshe, 1988.

Guo Yanli. *Zhongguo jindai wenxue fazhan shi*. Jinan: Shandong jiaoyu chubanshe, 1990.

Haipu zhuren. *Xu Honglou meng xinbian*. Beijing: Beijing daxue chubanshe, 1990.

Haitian duxiaozi. *Nüwa shi*. In Lingnan yuyi nüshi et al., *Dongou nühaojie* [etc.]. Nanchang: Baihuazhou wenyi chubanshe, 1991.

Hakansson, Thomas. "Family Structure, Bridewealth, and Environment in Eastern Africa: A Comparative Study of House-Property Systems." *Ethnology* 28.2 (1989): 117–134.

Han Bangqing. *Haishanghua liezhuan*. Changsha: Hainan chubanshe, 1997 (originally 1925).

————. Eileen Chang, trans. (revised and edited by Eva Hung). *Singsong Girls of Shanghai*. New York: Columbia University Press, 2005.

Hanan, Patrick. "The Bible as Chinese Literature: Medhurst, Wang Tao, and the Delegates' Version." *Harvard Journal of Asiatic Studies* 63.1 (2003): 197–239.

————. *"Fengyue Meng* and the Courtesan Novel." *Harvard Journal of Asiatic Studies* 58.2 (1998): 345–372.

Hanshang Mengren. *Fengyue meng.* Beijing: Beijing daxue chubanshe, 1990.

Hawkes, David, trans. *The Story of the Stone.* Harmondsworth: Penguin Books, 1977.

Henriot, Christian. *Belles de Shanghai: Prostitution et sexualité en Chine aux XIXe–XXe siècles.* Paris: CNRS Editions, 1997.

Hershatter, Gail. *Dangerous Pleasures: Prostitution and Modernity in Twentieth-Century Shanghai.* Berkeley: University of California Press, 1997.

Howland, D. R. *Borders of Chinese Civilization: Geography and History at Empire's End.* Durham, N.C.: Duke University Press, 1996.

Hsia, C. T. "Hsu Chen-ya's *Yu-li hun:* An Essay in Literary History and Criticism." *Renditions* 17 and 18 (1982): 199–240.

Hu Shi. "Hu Shi xu." In Han Bangqing, *Haishanghua liezhuan,* pp. 1–18.

Hu Siaochen. *Cainü cheye weimian.* Taibei: Maitian renwen, 2003.

————. "Pinfan riyong yu daotong lunli—lun *Ernü yingxiong zhuan.*" In Wang Ayling, ed. *Ming Qing wenxue yu sixiang zhong zhi zhuti yishi yu shehui, wenxue pian,* pp. 589–638. Taipei: Institute of Chinese Literature and Philosophy, 2004.

Hu Ying. "Re-Configuring Nei/Wai: Writing the Woman Traveler in the Late Qing." *Late Imperial China* 18.1 (1997): 72–99.

————. *Tales of Translation: Composing the New Woman in China, 1899–1918.* Stanford, Calif.: Stanford University Press, 2000.

Huang Jinzhu. "*Honglou meng* de jindai xushu." *Taibei Shiyuan xuebao* 9 (1996): 171–196.

Huang, Martin. "From Caizi to Yingxiong: Imagining Masculinities in Two Qing Novels, *Yesou puyan* and *Sanfen meng quan zhuan.*" *Chinese Literature: Essays, Articles, and Reviews* 25 (2003): 61–100.

————. *Literati and Self-re/presentation: Autobiographical Sensibility in the Eighteenth-century Chinese Novel.* Stanford, Calif.: Stanford University Press, 1995.

————. *Negotiating Masculinities in Late Imperial China.* Honolulu: University of Hawai'i Press, 2006.

————. "Sentiments of Desire: Thoughts on the Cult of Qing in Ming-Qing Literature." *Chinese Literature: Essays, Articles, and Reviews* 20 (1998): 153–184.

————, ed. *Snakes' Legs: Sequels, Continuations, Rewritings, and Chinese Fiction.* Honolulu: University of Hawai'i Press, 2004.

Huayue chiren. *Honglou huanmeng.* Beijing: Beijing daxue chubanshe, 1990.

Hummel, Arthur W. *Eminent Chinese of the Ch'ing Period.* Washington, D.C.: U.S. Government Printing Office, 1943.

Huntington, Rania. "Foxes and Sex in Late Imperial Chinese Narrative." *Nan Nü: Men, Women, and Gender in China* 2.1 (2000): 78–128.

Huters, Ted. *Bringing the World Home: Appropriating the West in Late Qing and Early Republican China.* Honolulu: University of Hawai'i Press, 2005.

Idema, Wilt, and Beata Grant. *The Red Brush: Writing Women of Imperial China.* Cambridge, Mass.: Harvard University Press, 2004.

Jaschok, Maria. *Concubines and Bond-servants: A Social History.* London: Zed Books, 1988.

Judge, Joan. "Blended Wish Images: Chinese and Western Exemplary Women at the Turn of the Twentieth Century." *Nan Nü: Men, Women, and Gender in China* 6.1 (2004): 102–135.

———. "The Culturally Contested Student Body: *Nü Xuesheng* at the Turn of the Twentieth Century." In Doris Croissant, Catherine Vance Yeh, and Joshua S. Mostow, eds., *Performing "Nation": Gender Politics in Literature, Theater, and the Visual Arts of China and Japan, 1880–1940,* pp. 105–132. Leiden and Boston: Brill, 2008.

Kang, Wenqing. *Obsession: Male Same-Sex Relations in China, 1900–1950.* Hong Kong: Hong Kong University Press, 2009.

Karl, Rebecca. *Staging the World: Chinese Nationalism at the Turn of the Twentieth Century.* Durham, N.C.: Duke University Press, 2002.

Kay, Sarah. "Desire and Subjectivity." In Simon Gaunt and Sarah Kay, eds., *The Troubadours: An Introduction,* pp. 212–227. Cambridge, Mass.: Cambridge University Press, 1999.

———. *Subjectivity in Troubadour Poetry.* Cambridge, Mass.: Cambridge University Press, 1990.

———. *Žižek: A Critical Introduction.* London: Polity, 2003.

Kircher, Francois (pseudonym of Francois Wildt). *Les trente-six stratagèmes: traité secret de stratégie chinoise.* Paris: Editions du Rocher, 2001.

Ko, Dorothy. *Cinderella's Sisters: A Revisionist History of Footbinding.* Berkeley: University of California Press, 2005.

———. *Every Step a Lotus: Shoes for Bound Feet.* Berkeley: University of California Press, 2001.

———. *Teachers of the Inner Chamber.* Stanford, Calif.: Stanford University Press, 1994.

———. "The Written Word and the Bound Foot." In Widmer and Chang, eds., *Writing Women in Late Imperial China,* pp. 74–100. Stanford, Calif.: Stanford University Press, 1997.

Lacan, Jacques. Alan Sheridan, trans. *Écrits: A Selection.* New York: W. W. Norton, 1977.

———. *Encore.* Paris: Editions du Seuil, 1975.

———. Alan Sheridan, trans. *The Four Fundamental Concepts of Psychoanalysis.* New York: W. W. Norton, 1981.

———. Bruce Fink, trans. *On Feminine Sexuality: The Limits of Love and Knowledge.* New York: Norton and Company, 1998.

Langhuan shanqiao. *Bu Honglou meng.* Beijing: Beijing daxue chubanshe, 1988.

————. *Zengbu Honglou meng.* Beijing: Beijing daxue chubanshe, 1988.

Lei Yong. "Xiaxie xiaoshuo de yanbian ji qi chuangzuo xintai." *Zhongguo gudai jindai wenxue yanjiu* 2 (1997): 131–136.

Li Boyuan. *Haitian hongxue ji.* In *Li Boyuan quanji*, vol. 3. Nanjing: Jiangsu guji chubanshe, 1997.

Li Fang. *Taiping guangji.* Beijing: Zhonghua shuju, 1986.

Li Ting. "Lun *Ernü yingxiong zhuan* zhong de manzu nüxingguan." *Manzu yanjiu* 2 (2003): 72–78.

Li, Wai-yee. *Enchantment and Disenchantment: Love and Illusion in Chinese Literature.* Princeton, N.J.: Princeton University Press, 1993.

————. "Heroic Transformations: Women and National Trauma in Early Qing Literature." *Harvard Journal of Asiatic Studies* 59.2 (1999): 363–443.

————. "The Late Ming Courtesan: Invention of a Cultural Ideal." In Widmer and Chang, eds., *Writing Women in Late Imperial China*, pp. 46–73. Stanford, Calif.: Stanford University Press, 1997.

Li, Xiaorong. "Engendering Heroism: Ming-Qing Women's Song Lyrics to the Tune Man Jiang Hong." *Nan Nü: Men, Women, and Gender in China* 7.1 (2005): 1–39.

Li Zhongchang. *Gudai xiaoshuo xushu manhua.* Shenyang: Liaoning jiaoyu chubanshe, 1993.

Lin Wei. *Qingdai xiaoshuo lungao.* Beijing: Beijing guangbo xueyuan chubanshe, 2000.

Lin Yixuan. *Wu cai ke bu tian: Honglou meng xushu yanjiu.* Taibei: Wenjin chubanshe, 1999.

Lingnan yuyi nüshi, et al. *Dongou nühaojie etc.* Nanchang: Baihuazhou wenyi chubanshe, 1991.

Liu Bannong. "Du *Haishanghua liezhuan*." In Han Bangqing, *Haishanghua liezhuan*, pp. 19–33. Changsha: Hainan chubanshe, 1997 (originally 1925).

Liu, Lydia. *Translingual Practice: Literature, National Culture, and Translated Modernity: China, 1900–1937.* Stanford, Calif.: Stanford University Press, 1995.

Liu Oubo. "Huayue hen zuozhe zhi sixiang." In Wang Junnian, ed., *Zhongguo jindai wenxue lunwenji, 1919–1949, xiaoshuo juan,* pp. 182–193. Beijing: Zhongguo shehui kexue chubanshe, 1988.

Liu Shide et al. *Zhongguo gudai xiaoshuo baike quanshu.* Beijing: Zhongguo dabaike quanshu, 1993.

Liu Yiqing. *Shishuo xinyu jiaojian.* Beijing: Zhonghua shuju, 1984.

Lu Dahuang, ed. *Pu Songling ji.* Beijing: Zhonghua shuju, 1962.

————. *Pu Songling nianpu.* Jinan: Qilu shushe, 1980.

Lu Xun. *A Brief History of Chinese Fiction.* Beijing: Foreign Languages Press, 1976.

————. *Erxin ji.* Shanghai: Hezhong shudian, 1932.

Ma Ruifang. *Pu Songling zhuan.* Beijing: Renmin chubanshe, 1986.

Mackerras, Colin. *Chinese Drama: A Historical Survey.* Beijing: New World Press, 1990.

———. *Chinese Theater: From Its Origins to the Present Day*. Honolulu: University of Hawai'i Press, 1983.

———. *The Chinese Theatre in Modern Times: From 1840 to the Present Day*. London: Thames and Hudson, 1975.

Mann, Susan. *Precious Records: Women in China's Long Eighteenth Century*. Stanford, Calif.: Stanford University Press, 1997.

Mather, Richard B. *A New Account of Tales of the World*. Minneapolis: University of Minnesota Press, 1976.

McMahon, Keith. *Causality and Containment in Seventeenth-century Chinese Fiction*. Leiden: Brill Publishers, 1988.

———. "The Concept of Chinese Polygamy." In Olga Lomova, ed., *Paths to Modernity*, pp. 127–147. Prague: Karolinum Press, 2008.

———, trans. Li Yuzhen, ed. "Cong Lagangde xingbie chayi lilun kan wanQing Zhongguo" [Lacan's Theory of Sexual Difference in Late Imperial China]. *Tsinghua Journal of Chinese Literature* 1 (Sept., 2007): 294–313.

———. "Cultural Destiny and Polygynous Love in Zou Tao's *Shanghai Dust*." *Chinese Literature: Essays, Articles, and Reviews* 27 (2005): 117–135.

———. "Eliminating Traumatic Antinomies: Sequels to *Honglou meng*." In Martin Huang, ed., *Snakes' Legs: Sequels, Continuations, Rewritings, and Chinese Fiction*, pp. 98–115. Honolulu: University of Hawai'i Press, 2004.

———. *The Fall of the God of Money: Opium Smoking in Nineteenth-century China*. Lanham, Md.: Rowman and Littlefield, 2002.

———. "Fleecing the Male Customer in Shanghai Brothels of the 1890s." *Late Imperial China* 23.2 (2002): 1–32.

———. "*Huayue hen* zhongde aiqing yu wenhua fuxin." In Chen Pingyuan, Wang Dewei, and Shang Wei, eds., *Lishi chuancheng yu wenhua chuangxin*, pp. 314–322. Wuhan: Hubei jiaoyu chubanshe, 2001.

———. "Love Martyrs and Love Cheaters at the End of the Chinese Empire." In Doris Croissant, Catherine Vance Yeh, and Joshua S. Mostow, eds., *Performing "Nation": Gender Politics in Literature, Theater, and the Visual Arts of China and Japan, 1880-1940*, pp. 135–142. Leiden and Boston: Brill, 2008.

———. *Misers, Shrews, and Polygamists: Sexuality and Male/Female Relations in Eighteenth-century Chinese Fiction*. Durham, N.C.: Duke University Press, 1995.

———. "Opium and Sexuality in Late Qing Fiction." *Nan Nü: Men, Women, and Gender in Early and Imperial China* 2.1 (2000): 1–51.

———. "Opium Smoking and Modern Subjectivity." *Postcolonial Studies* 8.2 (2005): 165–180.

———. Xu Huilin, trans., Li Yuzhen, ed. "Qinüzide nanban yu nüxing qizhide bentilun" [The Male Consort of the Remarkable Woman and the Ontology of the Feminine]. *Tsinghua Journal of Chinese Literature* 1 (Sept. 2007): 315–326.

———. "The Remarkable Woman in Pu Songling's *Liaozhai zhiyi*." In Paolo Santangelo (with Donatella Guida), ed., *Love, Hatred, and Other Passions: Questions and Themes on Emotions in Chinese Civilization*, pp. 212–228. Leiden: Brill, 2006.

——. Review of Dorothy Ko, *Cinderella's Sisters: a Revisionist History of Footbinding*. *Nan Nü: Men, Women and Gender in Early and Imperial China* 9.2 (2007): 395–400.

——. Liu Mengzhe, trans. "Xiandai Zhongguo qianxide xingxiang jiegou—Zhongguo nanxingde duoqi zhengzhi" [The Structure of Sexuality in China on the Verge of Modernity]. *Tsinghua Journal of Chinese Literature* 1 (Sept. 2007): 327–349.

Meng, Liuxi. *Poetry as Power: Yuan Mei's Female Disciple Qu Bingyun (1767–1810)*. Lanham, Md.: Lexington Books, 2007.

Mengmeng xiansheng. *Honglou yuanmeng*. Beijing: Beijing daxue chubanshe, 1988.

Ouyang Jian. *WanQing xiaoshuo shi*. Hangzhou: Zhejiang guji chubanshe, 1997.

—— et al., eds. *Zhongguo tongsu xiaoshuo zongmu tiyao*. Beijing: Zhongguo wenlian chubanshe, 1990.

Pflugfelder, Gregory M. *Cartographies of Desire: Male-Male Sexuality in Japanese Discourse, 1600–1950*. Berkeley: University of California Press, 1999.

Pruitt, Ida. *A Daughter of Han: The Autobiography of a Chinese Working Woman*. Stanford, Calif.: Stanford University Press, 1967.

Pu Songling. Zhang Youhe, ed. *Liaozhai zhiyi*. Shanghai, Shanghai guji chubanshe, 1978.

——. Denis C. Mair and Victor H. Mair, trans. *Strange Tales from Make-do Studio*. Beijing: Foreign Languages Press, 1989.

Qian Mu. *Zhongguo jin sanbai nian xueshu shi*. Taipei: Shangwu yinshu guan, 1976 (originally 1937).

Qian, Nanxiu. "'Borrowing Foreign Mirrors and Candles to Illuminate Chinese Civilization': Xue Shaohui's Moral Vision in the *Biographies of Foreign Women*." *Nan Nü: Men, Women, and Gender in China* 6.1 (2004): 60–101.

Qian Zhonglian. *Mengtiao'an zhuanzhu erzhong*. Beijing: Zhongguo shehuikexue chubanshe, 1984.

—— and Qian Xuezeng. *Qingshi sanbaishou*. Changsha: Yuelu shushe, 1994.

Qin Zichen. *Xu Honglou meng*. Beijing: Beijing daxue chubanshe, 1988.

Rong Zhaozu. "*Huayue hen* de zuozhe Wei Xiuren zhuan." In Wang Junnian, ed., *Zhongguo jindai wenxue lunwenji, 1919–1949, xiaoshuo juan*, pp. 194–206. Beijing: Zhongguo shehui kexue chubanshe, 1988.

Sanderson, Stephen K. "Explaining Monogamy and Polygyny in Human Societies: Comment on Kanazawa and Still." *Social Forces* 80.1 (2001): 329–335.

Santangelo, Paolo (with Donatella Guida), ed. *Love, Hatred, and Other Passions: Questions and Themes on Emotions in Chinese Civilization*. Leiden: Brill, 2006.

Shang, Wei. *Rulin waishi and Cultural Transformation in Late Imperial China*. Cambridge, Mass.: Harvard University Press, 2003.

Shen Fu. *Fusheng liuji*. Beijing: Renmin wenxue chubanshe, 1980.

——. Leonard Pratt and Chiang Su-hui, trans. *Six Records of a Floating Life*. Harmondsworth: Penguin Books, 1983.

Shu Wu. *Shuo meng lu*. Shanghai: Guji chubanshe, 1982.

Sommer, Mathew. "Making Sex Work: Polyandry as Survival Strategy in Qing Dynasty

China." In Bryna Goodman and Wendy Larson, eds., pp. 29–54. *Gender in Motion: Divisions of Labor and Cultural Charge in Late Imperial and Modern China*. Lanham, Md.: Rowman and Littlefield, 2005.

———. "The Penetrated Male in Late Imperial China: Judicial Constructions and Social Stigma." *Modern China* 23.2 (1997): 140–180.

———. *Sex, Law, and Society in Late Imperial China*. Stanford, Calif.: Stanford University Press, 2000.

Soulié de Morant, George. Gerald Fabian and Guy Wernham, trans. *Pei Yu Boy Actress*. San Francisco: First Alamo Square Press, 1991.

Starr, Chloe. *Red-light Novels of the Late Qing*. Leiden: Brill, 2007.

———. "Shifting Boundaries: Gender in *Pinhua baojian*." *Nan Nü: Men, Women, and Gender in China* 1.2 (1999): 268–302.

Sun Jiazhen. *Haishang fanhua meng*. Changchun: Shidai wenyi chubanshe, 1993.

Sun Kaidi. *Zhongguo tongsu xiaoshuo shumu*. Beijing: Renmin wenxue chubanshe, 1982.

Sun Qinshan, ed. *Gong Zizhen shi wen xuan*. Beijing: Renmin wenxue chubanshe, 1993.

Szonyi, Michael. "The Cult of Hu Tianbo and the Eighteenth-century Discourse of Homosexuality." *Late Imperial China* 19.1(1998): 1–25.

Tian Zechang. "Pu Songling he Chen Shuqing." *Pu Songling yanjiu jikan* 1 (1980): 264–280.

Tran, Lisa. "Concubines Under Modern Chinese Law." Ph.D. dissertation, University of California, Los Angeles, 2005.

Vitiello, Giovanni. "Exemplary Sodomites: Chivalry and Love in Late Ming Culture." *Nan Nü: Men, Women, and Gender in China* 2.2 (2000): 207–257.

———. "The Fantastic Journey of an Ugly Boy: Homosexuality and Salvation in Late Ming Pornography." *Positions* 4.2 (1996): 291–320.

———. "The Forgotten Tears of the Lord of Longyang: Late Ming Stories of Male Prostitution and Connoisseurship." In Peter Englefriet and Jan de Meyer, eds., *Linked Faiths: Essays on Chinese Religions and Traditional Culture in Honour of Kristofer Schipper*, pp. 227–247. Leiden: Brill, 2000.

Volpp, Sophie. "The Male Queen: Boy Actors and Literati Libertines." Ph.D. dissertation, Harvard University, 1995.

Wang, David Der-wei. *Fin-de-siècle Splendor: Repressed Modernities of Late Qing Fiction, 1849–1911*. Stanford, Calif.: Stanford University Press, 1997.

Wang Lanzhi. *Qilou chongmeng*. Beijing: Beijing daxue chubanshe, 1990.

Wang Qiongling. *Qingdai sida caixue xiaoshuo*. Taipei: Taiwan Shangwu yinshuguan, 1997.

Wang Tao. Wang Bin, Chen Fu, Guo Yinghai, and Li Siying, eds. *Hou liaozhai zhiyi quanyi xiangzhu*. Harbin: Heilongjiang chubanshe, 1988.

———. *Taoyuan wenlu waibian*. Shenyang: Liaoning renmin chubanshe, 1994.

Wang Zhenyuan. *Jianqi xiaoxin: xi shuo Gong Zizhen shi*. Beijing: Zhonghua shuju, 1990.

Wang Zhizhong. *Pu Songling lunji*. Beijing: Wenhua yishu chubanshe, 1990.

Wang Zhongxian. *Shanghai suyu tushuo*. Shanghai: Shanghai shudian, 1999 (original edition 1935).

Watson, Rubie. "Wives, Concubines, and Maids: Servitude and Kinship in the Hong Kong Region, 1900–1940." In Rubie S. Watson and Patricia Buckley Ebrey, eds., *Marriage and Inequality in Chinese Society*, pp. 231–255. Berkeley: University of California Press, 1991.

—— and Patricia Buckley Ebrey, eds. *Marriage and Inequality in Chinese Society*. Berkeley: University of California Press, 1991.

Wei Zi'an (Xiuren). *Huayue hen*. Fuzhou: Fujian renmin chubanshe, 1981.

Wen Kang. *Ernü yingxiong zhuan*. Jinan: Qilu shushe, 1989.

White, Douglas R. "Rethinking Polygyny: Co-wives, Codes, and Cultural Systems." *Current Anthropology* 29.4 (1988): 529–558.

Widmer, Ellen. *The Beauty and the Book: Women and Fiction in Nineteenth-century China*. Cambridge, Mass.: Harvard University Press, 2006.

——. "*Honglou meng* Sequels and Their Female Readers in Nineteenth-century China." In Martin Huang, ed., *Snakes' Legs: Sequels, Continuations, Rewritings, and Chinese Fiction*, pp. 116–142. Honolulu: University of Hawai'i Press, 2004.

——. "Inflecting Gender: Zhan Kai/Siqi Zhai's New Novels' and Courtesan Sketches." *Nan Nü: Men, Women, and Gender in China* 6.1 (2004): 136–168.

——. "Ming Loyalism and the Woman's Voice in Fiction after *Honglou meng*." In Ellen Widmer and Kang-i Sun Chang, eds., *Writing Women in Late Imperial China*, pp. 366–396. Stanford, Calif.: Stanford University Press, 1997.

——. "Xiaoqing's Literary Legacy and the Place of the Woman Writer in Late Imperial China." *Late Imperial China* 13.1 (1992): 111–155.

—— and Kang-i Sun Chang, eds. *Writing Women in Late Imperial China*. Stanford, Calif.: Stanford University Press, 1997.

Wong, Shirleen. *Kung Tzu-chen*. Boston: Twayne Publications, 1975.

Wu Cuncun. *Ming Qing shehui xing'ai fengqi*. Beijing: Renmin wenxue chubanshe, 2000.

——. "Qingdai shiren xiayou xutong fengqi xulue." *Zhongguo wenhua* 15, 16 (1997): 231–241.

Wu Liansheng et al., eds. *Wu fangyan cidian*. Beijing: Hanyu da cidian chubanshe, 1995.

Wu Weiye. *Meicun jiacangji*. Sibu congkan jibu (1680–1683). Shanghai: Shangwu yinshuguan, 1922.

Wu, Yenna. *The Chinese Virago: A Literary Theme*. Cambridge, Mass.: Harvard University Press, 1995.

Xia Jingqu. *Yesou puyan*. 1881 Piling huizhen lou edition. Beijing University Library.

Xiaoyaozi. *Hou Honglou meng*. Beijing: Beijing daxue chubanshe, 1988.

Xin Ping. *Wang Tao pingzhuan*. Shanghai: Huadong shifan daxue chubanshe, 1990.

Xu, Gary Gang. "*Flowers of Shanghai*: Visualising Ellipses and (Colonial) Absence." In

Chris Berry, ed., *Chinese Films in Focus: 25 New Takes,* pp. 104–110. London: British Film Institute, 2003.

Yang Yi. *Zhongguo xiandai xiaoshuo shi.* Beijing: Renmin chubanshe, 1986.

Yeh, Catherine Vance. "Cong shijiu shiji Shanghai ditu kan dui chengshi weilai dingyi de zhengduozhan." *Zhongguo xueshu* 1.3 (2000): 88–121.

———. "The Life-style of Four *Wenren* in Late Qing Shanghai." *Harvard Journal of Asiatic Studies* 57.2 (1997): 419–470.

———. "Reinventing Ritual: Late Qing Handbooks for Proper Customer Behavior in Shanghai Courtesan Houses." *Late Imperial China* 19.2 (1998): 1–63.

———. *Shanghai Love: Courtesans, Intellectuals, and Entertainment Culture, 1850–1910.* Seattle: University of Washington Press, 2006.

Yen, P'ing Hao. "Changing Chinese Views of Western Relations, 1840–95." In John K. Fairbank and Kwang-ching Liu, eds., *The Cambridge History of China,* vol. 11, part 2, pp. 142–201. Cambridge, Mass.: Cambridge University Press, 1989.

Yisu. *Honglou meng juan.* Taibei: Liren shuju, 1981.

———. *Honglou meng shulu.* Shanghai: Shanghai guji chubanshe, 1981.

Yu, Anthony. *Rereading the Stone: Desire and the Making of Fiction in* Dream of the Red Chamber. Princeton, N.J.: Princeton University Press, 1997.

Yu Da. *Qinglou meng.* Beijing: Beijing daxue chubanshe, 1990.

Yu Huai. Howard Levy, trans. *A Feast of Mist and Flowers.* Mimeograph. Yokohama, 1966.

Yuan Jin. "Fuchen zai shehui lishi dachaozhong—lun *Huayue hen* de yingxiang." *Shehui kexue* 4 (2005): 112–118.

Zamperini, Paola. "But I Never Learned to Waltz: The Real and Imagined Education of a Courtesan in the Late Qing." *Nan Nü: Men, Women, and Gender in China* 1.1 (1999): 107–144.

———. "Clothes That Matter: Fashioning Modernity in Late Qing Novels." *Fashion Theory* 5.2 (2001): 1–20.

———. "Lost Bodies: Images and Representations of Prostitution in Late Qing Fiction." Ph.D. dissertation, University of California, Berkeley, 1999.

Zarrow, Peter. "He Zhen and Anarcho-Feminism in China." *Journal of Asian Studies* 47.4 (1988): 796–813.

Zeitlin, Judith. *Historian of the Strange: Pu Songling and the Chinese Classical Tale.* Stanford, Calif.: Stanford University Press, 1993.

Zeng Pu. *Niehai hua.* Taibei: Sanmin shuju, 1998.

Zhang Ailing, trans. *Haishanghua kai, Haishanghua luo.* Taibei: Huangguan congshu, 1997.

———. *Zhang Ailing wencui.* Beijing: Wenhua yishu chubanshe, 2003.

Zhang Chunfan. *Jiuwei gui.* Nanchang: Baihua wenyi chubanshe, 1993.

Zhang Cixi. *Qingdai yandu liyuan shiliao.* Beijing: Zhongguo xiju chubanshe, 1991.

Zhang Hailin. *Wang Tao pingzhuan.* Nanjing: Nanjing daxue chubanshe, 1993.

Zhang Jiarong. "Guoqu guoqu yizhi lai: 80 niandai nüxing xiaoshuode qingfu shuxie." M.A. thesis, National Tsinghua University, 2006.

Zhang, Jingyuan. *Psychoanalysis in China: Literary Transformations 1919–1949*. Ithaca, N.Y.: Cornell University Press, 1992.

Zhang Yaosun. *Xu Honglou meng gao*. Beijing: Beijing daxue chubanshe, 1990.

Zhao Botao. "*Honglou meng ying* de zuoshe ji qita." *Honglou meng xuekan* 4.1 (1989): 243–251.

Zhao Jianzhong. "*Honglou meng* xushu de yuanliu shanbian ji qi yanjiu." *Honglou meng xuekan* 4 (1992): 301–335.

———. *Honglou meng xushu yanjiu*. Tianjin: Tianjin guji chubanshe, 1997.

Zhao Jingshen. *Zhongguo xiaoshuo congkao*. Jinan: Qilu shushe, 1980.

Zhu Jieqin, ed. *Gong Dingan yanjiu*. Hong Kong: Chongwen shudian, 1971.

Zhu Yixuan. *Honglou meng ziliao huibian*. Nanjing: Nankai daxue chubanshe, 1985.

———, ed. *Liaozhai zhiyi ziliao huibian*. Zhengzhou: Zhongzhou guji chubanshe, 1985.

Žižek, Slavoj, ed. *Cogito and the Unconscious*. Durham, N.C.: Duke University Press, 1998.

———. "Four Discourses, Four Subjects." In Žižek, ed., *Cogito and the Unconscious*, pp. 74–113. Durham, N.C.: Duke University Press, 1998.

———. *Looking Awry: An Introduction to Jacques Lacan through Popular Culture*. Cambridge, Mass.: MIT Press, 1997.

———. *The Metastases of Enjoyment: On Women and Causality*. London: Verso, 2005.

———. *Tarrying with the Negative: Kant, Hegel, and the Critique of Ideology*. Durham, N.C.: Duke University Press, 1993.

Zou Tao. *Haishang chentian ying*. Nanchang: Baihuazhou wenyi chubanshe, 1993.

Zou Zongliang. "Dui Pu Songling yu Chen Shuqing" yiwende jidian zhiyi." *Pu Songling yanjiu jikan* 3 (1982): 229–247.

Index

modern, 127–128, 137, 145–147;
resistance to polygamy, 5, 137,
138; wanton, 18–19, 128, 137,
152. *See also* agency, female;
remarkable woman
women writers: *ci*-lyrics, 158n10;
concubines, 141–142; in Ming
and Qing, 19–21; novelists, 38;
polygyny and, 139–141; pride,
140; *tanci* rhyme-narratives, 20–
21, 32, 36, 38–39, 98–99, 139–141
Wu Weiye, 21, 22–23, 52
Wu Xuexiang (*Flowers of Shanghai*),
107–108, 113

Xia Jingqu. See *Old Man's Radiant Words,
An*
Xiaoyaozi. See *Hou Honglou meng*
Xi Shiyi (*Precious Mirror of Boy
Actresses*), 59, 61, 62, 63, 66, 148
Xue Baochai (*Dream of the Red
Chamber*), 10, 37, 39, 44, 46, 64,
122
Xue Baochai (*Dream of the Red Chamber
sequels*), 41, 42, 43, 123
Xu Honglou meng (*Sequel to Dream of the
Red Chamber*; Qin Zichen), 40
Xu Honglou meng gao (*Draft Sequel
to Dream of the Red Chamber*;
Zhang Yaosun), 164n24, 165n27
Xu Honglou meng xinbian (*New Sequel to
Dream of the Red Chamber*; Haipu
zhuren), 163n20, 164n24

Yang Shuangqiong (*Shanghai Dust*), 118,
120, 122

Yangzhou, 51, 55–56, 169n17
Yesou puyan. See *Old Man's Radiant
Words, An*
yin and yang, 9–10, 36
Yuan Mei, 105
Yu Da, 85, 115, 175n2; *Courtesan
Chambers* (*Qinglou meng*), 84,
85–90, 99, 150
Yu Dafu, 124
Yuesu (*Courtesan Chambers*), 87–88, 89
Yuli Hun. See *Jade Pear Spirit*
Yun (wife of Shen Fu; *Six Records of a
Floating Life*), 142–143

Zeitlin, Judith, 30
Zengbu Honglou meng (*Sequel to Patching
the Dream of the Red Chamber*;
Langhuan shanqiao), 164n24,
165n27
Zeng Pu. See *Flower in a Sea of Karma*
Zhang Chunfan, 180n1. See also *Nine-
times Cuckold*
Zhang Qiugu (*Nine-times Cuckold*),
126–127, 129–132, 133–135, 137,
147, 149
Zhang Yaosun. See *Xu Honglou meng gao*
Zhang Zhupo, 19
Zhou Shuangyu (*Flowers of Shanghai*),
103, 108–109, 111–112
Zhu Shuren (*Flowers of Shanghai*), 103,
108–109, 111–112
Zou Tao, 115, 175n2, 180n1;
commentary on *Courtesan
Chambers*, 85, 87, 88. See also
Shanghai Dust

About the Author

Keith McMahon is professor of Chinese language and literature at the University of Kansas, where he teaches Chinese language, the history of literature, and the history of sexuality in China. He has published three books—*Causality and Containment in Seventeenth-century Chinese Fiction* (1988), *Misers, Shrews, and Polygamists: Sexuality and Male-Female Relations in Eighteenth-century Chinese Fiction* (1995), and *The Fall of the God of Money: Opium Smoking in Nineteenth-century China* (2002)—and is currently working on a history of imperial polygamy from ancient times to the end of the Qing empire.